ACTING IN
SHAKESPEARE

ACTING IN SHAKESPEARE

ROBERT COHEN
University of California, Irvine

Mayfield Publishing Company
Mountain View, California
London · Toronto

Library of Congress Cataloging-in-Publication Data
Cohen, Robert
    Acting in Shakespeare/by Robert Cohen.
        p.   cm.
    Includes bibliographical references and index.
    ISBN 0-87484-951-9
    1. Acting.   2. Shakespeare, William, 1564–1616 — Dramatic production.   I. Title.
PN2061.C577   1990
792.9 — dc20   90-36912
                                         CIP

Manufactured in the United States of America

10 9 8 7 6 5 4 3 2 1

Mayfield Publishing Company
1240 Villa Street
Mountain View, California 94041

Sponsoring editor, Janet M. Beatty; managing editor, Linda Toy; production editor, Carol Zafiropoulos; manuscript editor, Carol Dondrea; text and cover design, Cynthia Bassett Bogue. This text was set in 10½/12 Galliard by Thompson Type and printed on 50# Finch Opaque by Quinn-Woodbine. Photographs © 1989 Judy Davis.

CONTENTS

PREFACE   ix

INTRODUCTION   xiii

PART ONE

THE INGREDIENTS

LESSON 1
Who Was Shakespeare and Why Study Him?   1

LESSON 2
Speech Acts   5

LESSON 3
Calculated Effects   12

LESSON 4
Oppositions and Builds   19

LESSON 5
Antithesis   25

LESSON 6
The Demands of Shakespeare   33

LESSON 7
The Straight Build   38

LESSON 8
The Nature and Structure of Builds   44

LESSON 9

Platforms, Cutbacks, and Interpretation   51

LESSON 10

Shared Builds   58

LESSON 11

Physical Shakespeare   65

■▨▨■ PART TWO

THE CHARACTERS

LESSON 12

Costume and Character   72

LESSON 13

A Gallery of Shakespearean Characters   77
Cassius, *Julius Caesar*   78
Doll Tearsheet, *2 Henry IV*   80
Richard II, *Richard II*   81
Hermione, *The Winter's Tale*   83
Gremio, *The Taming of the Shrew*   84
Calpurnia, *Julius Caesar*   85
Troilus, *Troilus and Cressida*   87
Queen Elizabeth, *Richard III*   88
Grumio, *The Taming of the Shrew*   90
Isabella, *Measure for Measure*   91
Richard III, *Richard III*   92
Abbess, *Comedy of Errors*   94
Mercutio, *Romeo and Juliet*   96
Katherine, *The Taming of the Shrew*   97
Sir Andrew Aguecheek, *Twelfth Night*   99
Olivia, *Twelfth Night*   100
Thersites, *Troilus and Cressida*   102
Cassandra, *Troilus and Cressida*   104
Launcelot, *The Merchant of Venice*   105
Old Gobbo, *The Merchant of Venice*   107
Launce, *Two Gentlemen of Verona*   108
Luciana, *Two Gentlemen of Verona*   110
Mark Antony, *Julius Caesar*   111

Viola, *Twelfth Night*   113
Benvolio, *Romeo and Juliet*   114
Joan of Arc, *1 Henry VI*   116
Petruchio, *The Taming of the Shrew*   117
Charmian, *Antony and Cleopatra*   120
Gloucester, *King Lear*   121
Margaret, *Richard III*   123
Soothsayer, *Antony and Cleopatra*   125
Toby Belch, *Twelfth Night*   126

PART THREE

THE WORKINGS

LESSON 14

Shakespearean Language   *129*

LESSON 15

Word Choice   *138*

LESSON 16

Scansion: A Primer   *143*

LESSON 17

Using Scansion   *155*

LESSON 18

Shakespearean Rhetoric   *168*

LESSON 19

Speeches into Scenes   *183*

LESSON 20

Storytelling   *196*

LESSON 21

A Dream of Passion   *209*

APPENDIX

Variant Versions   *217*

GLOSSARY   *221*

ANNOTATED BIBLIOGRAPHY   *225*

INDEX   *227*

P R E F A C E

This book outlines a step-by-step approach to acting in the plays of Shakespeare.

It is step by step because I think that is the best way to proceed with a difficult subject. Acting Shakespeare *is* difficult—let's face it. His verse is not the language of our everyday American speech; the costumes in which he visualized his characters are not the clothing of everyday American life. Playing Shakespeare means living in a very different world from the one we normally inhabit.

Shakespeare's vocabulary, his use of rhetoric, his basic notions of theatre: these are all substantially different from their contemporary counterparts, and our normal methods of discourse and performance do not train us to handle (much less master) Shakespearean language or Shakespearean dramatic texts.

It does no one any good to sweep these differences under the carpet and pretend they don't exist—to assume, for example, that Shakespeare is simply "our contemporary" and that we can treat him as such—for among other things the differences stem from Shakespeare's very greatness as an artist and his importance as a creator of great dramatic roles. To simplify Shakespeare, to remove his complexity and difficulty, is simply to diminish his genius and eliminate the challenge of rising to the level of his accomplishment. In this book, we will explore the differences between Shakespeare's world and ours, and the brilliance of his achievement, with the goal of growing toward his greatness rather than reducing that greatness to an easy-to-master mediocrity. To do this, we will work slowly.

We will begin by working on single Shakespearean lines, then move up, step by step, to short speeches. Finally, we will take a look at short scenes and the development of whole parts.

Don't be impatient. As a beginning acting student, no matter how talented, to jump headlong into (or off) the balcony scene in *Romeo and Juliet* is to crash into more problems than you can effectively cope with at one time. It is somewhat like calculating with Einstein's theorems without knowing basic algebra. The step-by-step process of this book will guide you into a complex subject in basic, teachable (or self-teachable) units.

The single lines will be hard enough—at first, anyway. When you can do them authoritatively and with confidence, you will be ready to move along.

This is not simply a book about Shakespearean acting, however. It's about acting with texts, with style, and with dramatic authority. In this text, Shakespeare's plays are employed as a vehicle for an advanced level of acting study, a level beyond theatre games, improvisations, and contemporary naturalistic scenes.

Acting in Shakespeare deals with acting in plays; specifically, it deals with plays of great literary art and theatrical genius. Plays from times other than our own. Plays celebrated for their brilliantly shaped texts and for their innovative, lyrical, and imaginative theatrical "style." How do we animate such splendidly contrived works of art? How do we make them vividly alive on our modern stage? How do we make them represent or signify a dramatized reality that concerns our own lives?

It is not merely a matter of adopting a "Shakespearean style." Indeed, there is no such thing as a Shakespearean style, nor is there a form of acting that can be called Shakespearean acting. These phrases have cultivated a false mystique for many years, but they have simply no basis, historical or otherwise. Shakespeare wrote plays over a twenty-year period (from the late 1580s to about 1611), spanning two entire literary-historical periods (Elizabethan and Jacobean). Shakespeare's dramatic work included, in nearly equal amounts, plays in four separate and distinct genres: tragedy, comedy, romantic tragicomedy, and history. His plays contain every sort of dramatic writing: blank verse, rhymed couplets, Italian and English sonnets, satirical doggerel, prose, mime, dance, songs, bawdry, slapstick, wit, foolishness, fantasy, cynicism, puns, jokes, parody, and scatology. His settings run the gamut from ancient Rome and Athens to medieval England and Denmark, to Renaissance France and Italy, to 17th-century London and Vienna, to fantasy islands and forests that exist outside of space and time. His plays comprise no single style but rather a staggering variety of modes, tones, attitudes, locales, and ideas. And the acting in his plays encompasses every possible manner and fashion.

Modern producers have tended to exaggerate, rather than restrict, Shakespeare's near-infinite variety, to the extent that Shakespeare's plays are now professionally presented in every imaginable form, from Kabuki to Commedia, from Epic to Absurd, from Circus Act to Philosopher's Pit to Street Theatre. Even the rare "traditional" staging of Shakespeare poses more questions than answers, for what is traditional anymore? Generally, when literary critics speak of a traditional production of Shakespeare, they are really speaking of a 19th-century type of production, with painted backdrops and arch, pseudo-British "rounded tones" from the actors. This production style is rarely seen on professional stages anywhere in the world today—*particularly* not in England.

No, what is remarkable about acting in Shakespeare (as opposed to "Shakespearean-style acting") is not its regimentation through some sort of stylistic codification but its brilliant vigor, its extraordinary diversity, its unpredictability, and its continuous capacity for surprise and amazement. Actors should approach all this not through following rules or imitating techniques but through the development of deep literary understandings and superior performance skills.

ACKNOWLEDGMENTS

Among the Shakespeare enthusiasts who have, over the years, lent me their inestimable wisdoms have been:

Miss Margaret Casey, my high school English teacher at Bethesda-Chevy Chase High School;

My college and university professors, particularly: Henry B. Williams, George Schoenhut, and John Finch at Dartmouth College; Travis Bogard, Jonas Barish, Harry Ritchie, and William T. Oliver at the University of California at Berkeley; and John Gassner, Nikos Psacharopolous, Frank McMullan, and Alois Nagler at the Yale Drama School;

My theatrical colleagues, particularly Stacy Keach, Adolph Caesar, Jerry Turner, Liz Huddle, Peter MacLean, Ed Brubaker, and Angus Bowmer at the Oregon Shakespeare Festival; Jack Crouch, Michael Moriarity, K. Lype O'Dell, Jim Symonds, Dan Yang, David Anthony, David Knight, Gavin Cameron-Webb, Cal Winn, Roger and Sally Mitchell, Doug and Chuck Goheen, Jim Berton Harris, Dudley Knight, Katherine Fitzmaurice, Richard Devin, Joel Fink, and Jim Sandoe at the Colorado Shakespeare Festival; Fred Adams, Cam Harvey, Doug Cook, Monica Bell, Laurie Birmingham, Jan Gist, Patrick Page, Sandy Robbins, Leslie Reidel, Kent Thompson, Jim Edmonsen, Howard Jensen, Charlie Antaloski, Barry Kraft, Ron Ranson, Beth Novak, Liz Stillwell, Carey Lawless, Christine Frezza, Dennis Rees, and Michael Finlayson at the Utah Shakespearean Festival; Patrick Stewart, Richard Pasco, Lisa Howell, Sheila Allen, Ben Kingsley, and Brewster Mason of the Royal Shakespeare Company; Bill Needles of the Canadian Shakespeare Festival; and Keith Fowler, Ray Reinhardt, Ashley Carr, Clayton Garrison, Stuart Duckworth, Eli Simon, John Harrop, Michael Addison, Mary Corrigan, Arthur Wagner, Audrey Stanley, Richard Risso, Michael Edwards, Bob Goldsby, and Curt Conway of the University of California theatre faculties;

My scholarly colleagues at the University of California, particularly: Edgar Schell, James Calderwood, Hugh Richmond, Homer Swander, Murray Kreiger, Robert Folkenflik, Stephen Barney, David McDonald, Stephen Barker, Franco Tonelli, and Judd Hubert;

The fine actors in the photographs: Sarah Salisbury and Philip Thompson; and the excellent photographer: Judy Davis.

I am grateful to my colleagues who reviewed the manuscript and provided valuable comments and suggestions: Robert Barton, University of Oregon; Tom Markus, University of Utah; James Norwood, University of Minnesota, and Lorna Cohen.

INTRODUCTION

The problems in acting Shakespeare are not separable from basic acting fundamentals. In acting Shakespeare, your need to pursue a goal (a victory, an objective) for your character, to interact vigorously with other people (other characters), to use a wide range and variety of tactics in pursuit of your goal(s), and to allow your character to be drawn by expectations of victory (and shaken by fears of defeat) is every bit as important as in acting Arthur Miller or David Mamet.

Shakespearean acting, in other words, is real acting. It is not some kind of great leap backward into ancient times or artificial manners; and the need to deal with text, historical period, and theatrical style does not signal a retreat from dealing with yourself, your acting partners, and your basic acting approach.

Shakespeare's characters, like any in drama, must be seen to live, to breathe, to threaten, to seduce, to fall in love, to fear, to care, to suffer, to fail, and to die. That Shakespearean texts are for the ages does not mean that Shakespearean acting is not for the moment. To study Shakespearean drama is to study life; and to study Shakespearean acting is to study living.

ORDER OF LESSONS

The lessons that follow are arranged in a step sequence. They begin with what will certainly appear as the simplest of assignments. You are urged not to skip over these early exercises or to skimp on the time allotted to them. No exercise in this book is beneath the attention of any acting student; indeed, veteran professional actors have found these apparently simple challenges to be stimulating and thought-provoking.

PARTNERS AND GROUPS

Most exercises ask that you say something, or do something, to a partner. This is someone who's studying with you, or at least willing to experiment with you. However, in most cases and without any loss of effectiveness, your partner can be an imaginary person.

Similarly, if the exercise asks that you address a group, you may, having no warm bodies at your immediate disposal, create such a group solely in your imagination. Acting takes large amounts of imagination anyway, so these solo ventures won't prove too difficult.

By using imaginary partners and/or groups, almost all the exercises in this book can be explored by a reader studying in private. Even the student exploring this material as part of formal classroom study should learn to work, between classes, with imagined partners and groups (just as, on stage, you work with imagined tyrants, witches, and armies).

MEMORIZATION

Each exercise in the book requires that you memorize a section of Shakespearean text. It is essential that the words be memorized precisely, with no paraphrases or simplifications. The text sections are usually brief enough that you can do this in a short time — but don't let the shortness of the text deceive you into taking further shortcuts in learning the words. Learn them *exactly* as they appear here, which is to say, exactly as Shakespeare wrote them.*

Most unfamiliar words are explained where they appear. If you still do not know what a word means, or how it is pronounced, try looking it up in the footnotes of a published edition of the play, or in a Shakespearean glossary (for meaning), or in a pronouncing dictionary (for pronunciation); the bibliography in this book lists several sources or you can ask your instructor.

But go ahead and memorize the word anyway, even before you know what it means or how it is pronounced. Often the meaning and pronunciation will come out of what you learn in the exercise. Feel free to stumble around a bit with the language; you're not on stage yet, and learning begins as much by *doing* as by any other form of investigation.

Remember, no one expects you to be a Shakespearean scholar, and, indeed, you may very well come up with meanings of words in your exercise that are superior "definitions" than are in many scholarly footnotes or glossaries. Definitions and pronunciations in Shakespeare are often variable, depending on the dramatic situation and the speaking context, and experts (as well as glossaries) often disagree about individual readings of Shakespeare's lines.

READINGS ARE BOTH NATURAL AND DRAMATIC

In many of the exercises that follow, certain "readings" are suggested. "Readings" in this sense simply means "ways to say a line," which might include inflections of pitch (up, down), dynamic range (loud, quiet),

---

*Well, maybe not *exactly* as Shakespeare wrote them. See an expanded note on this delicate matter in the appendix.

speed of delivery (fast, slow), and possible movements, gestures, and expressions. These suggested readings are not merely technical instructions; rather they are responses to *two* general demands:

1. The reading should ordinarily conform to a character's *natural* speaking pattern for the situation, and

2. the reading should be *dramatic,* which is to say, it must both stimulate and inform.

Both are critically important; that is, every dramatic reading should be *both natural and dramatic.*

"Natural" does not mean that it must sound like 20th-century American conversation; rather it means that the line should sound as though the character thought it up and decided to say it that way.

"Dramatic" does not mean that the reading must be gaudy or eloquent or "Shakespearean," but that it should stimulate its hearers to some sort of action or change of attitude; it should provoke dramatic values (suspense, humor, excitement, empathy) in the characters on stage — and, through them, to an audience.

Notice that what is required is not one or the other of these demands, but both. Every discussion in this book will consider, explicitly or implicitly, both the naturalness or lifelikeness of the suggested readings, plus the reading's dramatic impact or theatricality.

SUGGESTED READINGS ARE NOT RULES, BUT . . .

Notice also that what will be discussed are only suggested readings, not mandatory ones, for there simply are no definitive ways to play any given line, much less any given character. In fact, a nearly infinite number of possible readings for Shakespearean lines exist, and great actors will have a huge palette of choices to make in building their parts. Were you to compare recordings, say, of Laurence Olivier and John Gielgud in the same roles, you would hear enormous variation in the way they produced the same speeches. But you would also discern certain underlying principles to which both these actors — like all fine performers — would have adhered.

Think of the game of chess. Of the many possible opening chess moves, no one has yet found a move that is in all cases "right." Every expert chess player has favorite moves, and no two experts play the same ones in the same order. Still, certain principles of chess *suggest* the moves the experts choose. It is important to control the center of the board, for example, and therefore it is almost always better to start the game with the king's pawn than the rook's pawn. While there is no single right opening move, the beginner has to learn the strongest (and therefore the most obvious) moves before going on to discover the expert's variations.

It is the same with acting. The exercises in this book will pose certain challenges. Your job should be to meet these challenges in the most effective way possible, not the most attention-getting and show-offy way. There may be a time for that later on, but only when you have demonstrated your power and skill on the "king's pawn" approaches.

READINGS AND STAGINGS

Some of the exercises ask for "readings," but you must understand that in the theatre the word *readings* means everything you do when speaking, including movement, posture, tone of voice, gesture, expression, handling of props, and so forth. At least it does in this book. One can discuss the specifically verbal aspects of reading more easily in a book than you can show the physical aspects, so this book is a bit weighted toward the sound of Shakespeare rather than the visual picture. Nevertheless, you must always remember that they go absolutely hand in hand at acting time, and are never to be thought of as separate in any way.

DON'T GIVE UP

A final word: Although these exercises follow a step-by-step approach, you won't necessarily make step-by-step progress. Learning to act Shakespeare is a slow process characterized by long stagnant periods followed by quantum leaps, as certain notions, or feelings, or rhythms click in. These leaps come when discovery is joined by confidence, and they *will* occur in your progress if you are persistent in seeking them. Don't be deceived by the apparent simplicity of the exercises or the seeming snail's pace of your day-by-day achievements. To get to the end of this book, and to understand and be able to apply the principles herein, is to take giant steps toward learning how to perform Shakespeare with power and authority.

To Lorna Cohen

*ACTING IN
SHAKESPEARE*

Who Was Shakespeare and Why Study Him?

We begin our study with an overview of some fairly well-known facts about Shakespeare the man, and with some generally accepted assessments of his life and work.

Shakespeare is, first of all, the most successful playwright who ever lived. Success isn't everything, of course, but in this case, it is an important starting point.

His plays are the most produced dramatic works not only in most English-speaking countries (England, Canada, Australia, the United States), but in much of continental Europe as well, including Germany, Hungary, and the Soviet Union. In the United States, in addition to the hundreds of productions of his works that appear annually in the professional and academic theatre, there are entire festivals devoted to presenting his plays, including major festivals in the states of New York, Oregon, Colorado, Idaho, Georgia, Alabama, Vermont, Texas, Virginia, Ohio, Wisconsin, Pennsylvania, Maine, New Jersey, Connecticut, and Illinois. There are two in Utah and at least four in California. There are even two in Dallas–Fort Worth, so that the citizens of neither of these neighboring cities should feel neglected.

In England, Shakespeare's birthplace is the country's most visited national shrine, and the theatre ensemble that bears his name (the Royal Shakespeare Company) is the country's most celebrated dramatic organization.

In addition, Shakespeare's plays do not exist solely on the stage; they comprise a major part of the curriculum in literature wherever English is spoken, and the scholarly study of his works is a virtual industry. Whole libraries are devoted to his works and the commentaries on them. For Shakespeare is not merely thought of as the finest playwright of all time, but usually as the greatest *writer* as well.

And yet much of his life and work remain a mystery to us.

He was born in Stratford-upon-Avon, a pretty village in southcentral England, in the spring of 1564. In 1582 he married a local woman, Anne Hathaway, eight years his senior, and by 1585 he and Anne were the parents of three small children. The next seven years of his life, however, are lost to history, for the next known fact in his biography is his appearance in 1592 as a popular London playwright. This appearance is not particularly pleasant, for it is an attack on Shakespeare. In a deathbed pamphlet, the expiring writer Robert Greene calls attention to an unnamed young playwright currently becoming "an upstart crow, beautified with our feathers." The playwright Greene is speaking of is Shakespeare, who, Greene says, "with his *Tiger's heart wrapt in a player's hide* supposes he is as well able to bombast out blank verse as the best of you, and being an absolute Johannes-factotum, is in his own conceit the only Shake-scene in a country." If "Shake-scene" didn't quite identify young Will to Greene's readers, the "Tiger's heart" reference did, for it was a direct parody of a line from Shakespeare's then-popular *Henry VI, Part III*. When Polonius, in Shakespeare's *Hamlet,* says that "beautified is a vile phrase," one suspects Shakespeare was remembering Greene's intemperate jealousy.

By that time — and probably even by 1590 or 1591 — Shakespeare was a London theatre professional. He acted, he wrote plays, he directed, and he was a major co-owner of London's leading theatre company, the Lord Chamberlain's Men, to which he contributed about two plays every year.

Shakespeare seems to have been immensely popular well within his own lifetime. In 1598, an essayist praised him as the greatest dramatic writer who had ever lived, both in comedy and tragedy, although his greatest plays in both fields were still to be written. He apparently became wealthy and socially respected, able to purchase the biggest house in Stratford for his retirement, and earning a gentleman's coat of arms for his family. In 1603, when Queen Elizabeth died, King James took over personal patronage of Shakespeare's theatre troupe, which was consequently renamed The King's Men.

Little else is known of Shakespeare's life. His wife and children apparently remained in Stratford, where he seems to have retired in 1611, dying on (or close to) his fifty-second birthday, in 1616.

Where and with whom he lived during his career, where he may have traveled, what he read and studied, and what he thought about life, love, marriage, religion, politics, or the theatre can only be deduced, if at all, in and between the lines of his 37 plays, his 114 sonnets, and his 2 longer poems, plus a handful of controversial court records, dedicatory epistles, and contemporary references of varying authenticity and importance.

What is certain is that Shakespeare was a man of the theatre, an actor-playwright and theatre owner who created dramatic works of such brilliance, depth, and power that a lifetime of study would suffice to probe only a small portion of his accomplishment.

SHAKESPEAREAN DRAMA

The English drama of Shakespeare's time was as vigorous a cultural art form as has ever existed; it is said that if Shakespeare had never lived, the Elizabethan drama would still be one of mankind's supreme intellectual and artistic achievements.

It was, above all else, entertainment—for the masses and for the privileged elite. Although they demonstrate profound literary and intellectual subtlety, Shakespeare's plays were performed to a large and often rambunctious public. Outdoor public playhouses, three tiers high and open to the sun and rain, held up to 3,000 spectators, not all of whom came to the theatre strictly to see a play. Eating, drinking, and even socializing went on during the performances, which were usually followed by music and dancing. Since admission to the ground level was only a penny (the price of a glass of beer), the public playhouse was immensely popular with 16th- and 17th-century Londoners—indeed, too popular, according to some city officials who railed against the playhouses for distracting workers from their official duties. Public playhouses were thus banned by local ordinance during Shakespeare's lifetime to the suburbs (across the Thames or north of the city wall).

But Shakespeare's troupe played in more intimate and elegant indoor spaces as well: at court, in the city and country palaces of Queen Elizabeth and King James, and in "private" theatres built within royal homes, inns of court, and abandoned monasteries in and out of London and Westminster. It also played on tour: in the universities to the north (Cambridge and Oxford), in market towns and street fairs, and in the country manors of the nobility.

Thus, kings and queens were the patrons of the Shakespearean theatre—but so were intellectuals, laborers, apprentices, shop owners, lawyers, students, prostitutes, and peasants. It was dramatic entertainment for the enormously rich blend of people who made up the English public—entertainment that was as varied as its patrons. During the quarter century of Shakespeare's career (1587–1612), literally thousands of comedies, tragedies, historical pageants, court masques, literary satires, melodramas, and classical translations flowed from the pens of dozens of dramatic authors, many of whose works are still being performed today, nearly 400 years after their times. No other period of world drama has left such a glittering heritage.

Shakespearean drama is shaped by several *literary* antecedents as well. It owes some of its outer form—a five-act structure, multilayered parallel plots, regular verse speeches—to the classical Roman theatre, particularly the comedies of Plautus and the tragedies of Seneca. It owes much of its earthy theatrical vigor, and much of its humor and bawdiness, to the English pageant plays of the Middle Ages, and to the mimes, mimics, and jongleurs that performed on the streets and in the manors and innyards of medieval England. It owes its wide-ranging exoticism to the romantic novellas and tales coming out of the European Renaissance, particularly from France and Italy. And it owes its skeptical, secular objectivity to the beginnings of empirical science and detailed political history that characterized Tudor England.

By the time Shakespeare came on the scene, there was one more literary antecedent: Elizabethan drama itself. From the 1560s drama flourished in England, and by the 1580s an entire English Renaissance had taken place in the world of drama and theatre production. Shakespeare himself drew on these sources; his *Hamlet, King Lear,* and *The Taming of The Shrew* include at least some elements from earlier Elizabethan plays of the same names.

With all these influences, the Shakespearean actor in the author's own time was required to work with equal facility at two levels: first, to give a thrilling and charismatic performance capable of captivating mass audiences in the public arena; and second, to fulfill the aesthetic demands of exquisitely shaped literary texts, suitable for presentation at colleges and court.

The demands facing a modern actor in Shakespeare are exactly the same. No small task. But not an impossible one either, as hundreds of successful productions annually attest, year after year.

L E S S O N   2

Speech Acts

In this first practical lesson, we explore four very simple speech fragments — which will perhaps prove to be not quite as simple as they first appear.

You can memorize each fragment immediately; it may help to have the speech written on a blackboard if one is available.

EXERCISE 2-1

Memorize and say this line:

Peace, Kent!

Just two words, but each one of them speaks volumes.

The line is from the first scene of *King Lear,* the speaker is the king himself. You, King Lear, have just "disclaimed" (disowned) your daughter Cordelia in the presence of the court. The Earl of Kent, loyal to both Cordelia and you, tries to intercede with you, saying "Good my liege. . . ." You cut him off abruptly with this two-word line.

Say the two-word line to a partner, real or imaginary,[1] so as to stop your partner (the Earl of Kent) from speaking. Speak the line as forcefully as possible.

Think of the line as a **speech act,** that is, speech as action; where the speaker seeks with his or her words to create a specific change in the attitude, opinion, and behavior of the person spoken to. Not as a description or a narrative, but as an action that is intended to stop the Earl of Kent from speaking.

How does King Lear stop Kent? How do you stop your "Kent"? There are many ways, and we will suggest some of them.

First, Lear does it by the *violence* of the interjection. Notice that the speech is composed of two harshly stressed syllables, that elide together with

---

[1]Read in the preface about "imaginary" partners if you are trying this, or any of the following exercises, on your own.

a hiss (at the end of "peace"), and then explode with the **glottal** *k* that begins "Kent!" A glottal is a consonant caused by air held back and then suddenly released by a movement of the glottis.

Lear particularly focuses this violence by calling the earl by his abbreviated, one-syllable name, "Kent," thus stripping his loyal follower of his royal title along with his dignity, and subordinating him before the court. (When the Earl of Kent is introduced earlier in the scene, it is as "My Lord of Kent.")

Second, Lear emphasizes his own superiority by the *cleverness* of his word choice for "be silent." "Peace," implies that it is the Earl of Kent, not Lear, who is performing the violent deed. If Lear were simply to say "Shut up, Kent," he would confirm the court's suspicion that he was an old man losing his temper, and he would lose his regal authority. By demanding "peace," even violently, Lear poses as the royal peacemaker, and remains (for the time) unassailable.

Notice that in fact the two words stand in tonal opposition: "Peace," with its long, elongated vowel and hissing terminal consonant, is seemingly gentle but actually insidious, while "Kent!" with its clipped short vowel and abrasively hard consonants is abrupt, demeaning, arrogant, and cutting. These go in the proper order, too: The seemingly gentle "peace" becomes the setup for the more violent "Kent!" "Peace" disarms Kent (and the court), so that the subsequent "Kent!" then stuns him (and them) into awkward silence.

What happens when you are silenced by someone in authority? Generally, you feel small, anxious, undercut, frightened. You might even feel cold and nauseous; you might shiver, perspire, or become teary. You feel suddenly childlike, infantile. Your logic gives way, and you become terrified of speaking — for fear of saying something as infantile as you feel at the moment.

Try to make a variety of "Kents" (two or more different acting partners) really experience these psychophysiological states by the way you speak the line "Peace, Kent!" to them.

Try to make each "Kent" feel anxious, nauseous, and infantile. Try to make him or her shiver, perspire, or become teary. Acting is not pretending to *be* something, it is trying to *do* something, and the speech act of "Peace, Kent" is to try to make Kent speechless with anxiety.

It is a tall assignment, of course, and you will probably not succeed. But you should realize that a Dark Age king — who had been a successful king for many years — would almost certainly succeed. Your "job" in playing the role of Lear demands (among many other things, of course) that you be able to threaten; able, on occasion at least, to strike fear in the hearts of others with only a few well-chosen words. Shakespeare has given you words that are certainly well chosen; it's up to you to do the rest.

Try it.

Now take this exercise one step further. There is a (real or imaginary) group around you as you say "Peace, Kent." They are your "court," and they are anxious to know if you still have your old authority, or if you're losing it.

They could be awed by your power in silencing Kent—or they could start giggling behind your back if they realized you were simply blustering.

Perform your "Peace, Kent!" speech act to your Kent, but do so for the benefit of this "audience" of courtiers. Try to make Kent speechless with anxiety, and also to impress the court with your ability to command this earl to obedience.

A taller assignment yet. But one every aging king, or shop foreman, must do regularly.

▚▞▚▞▚ EXERCISE 2-2

KING LEAR: Peace, Kent!
　　　　　　Come not between the dragon and his wrath.

Yes, this is the same speech as in Exercise 2-1, but with the next line added in. Memorize it, and say it to a partner.

The second line adds a narrative dimension: You are to specify a precise instruction to "Kent." "Don't try to prevent me from getting angry; don't get in my way" you must tell your faithful earl.

But Lear doesn't simply "say" this. Rather, Lear speaks in a metaphor: "I am a dragon, and when a dragon is as wrathful as I am, anyone who comes too near gets burned by the fire of my breath!" This line both extends and elaborates the opening salvo of "Peace, Kent!"

In order for you to be successful with this second line, you must not only *say* that you're a dragon, you must *prove* to Kent that you are one; moreover, you must also prove this to the "court"—or some other "Earls" may just try to follow the trail that Kent has blazed.

That's not to say that you (or Lear) are going to prove successful. In fact, as the play shows, Lear is not. But he tries, and therefore you must too. Your job (the actor's job) with this speech act is to try to make Kent and your court think that you are a dragon breathing fire on anyone trying to stop you from disowning your daughter.

How do Shakespeare's words help? The glottal *c* in "Come" echoes the preceding glottal *k* in "Kent," thus allowing your first line to serve as an **alliterative** springboard to your second. Alliteration consists of two or more words beginning with the same sound, ordinarily a consonant.

The reversed negative imperative ("Come not," as opposed to the more ordinary and conversational "Don't come" or "Do not come") permits a violent and contradictory explosion of negation on "not," thus:

. . . come NOT . . .

This is also a setup, the word "come" first appearing as an inducement, and the "NOT" as a slap in the face: a shocking tonal reversal. It is also a formal rather than casual form of discourse, more typical of a kingly command than a casual warning, and particularly suitable for putting a subordinate in his or her proper place.

If you elongate the vowel in "come"—the elongation aided by the **nasal** coloring (in this context, a vowel made with air passing through the nose) which can be prolonged almost indefinitely—and then make the syllable "NOT" both loud and staccato, these two words take on a strongly stentorian regality.

. . . between the dragon . . .

Lear doesn't say that he is "like" a dragon, he states that he *is* a dragon: no longer a mere human being, but a violent and fantastical creature. Lear seeks, through these words, to become depersonalized, mythic, and invulnerable in the court's eyes, using the power of metaphor to attempt a transformation. And not just *a* dragon, either, but *the* dragon (or *The* Dragon)—a very specific and terrifying creature.

This requires some coloring of the word "dragon," which might mean drawing it out a bit and calling a little extra attention to Lear's dragonish ferocity, perhaps with a physical action. Shakespeare has helped here since saying the word "dragon" in a forceful manner requires baring the teeth. And if there's a little pause after "dragon"—to make certain everybody gets the point that you're a dragon—and the teeth are bared through the pause, they can remain bared for the next two words, "and his," thereby coloring in the dragon for all (Kent, the court, the audience at large) to see.

. . . and his wrath.

Notice how the last syllable actually becomes The Dragon's breath itself. Wrrrraaaaaaaaaaaathhhhh!

So, once again, try to terrify Kent and impress the court:

Peace—Kent!
Come NOT between The Dragon (*bared teeth*)—and his (*fire!*) wraaaaaaath!

◤◣◢◥ EXERCISE 2-3

This exercise should move you in quite the opposite direction.

Come, thick Night . . .

The speaker here is Lady Macbeth; it is in the first act, fifth scene of *Macbeth,* and the lady is alone on stage, calling Night about her, as if to shroud her murderous intentions. It is what we technically term an **apostrophe,** an appeal, often literary in tone, to a non-present being, real or imaginary.

But how does one call "Night" to one's side?

Basically, there are only two ways to make someone do what we want: to *threaten* (to order, to command, to force), or to *induce* (to lure, to invite, to seduce.) Threats and inductions (punishment and reward, we might say) are the tactics of human interaction, and, therefore, the basic content of a speech act—and of an acting performance.

Clearly Lear *threatens* Kent in the previous exercise, but the second tactic, *induction,* would be more appropriate in trying to bring Night (the spirit of night? the god of night?) down around one's shoulders. Surely, Night cannot be bossed or bullied by a mere human. Night must be lured, romanced, seduced: "Come, thick Night. . . ."

The three single-syllable words, each with its vowel in the middle, are almost equally stressed; together they make a steady and level incantation, to which darker spirits may hearken.

Is Night in fact "thick"? Perhaps, as in the sense of dense or impenetrable. The question, however, is not whether Night is or is not thick; the actor's key question is: "For what reason does Lady Macbeth *choose to tell Night* that it's thick?"

In speech act analysis, or in acting, it is never sufficient merely to understand what a given word or line "means," or to determine that such and such a line is (or isn't) "true." It is necessary to understand for what reason the character says the word or line to the person addressed. There must, in other words, be an *interpersonal* or *interactional* reason for each line of the play to be spoken.

Otherwise, characters simply wouldn't speak. Lady Macbeth is not put on the stage simply to tell us truths about nature, or she would go on with "the sky is blue" and "the floor is wood," and other truisms. Lady Macbeth calls Night "thick" because she has some *reason* for doing so.

Let us suggest that Lady Macbeth calls Night "thick" because she thinks Night will be pleased with this description. She is flattering Night. The word "thick" is part of her lure, part of her seduction of Night.

"Come, thick Night." Try to seduce "Night" with this line.

Move your arms toward the "Night," and draw Night down around you as you speak.

Writhe—with trunk, arms, and legs—on the word "Come," and subtly suggest a sexual double entendre as you say it.

Let your tongue *linger* between your teeth on the *th* of "thick" when you say the line.

 EXERCISE 2-4

Come, thick night,
And pall thee in the dunnest smoke of hell . . .

This, of course, is a continuation of the same speech. For context, know that the speech concludes:

That my keen knife see not the wound it makes,
Nor heaven peep through the blanket of the dark,
To cry 'Hold, hold!'

But work on just the two lines of the exercise.

The meaning of the line is both elusive and allusive: Literally, Lady Macbeth is asking Night to pall itself—that is, to put on a black funeral drape—in the dunnest (or most gray-brown) smoke of Hell.

But there are word plays here that create a broad texture of secondary and tertiary meaning as well. A "pall" is also the cloth used in Christian churches to cover the chalice (which holds the communion wine), thereby bringing in images not only of death but of eternal separation from holiness. "Pall" also suggests "appall" and "appalling," which certainly describe the deed that Lady Macbeth contemplates.

"Dunnest," an unusual word, suggests, by a pun, an ultimate finality, as "utterly done," "the most done deed." This proves a good prediction: Shortly Macbeth will say "If it were done when 'tis done, then 'twere well it were done quickly." And Lady Macbeth's last line in the play begins "What's done cannot be undone."

These secondary meanings cannot be directly "played" in the speech, of course, but the texture of the language is part of your seductive tactic and your overall speech act. Night loves appalling acts, done deeds, and ultimate finality; your puns will attract the darker spirits.

Continue the incantation of "Come, thick Night," by making the whole line an incantation to dark spirits. How do you create an incantation to night? Make it up! After all, nobody else knows either. Your imagination here is your best seductive weapon; it may prove your gift to the character of Lady Macbeth.

Try many approaches. Lie on your back, arching your body to the dark. Dance, whisper, coax, sing. Create a witches' ritual (Lady Macbeth may be allied with the witches in this play), a demonic chanting of your own devising.

Almost every vowel in English appears in this speech, and with them, *caress* the Night: Caress Night particularly with the long, steady, equally stressed vowels of "pall thee in the dunnest smoke. . . ." The repeated **sibilants** or hissing sounds of "dunnest smoke" bring in the serpent's hiss, don't they? Let Night hear the devil in your "esses." Night loves the devil, you (as Lady M) must imagine.

The glottal *k* in "smoke" lifts the word out of the speech ("smoke" is the first noun in the speech other than the identified hearer, "Night"); you can bring the whole speech up to real time with this word, implying the directive "and do it now!" as you say "smoke." "See" smoke at the precise moment that you say the word. Taste it at that moment; maybe you even choke on it. Make us—other spirits watching over you—see it, taste it, choke on it, too.

. . . of Hell.

Here is the upshot of the pall covering the chalice, and the serpent's hiss: The smoke you are calling is not just from a fire, but from Hellfire. Ask Night to cover herself in a pall of Hellfire smoke. Enlist the devil's aid.

Are you afraid when you bring Hell into this? Fine. Lady Macbeth might be as well; it depends on how you want to play her. But bring Hell in you must. Play the line two ways:

1.   Tantalize Night with the idea of joining forces with Hell, Night's natural ally.

2.   Realize, as you arrive at the word "Hell," where your line is taking you, but go ahead with it anyway. Rise above your terror.

SUMMARY OF LESSON 2

This lesson lays out the foundation for the rest of the work. You should clearly understand the following points before proceeding further.

1.   All lines on stage are *actions*. They are not merely descriptions, clever sayings, poetic flights of fancy, or jokes. From the character's point of view, they have a purpose, which is to compel some sort of behavior or attitude change from another person, or persons, or personified animal or object. All lines, in brief, are *speech acts,* whatever else they may be.

2.   Speech acts compel behavior or attitude change, either by some sort of threat or induction, or both. These are tactics; they may be exquisitely mild and subtle, but they can also be very powerful (and sometimes the subtler they are the more powerful they are also).

3.   With a playwright as gifted as Shakespeare, dramatic dialogue is married to dramatic action, not just in meaning but in sounds, rhythms, syntax, and imagery. You should study the words of a Shakespearean speech not merely for their semantic meanings, therefore, but for their whole tactical impact on the hearers — both those onstage and off.

4.   What does this speech try to *do*? How does it try to do it? And how do *I* try to do it? These are the fundamental questions.

Calculated Effects

Should acting be calculated or spontaneous?

This is a trick question. The answer can only be "it must be both." *Spontaneous* because the actor, like the character, must be seen to think on his or her feet; must be seen to be responding to the situation on a moment-to-moment basis. But, of course, the play is *rehearsed,* which means that the performance is, to some extent, calculated. Thus, much of what the audience sees as moment-to-moment spontaneity can only be achieved by suppressing a certain part of your consciousness — which some actors find almost impossible to suppress.

In classical or verse plays, this apparent spontaneity is even more difficult to achieve, both because the actions of the plays are often historically remote and/or fantastical and because the dramatic dialogue is wildly different from ordinary and spontaneous conversation.

How, then, with the performance rehearsed and the play's action clearly calculated, do you maintain any sense of spontaneity in Shakespeare? You do so by making clear that it is the *characters* who calculate their dramatic effects. Yes, you calculate, but you do so *in the person of your character*.

First, you have to understand that all people — meaning "real" people, "imaginary" people, or dramatic characters — try to calculate the effects of their actions. They seek to *plan* their acts (although their acts do not always go according to plan).

Just as we choose our clothes before going out for the day, or decide just how to stand and speak when answering a question from the podium, so dramatic characters frame their words and actions to their purposes. All people, dramatic characters included, "put on a face to meet the faces that they meet," in a paraphrase of T. S. Eliot's famous line. Sometimes consciously, sometimes unconsciously, we are always in a planning stage. We are always choosing or trying to choose how to behave. And so are dramatic characters. Except that you — the actor — must do the planning and the choosing for them.

Sometimes, of course, plans go awry. Your clothes, so carefully chosen, tear. Your fine phrase, delicately rehearsed at the podium, comes out garbled. The face you put on to greet your ex-lover dissolves, at the first angry word, into unexpected tears.

Acting is often most exciting when it is experienced in the tension between your character's calculated plan and your subsequent, spontaneous reaction to events outside that plan.

So, to the extent that you play a character, you also play your character choosing and contriving various actions and effects — as well as responding to the moment-to-moment actions of the play's situation and to the other characters and their choosings and contrivings.

Your ability to respond spontaneously and energetically gives your acting its naturalness and vigor. Your ability to plan, to choose, and to contrive actions and behaviors gives your acting its breadth, its specificity, and its dramatic variety.

Shakespeare gives you an extraordinary portfolio of characters who are defined, primarily, by the plans and choices they (and you, playing them) will make. These will ordinarily not be plans or choices you yourself would ever make in the real world (that's why the characters are extraordinary), so, in the exercises that follow, explore your imagination to the fullest.

▚▞▚▞ EXERCISE 3-1

GLOUCESTER: They do me wrong, and I will not endure it!

Gloucester is Richard, Duke of Gloucester, soon to be known as King Richard III, and the hero of the play bearing his name. In this, the first sentence of your first speech at the palace, you enter, accusing the present assembly — Queen Elizabeth, Lords Rivers, Grey, Buckingham, and Derby — of doing you wrong, of complaining to the king that you, Gloucester, are "stern and love them not."

The speech, and its opening line, prove a sterling example of the maxim "a good offense is the best defense," for indeed you *are* doing them wrong: You are plotting murders, seeding discontent, and planning to maneuver yourself onto the throne. But rather than defend yourself, you accuse the others of plotting against you, putting *them* on the defensive — and it works!

Your (character's) goal with this opening line is therefore simple. You want to intimidate weak courtiers into inaction and to impress the strong courtiers into allegiance. Both can be achieved if you seize the high ground for your own, and demonstrate bold, reckless, charismatic authority. You cannot rationally persuade your foes of your innocence, but you can certainly try to cow the weak into submission and convert the clever into subordination.

Memorize and play the line. Play it to a (real or imaginary) crowd of courtiers. Try to use the line to thrill and terrify your hearers with your inner conviction, your seizure of high moral ground, and your reckless courage.

Build the two negative words in the line so that the second ("not") becomes a little explosion of revolt, momentarily staggering and silencing the court:

They do me *wrong* and I will *NOT* endure it.

Why do you want the court silent? Because you have more to tell them, that's why. This first line, and the explosion on "NOT" sets them back on their heels, and gives you some breathing room. All but one of the words in this line are quite ordinary. The exception is "endure," which is, under the circumstances, a little refined. Pronounce the word with a liquid *u* sound on the second vowel (the *u* in "pure," rather than the *oo* in "poor") so as to temper the explosive violence of the "NOT" with the covering courtly sophistication of a crown prince.

They do me *wrong* and I will *NOT* (pause) enduuuure it.

This way you both boldly threaten the queen and her followers (with "NOT") and sagely induce them (with "endure"). Courtly behavior is, of course, by definition inductive (as in "to court," meaning "to romance").

▮▨▮▨▮ EXERCISE 3-2

Same line. Know that in the play Gloucester is considered physically deformed: "rudely stamped," in his own words; a "lump of foul deformity," an "elvish-marked, abortive, rooting hog," a "poisonous bunch-back'd toad," according to his enemies. Apparently, you have a withered hand, a club foot, and a hunched back: How can you use them in the service of your goal? Assume Gloucester's physical characteristics and practice walking about, in private, dealing with these particular deformities.

Now play Gloucester's line to the assembled court, using two different physical approaches to do so:

1. Try to *hide* your deformities. Try, in other words, to look your best: innocent, dignified, attractive, normal, hurt. Try to look heroic, for bearing up so bravely with your affliction.

Make the court feel guilty of thinking ill of so suffering a person as you. Stroll about as normally as one could possibly do with such tragic deformities.

2. Now try, conversely, to *parade* your deformities, and thereby intimidate the court with your ugliness. Make the courtiers queasy: Make it clear to them that you are quite disgusting already and not reluctant to get even more so if they continue to cross you. Make them afraid of you — afraid of your bestiality, your recklessness.

Exaggerate your hobble and put your withered arm right in their faces. Shame them for their cowardice when they turn away from you in revulsion.

Both of these lines of behavior — and there are an infinite variety of ways in which you can put them to practice — transform the line into a comprehensive speech act. Both lines will make you a "Richard" to be reckoned with. Neither line is "correct," and celebrated performances have taken off in each direction, for while the first is a solid "common sense" approach to the problem, Richard says in his opening speech that he will take "delight" when he can "descant on [that is, make music out of] mine own deformity." The latter interpretation holds highly theatrical potential, while remaining well within the bounds of "normally abnormal" human behavior.

◼▨◢▨◢◣ EXERCISE 3-3

CLEOPATRA: O happy horse, to bear the weight of Antony!

You are the Queen of Egypt, lying on your cushioned palace daybed, being fanned by Nubian eunuchs and attended by soothing confidantes. Antony, the greatest general and ruler of Rome, is your lover; he has just been called home, however, and has just departed for the ship that will bear him back to the capital. You have sent after for news of him, and now are speaking wistfully to Charmian, your maid. The build-up to your line is:

O Charmian,
Where think'st thou he is now? Stands he, or sits he?
Or does he walk? or is he on his horse?
O happy horse, to bear the weight of Antony.

Your assignment is only the last line. Memorize and say it to a real or imaginary "Charmian." What is the speech act of this line? For what reason does Cleopatra ask Charmian if Antony is standing or sitting? Obviously this is a **rhetorical question,** one asked to make a point rather than to receive an answer, rather than a real question.

What is Cleopatra's point? Let us say she is trying to impress her court with how much she is loved, particularly how much she is loved by a great Roman warrior and ruler. We can call this "bragging." Her act is to instill admiration and redoubled support.

We can also say she is trying to make up for Antony's absence by indulging in a revery of lovemaking. In her reveries, of course, she is the "horse"; her act is to vicariously experience, as a horse, being "mounted" by her absent lover. To get sexual pleasure, in other words.

Now play the line, both to brag about your heroic lover and to enjoy your lover's (absent) presence.

1.   Notice the alliteration (you can hardly miss it) of "happy horse." Let the repeated first aspirations of those words, the "ha . . . ho . . ." build as deepening sighs of erotic pleasure. "Taste" the two words as you say them, letting the court see your pleasure in tasting them, as if you were tasting wine before an "audience" of winemakers, each hanging on your taste "verdict."

Show your court how sophisticated your "taste" is—how much relish you can take in those words "happy" and (particularly) "horse." Show them that you *are* a happy horse, at least when Antony mounts you. Play the tastiness and playfulness of the words in the line.

2.   Shakespeare frequently combines animal imagery with human sexuality (thus, in *Othello*, sexual intercourse is described as "the beast with two backs," and in *Much Ado About Nothing*, a young woman accused of adultery is compared with "pampered animals that rage in savage sensuality.")[2] This line of Cleopatra's mentions one animal, but also includes the homonym of another ("bear"), which is also homonymous with "bare." That means that while "bear" does not mean bear literally, the word is *heard* by the audience with both bearish and bare-ish associations. Play the animalisms of the line. Be horsy on "horse" and bearish on "bear."

3.   How many feet has the line?

We will discuss meter in some detail later on (Lessons 16 and 17), but you perhaps already know that the standard blank verse line in Shakespeare consists of five "feet," each with two syllables. This is a six-foot line. Compare it with a regular five-foot construction; as:

O happy horse, to bear the weight of Jove.

Shakespeare's line is "weightier" at the end. The two extra syllables prolong the expected five-foot line. They slow it down, making it languid rather than heroic or military. Particularly in contrast to the broken-up verse that precedes it, this line, when it finally comes, expresses the long nights of prolonged boredom Cleopatra must face without her lover.

Play this "extra foot" as an elaboration of your despair, a public display of the weightiness of Antony's leavetaking, and your ability to rhapsodize sexily about it.

Can you laugh after the line, as if to make fun of your own sexual dependence on this man? How absurd—a queen, the richest woman in the world, wishing she were a horse! What a fool am I! you might imply to the court. What fools we mortals be!

---

[2]A wonderful discussion of this subject is given in James Calderwood, *Shakespeare and the Denial of Death* (Cambridge: University of Massachusetts Press, 1987), pp. 46–57.

◥◤◢◣ EXERCISE 3-4

> HENRY V: Once more into the breach, dear friends, once more.
>   Or close the wall up with our English dead.

You are leading your vastly outnumbered English army into the breached wall of a garrisoned French town. Chances are that many, if not most, of your troops will be killed moments after the attack begins. It is your task, King Henry that you are, to inspire your men to make their finest effort.

Why do men go into battle? Into near certain death? There is no simple answer, but certainly it is some combination of pressure (anxiety at being punished, or overridden, by the troops behind you) and desire (excitement at the prospects of the victory awaiting you). You, as King Henry, must supply both; you must put on the pressure and induce the desire — your speech, your posture, your delivery must constitute a complete and charismatic speech act, provoking men into deadly battle.

You may not simply stand on vague legal principles such as kingly authority. The law courts of England are a long way from the French battlefield. Face it: If your soldiers were simply to drop their arms and walk away, you couldn't do a thing about it. You, King Henry, stand alone — between each soldier's death and his desertion. You offer them your love ("dear friends"), you imply a military threat ("or close the wall up"), and you promise them a quick conclusion to their heroic efforts:

Once more . . . [*just*] once more.

Try it.

Kings are not just born, they are made. King Henry V was born a helpless baby, just like you were. Whatever personal powers he may or may not have over his troops are simply those he has learned; whatever powers you would have on such an occasion would be the ones you had learned, and those you could summon up to meet the situation. The only difference between Henry and you is that Henry learned his lessons in twenty-some years of tutelage and battlefield observation — and you will have to learn them in a few hours of class time or rehearsal.

Kings and tyrants, however, are not a different species from us. They are only individuals who have grown accustomed, as we probably have not done, to seizing and holding authority over thousands of other people. That authority undoubtedly gives them a confidence in leadership ordinary people don't usually have, but that confidence is something the actor must master to play Henry V — or Henry IV, or Richard III, or King Lear, or Lady Macbeth, or Cleopatra. The confidence to wheedle, to threaten, to reward, and to inspire. It can all be done with these two lines.

Remember, words are sometimes all that rulers have. Inspiring words at the right time have carried elections, won battles, generated social and political revolutions. Words were just about all that England had during the darkest days of World War II, and while Winston Churchill's words couldn't stop bombs from exploding over London, they kept hope alive (in the words of a contemporary American leader) until the tide could be turned.

Try it again. And again. *Rehearse* it. Once more into the breach — for you as well! Kings, after all, weren't made in a day, or in a single battle. They practiced at being kings, and you should too.

SUMMARY OF LESSON 3

Characters speak — even when spontaneously — to achieve calculated effects, which may be to terrify, to impress, to inspire, to induce. These are specific, intended, goal-oriented tactics, both verbal and physical. Characters try to parade virtues and hide defects. They often "rehearse" the calculated effects they want to achieve. You, too, should learn — by practice and rehearsal — how to speak and move with Shakespearean lines to impress, inspire, terrify, arouse, and intimidate your character's (real and imaginary) observers.

LESSON 4

Oppositions and Builds

BERNARDO: Who's there?

This is the first line of *Hamlet*. Bernardo, a soldier, is coming onto night-watch duty, relieving Francisco. It is midnight ("in the dead vast and middle of the night") and it is cold ("bitter cold," we are shortly given to understand). The setting is the outward wall of Elsinore, a castle on the eastern seacoast of Denmark; the historical period is late medieval Europe.[3]

1. Close your eyes, or blindfold yourself, and "play" the line into the subsequent darkness, trying to establish an answer to your question, "Who's there?"

2. Intensify the exercise: "Feel" the bitter cold and protect yourself against it. Now, while still pursuing the goal of finding who's there, try also with your line to "warm yourself" by challenging a possible enemy (which will get your adrenalin fired up), or by finding your fellow soldier (and going into his warming tent).

There is one immediate oddity in the line: It is you, the approaching guard, rather than Francisco, the on-duty one, who inquires "Who's there?"—a reversal of what would ordinarily be expected. Why is this?

Two factors could explain this. The first is that these are particularly anxious times: War seems imminent, and people could be especially touchy. Across the border, Fortinbras, the Norwegian prince, is gathering troops for an attack. Your own country's defense factories have gone into high gear, with the cannon factories and shipwrights working night and day, taking no holidays. Everyone is tense, including you.

---

[3]Setting and period, when given in this book, are as traditionally ascribed. Modern producers, of course, frequently choose to set Shakespearean plays in nontraditional locales and eras.

Second, and scarier yet, last night at this time you saw a "dreaded sight" on your watch — a "sight" that appeared to be in the form of the dead King Hamlet. You are pretty sure it was a ghost.

These apprehensions surely lie behind your asking "Who's there?" before you are asked yourself. You do so to seize control of the situation as best you can. If there's to be a military confrontation, you want the enemy identified fast. If there's a ghost in the neighborhood — particularly the ghost of a king — you want to put up a bold front.

3.   So, without necessarily *showing* anything:

"Feel" the cold and try to warm yourself against it.

"See" into the darkness, and try to penetrate it with your eyes.

"Think" of Fortinbras's army and try to anticipate its ambush.

"Remember" the ghost you saw last night and try to scare it away.

Now, using the line to warm yourself, to see through the darkness, to scout the enemy, and to scare a ghost, demand:

(YOU): Who's there?

Don't work to *show* anything, work to *do* these things: To warm, to see, to scout, to scare. Try it again.

Good. Notice that the line *reciprocates* the situation as you have imagined it. Notice how your delivery — your tone of voice, your bearing, your posture, your volume level, your inflections — has responded to real and imagined fears, hopes, and feelings. You don't have to "show" these things: The working to "do" things will bring the delivery out of you. The "doing" of actions makes you "deliver" a performance.

Notice how *rich* the line can be with meaning and import — and how much it can "say" beyond the mere literal question of the text.

EXERCISE 4-2

FRANCISCO: Nay, answer me: stand, and unfold yourself.

This is Francisco's response.

1.   Blindfolded, or with your eyes closed, and using the line both to "see" who's there and also to keep warm against the cold, "play" Francisco's line into the darkness.

2.   You have a miserable gnawing at your gut; you are cold and wet, and your fingers are numb; you have been out here for several hours; you have diarrhea. Don't try to *show* any of this, but rather try to make yourself feel better by the vigor of your response. Don't play the cold and the sickness; *respond* to it.

Use the line to "cure yourself."

Pay particular attention to the directive "Don't try to show this." You should not try to indicate that you're cold or sick; these are things Francisco, a soldier on duty, would try to hide, not show, at this point. If you try to indicate anything, indicate that you are fierce and ready for all comers. As an actor, you do not "play the obstacle" (being cold and sick, in this case), rather you play against the obstacle. You try to do what the character tries to do: to achieve your goals and overcome your obstacles. Just try to do *that*.

Two **structural characteristics** of Francisco's line bear further attention; these will define the foundation of much subsequent work in this book. (Structural characteristics are those that have to do with the patterns of action and dramatic language in a play's text.)

The first structural characteristic is that Francisco's line is in *disharmony* with Bernardo's. It may be considered a rebuke, or as the beginning of a possible argument; it defines a level of conflict. Drama, after all, is centered in conflict. So, for that matter, is human speech, which is ordinarily directed to changing the status quo in some way or other, and is therefore in some degree in conflict with things as they are.

As Francisco, you must rebuke this apparent stranger for asking who's there (that's *your* job!). You must also stop him from moving toward you—which you do by the command to "stand."

Finally, you must order him to explain *his* presence and identity, before you acknowledge yours.

3.   So, say into the darkness, and while trying to make yourself feel warmer and healthier, and more professionally soldierly:

"Nay," (Shut up, don't tell me what to do.)

"Answer *me*." (*You* tell *me*, rather than the other way around.)

"Stand, and unfold *yourself*!" (*I'm* certainly not going to unfold *myself*.)

Try to make the stranger shut up. Try to make him answer you. Try again, and try harder. Try to make him stop dead in his tracks. Try to make him terrified of you. Try to make him as cold and sick at heart as you are.

Try not only to warm yourself up, but to get stronger of heart in the process.

The structural characteristic involved here is *opposition*. Virtually every speech in every play—or in life—is in some way in opposition to the absolute status quo. "Peace, Kent" opposes Kent's speaking. "Come, thick night" opposes night's staying put. "Once more into the breach" opposes the soldiers' fatigue and fear. "They do me wrong" and "O happy horse" both oppose, in very different ways, the complacency of the respective courts addressed.

In this case, and in most, the opposition must be *focused* and *specified*. The speech is thus a challenge to the previous speaker—and here, of course, the challenge is quite literal.

Try it again.

4. *A three-step build*   Your speech also *builds,* which is a second structural characteristic. Play the speech as a three-step build:

(1)   Nay.

(2)   Answer *me*.

(3)   Stand, and unfold *YOURSELF*!

Each step is longer and more forceful than the last. The first, a one-syllable sentence, is essentially a prologue, reversing the speech flow, stopping Bernardo's speech and giving you the stage. The second is a three-syllable command, plainly expressed. The third is a six-syllable intensification and elaboration of the command, which has so far gone unanswered. It demands both a physical and verbal response, employing metaphorical language:

"stand" in lieu of "stay there" or "stop," and

"unfold" in lieu of "explain" or "identify."

Your speech builds in three steps because Bernardo fails to respond to your steps one and two. He could have responded to your "Nay," (as with "Hey, it's me, Bernardo!") and almost certainly should have answered your "Answer me." That you go to the third step is only occasioned by the fact that Bernardo has not responded to the first two: You *must* succeed with step three.

Play it in this building fashion: each step more forceful than the last.

Notice that your level of opposition (and the overall level of conflict) increases with each step, which are like the steps of a ladder. You will probably get louder and more insistent with each step.

Building does not require getting louder, of course, and it may often be played by growing quieter. A stepped **escalation,** or regular increase, of volume, however, is a normal and everyday response to conflict, and would be appropriate in this case.

But step three is not merely louder; it is also more linguistically complex, more elaborate in the actions demanded, and more metaphorical in expression. Thus the line builds in a broad sweep.

Try Francisco's speech again several times, playing toward all the goals cited earlier, but building its three steps in different ways.

5. *A four-step build*   Now try Francisco's speech with a four-part build:

(1)   Nay!

(2)   Answer *me*!

(3)   Stand! . . .

(4)   And unfold *YOURSELF*!

Notice that this too is a regular build pattern, broken into two units of two "lines" each, or:

(1)   Nay!

(2)   Answer *me*!

(3)   Stand! . . .

(4)   And unfold *YOURSELF*!

In this structure, both "Nay" and "Stand" are one-syllable negative demands ("don't speak" and "don't move") followed by, first, a three-syllable demand to explain, and, second, a five-syllable demand to explain. In terms of building, line three builds from line one, and line four from line two, although line three can be "beneath" line two.

Oppositions and builds are the basic patterns of dramatic action. In dramas, conflict escalates until some sort of final explosion (climax) and resolution (denouement). The escalation is not always straight-line and direct, and, in fact, is often quite complexly configured. Nonetheless the underlying intensification of characters' drives — and the conflicts they precipitate — determines the basic pattern of drama. Even this simple exchange from the first two lines of *Hamlet* illustrates this.

▚▞▚▞ EXERCISE 4-3

With a partner, play the first six lines of this scene.

BERNARDO: Who's there?

FRANCISCO: Nay, answer me. Stand, and unfold yourself.

BERNARDO: Long live the King.

FRANCISCO: Bernardo?

BERNARDO: He.

FRANCISCO: You come most carefully upon your hour.

It is usually understood that "Long live the King" is the guard's password, for through Bernardo's saying it, Francisco recognizes his partner. On the other hand, as the king is Claudius, it could be that Bernardo is simply making a sarcastic crack about a disliked ruler, intending that Francisco recognize him by his voice and expressed attitude. Bernardo, being a friend of young Hamlet, may be presumed to dislike Claudius, and this could be common barracks knowledge.

Notice the extreme economy of:

Bernardo?

He.

After the near-panic of escalating challenges in the dark, the calm simplicity of revealed identity is welcoming in the extreme.

And the last lines: Are they sincere or sarcastic? Is Francisco encouraging (inducing) Bernardo's friendship with his "most carefully" remark, praising his colleague's promptness? Or is he rebuking Bernardo (and thereby defending his inattention) with these words, suggesting Bernardo was *too* careful, too silent. "You snuck up on me, you jerk; that's why I didn't challenge you first."

"Most carefully" could even imply that Bernardo was unwarrantedly early. (Indeed, Bernardo seems to defend himself with his subsequent response, "'Tis now struck twelve.")

Play Francisco's last line not merely as a statement of fact (almost *no* line in drama should be played as a mere statement of fact), but as a beginning gambit: either of a rebuilt friendship, after a scare, or the start of a new argument. (Bernardo will pick up on neither of these, as he's preoccupied with the ghost, but you, Francisco, don't know anything about that at this point, and you probably never will.)

Through this brief analysis, you should see a new complexity of potential detail in these opening lines, and a vast realm of possible relationships between the characters. They are all yours for the playing. Try them.

Play the lines in the dark, and get flashlights for you and your partner. "Find" each other on the exchange "Bernardo?" "He." Find each other on an earlier line. On a later. What difference does the timing—of the visual discovery of the "other" character—make in the speech acts you play on your individual lines?

Play the scene with Francisco asleep at his post at the beginning, and Bernardo tripping in the dark, awakening him.

Play it with Francisco going behind the bushes to relieve himself (or herself). Play it with Bernardo hard of hearing.

Play it in several new situations of your, and your partner's, own invention. How do the speech acts change?

SUMMARY OF LESSON 4

1.   Stage actions, like life actions, have multiple purposes, some of which are obvious in the specific text, and others more embedded in the general human situation. To seek warmth and well-being, for example, even when they are not immediately specified in the text, are powerful goals to pursue. They work together with the more text-specific goals.

2.   Obstacles to your goals must be played against, rather than demonstrated.

3.   Speeches and stage actions engage you in opposition—often to other characters, and often (if not always) to the status quo. To act is, therefore, usually to *oppose* something; and it is from this opposition that the conflict underlying all drama derives.

4.   As a general rule, conflict (in life and on the stage) *escalates,* although not necessarily in a straight line, until someone wins or until there is some other sort of resolution. In life, conflict is often resolved in compromise; in drama, the resolution is more often climactic. In the theatre, therefore, most stage actions and speeches *build* toward a dramatic climax.

LESSON 5

Antithesis

Antithesis is a way of making points through opposites: of clarifying what is by disposing of what is not.

"No shepherdess, but Flora . . . ," Florizel says of Perdita, in *The Winter's Tale*. He is explaining that his new girlfriend is no longer simply a shepherd's daughter but is now the goddesslike (Flora-like) hostess of a sheep-shearing festival. "No shepherdess, but Flora" — not this, but that. This is one simple form of antithesis, which means, essentially, defining by opposites:

> LYSANDER: "Not Hermia, but Helena I love."
> (*A Midsummer Night's Dream*, II.ii.113)[+]

Antithesis is a powerful speaking tool because, by showing what "is" in direct contrast to what "is not," it focuses and emphasizes a precise meaning. Shakespeare uses it often:

> MARK ANTONY: I come to bury Caesar, not to praise him.
> (*Julius Caesar*, III.ii.74)

> HAMLET: Let me be cruel, not unnatural.
> (*Hamlet*, III.ii.395)

Often, antithesis is a parallel expression of opposites:

> OLIVIA: Love sought is good, but given unsought is better.
> (*Twelfth Night*, III.i.156)

> ROMEO: Here's much to do with hate, but more with love.
> (*Romeo and Juliet*, I.i.175)

> ROMEO: Arise fair sun, and kill the envious moon . . .
> (*Romeo and Juliet*, II.ii.4)

[+]Quotations from Shakespeare's plays are described in this fashion. The numbers refer, respectively, to the act, the scene, and the line or lines.

Or a parallel contradiction:

DEMETRIUS: For I am sick when I do look at thee.

HELENA: And I am sick when I look not on you.
(*A Midsummer Night's Dream*, II.i.212–213)

KATHERINE: Asses are made to bear, and so are you.

PETRUCHIO: Women are made to bear, and so are you!
(*Taming of the Shrew*, II.i. 200–201)

Or a combination of all of these:

LYSANDER: Content with Hermia? No, I do repent
The tedious minutes I with her have spent.
Not Hermia but Helena I love:
Who will not change a raven for a dove?
(*A Midsummer Night's Dream*, II.ii.111–114)

In this last case, notice the three specific antitheses: one made sharper by rhyme (content/repent); one by assonance and part of speech (the proper names Hermia and Helena); and one by color (raven, a black bird, and dove, a white bird).

◼◤◢◤◢◼ EXERCISE 5-1 SIMPLE ANTITHESES

"Play" the above antithetical lines by speaking them to or with (as the occasion determines) a partner.

Give the contrasting words (or, in the Demetrius/Helena exchange, the negative "not") sufficient emphasis to drive the antithesis home, to make your point in the sharpest, most final way possible.

Both alternate words of an antithesis will need some emphasis, but the preferred alternate (the one you are favoring) will usually have the stronger stress, regardless of where it may come in the phrase, as

"It's not *Mary* who's in trouble, but *JOHNNY*" and "*JOHNNY*'s in trouble, not *Mary*."

Therefore, normally:

I come to *BURY* Caesar, not to *praise* him.

I must be *CRUEL*, not *unnatural*.

Love *sought* is good, but given *UNSOUGHT* is better.

Here's much to do with *hate*, but more with *LOVE* . . .

Arise fair *SUN*, and kill the envious *moon*.

and

Content with Hermia? No, I do *REPENT*

The tedious minutes I with her have spent.
Not *Hermia* but *HELENA* I love:
Who will not change a *raven* for a *DOVE?*

In the Demetrius/Helena exchange, the strongest emphases (the highest stresses) would come on Helena's line, which is the second, or answering, speech. Helena's line builds on Demetrius's:

DEMETRIUS: For I am sick when I do look at thee.

HELENA: And *I* am sick when I look *NOT* on *YOU.*

How do you give a strong emphasis? Or highly stress a word? The most common way is with a changed *pitch inflection,* which is almost always a change upward.

Johnny."

Mary

"It's not   who's in trouble, but

and

"Johnny's

Mary."

in trouble, not

"Johnny," being the stressed noun (Johnny's the one in trouble) is given with a higher pitch than "Mary," which itself is given with a higher pitch than other words in the sentence.

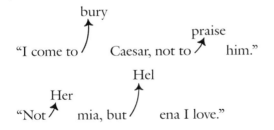

bury

praise

"I come to   Caesar, not to   him."

Hel

Her

"Not   mia, but   ena I love."

A second way of stressing a word is a change in *volume.* A very tiny increase in volume can make the emphasis—if you mean what you say when you do it.

Put these together and you get:

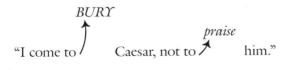

BURY

praise

"I come to   Caesar, not to   him."

and

"Not mia, but ena I love."

Spoken in this fashion, there should be no question what you intend to do with Caesar, or with which lady you're in love.

The change in volume can be a reduction as well. In Romeo's "but more with *LOVE*," volume is not particularly effective in emphasizing the notion of love; a hand on the heart might make the antithesis more powerfully.

An increased sharpness in *articulation,* together with a slight drawing out of the vowel or vowels, can also provide emphasis. So also can gesture, tone of voice, and general expression. A gesture to the ground on "bury," or to your heart on "Helena" makes the antithesis even clearer, and may stimulate the feelings (of you and those around you) as well.

How do you figure out which word to stress? Generally, you do so by determining which words are being contrasted, and which one is your (the speaker's) preferred alternative. You will quickly find that this becomes automatic.

And *make your character's point* when you speak your line. This in itself, if you are engaged in a speech act communication with another actor or actors, will probably bring the proper stress into play. If you are really trying to tell a Roman mob that you are here to bury Caesar not to praise him, you will probably stress "bury" without even thinking about it.

EXERCISE 5-2

Work up a reading of the following four speech fragments:

1.   FALSTAFF: Thou art fitter to be worn in my cap than to wait at my heels.

(*2 Henry IV,* I.ii.14. Falstaff is speaking to his page, essentially calling him as small and useless as a feather.)

2.   NURSE: Go, girl, seek happy nights to happy days.

(*Romeo and Juliet,* I.iii.114. The nurse is telling Juliet that when she marries Count Paris she will have happy nights, which will lead to happy days.)

3.   KING OF FRANCE: Fairest Cordelia, that art most rich, being poor, Most choice, forsaken; and most loved, despised . . .

(*King Lear,* I.i.252–253. The king is taking up Cordelia, who has just been disowned and disinherited by her father, but whom he will shortly marry. He tells her that the poorer she is in the world's eyes, the richer she is in his.)

4.   LUCIANA: Though others have the arm, show us the sleeve.

(*Comedy of Errors,* III.ii.22. Luciana is trying to persuade Antipholus to pretend that he loves Adriana—whom Luciana believes is Antipholus's wife—and to dress the part of a faithful husband.)

◼◪◪◪ EXERCISE 5-3

Luciana's speech in Exercise 5-2 includes several antitheses, in-cluding this quatrain:

Apparel vice like virtue's harbinger
Bear a fair presence, though your heart be tainted;
Teach sin the carriage of a holy saint
Be secret-false: what needs she be acquainted?

In this quatrain (a four-line, rhymed poetic unit) three antitheses *build*. Try reading Luciana's quatrain with an escalation of the three individual an-titheses: vice/virtue, fair presence/tainted heart, and sin/saint.

◼◪◪◪ EXERCISE 5-4

ROMEO: Here's much to do with hate, but more with love:
Why, then, O brawling love! O loving hate!
O any thing, of nothing first create!
O heavy lightness! serious vanity!
Mis-shapen chaos of well-seeming forms!
Feather of lead, bright smoke, cold fire, sick health!
Still-waking sleep, that is not what it is!
This love feel I, that feel no love in this.
Dost thou not laugh?
BENVOLIO: No, coz, I rather weep.
(*Romeo and Juliet*, I.i.167ff.)

This is an extension of Romeo's line in Exercise 5-1. Having heard of a street fight, and having told his friends of his passionate love (for Rosaline), Romeo now tells his friends his confusion through a series of antitheses — which have the character of wordplay rather than persuasive argument.

A noun modified by a contradictory adjective (as "heavy lightness") is called an **oxymoron**. Shakespeare often uses such devices, often in a comic way, to show confusion, neurosis, or, as here, a character topsy-turvy in love.

Play with the line, and try to entertain your friends with it. Entertain them with your wordplay, your clever verbal inventiveness. Let the entertain-ment build, like any good comic act. *Create* — don't merely recite — this list of escalating oxymorons.

If you have a partner, have him or her play Benvolio to make the final antithesis answering yours.

Want to try it with Juliet instead of Romeo?

JULIET: Beautiful tyrant! Fiend angelical!
Dove-feathered raven! Wolvish-ravening lamb!

Despised substance of divinest show!
Just opposite to what thou justly seem'st —
A damned saint, an honorable villain!

EXERCISE 5-5

Read the following dialogues to determine the antitheses, and give them their needed emphasis:

1.   LIGARIUS: . . . What's to do?
BRUTUS: A piece of work that will make sick men whole.
LIGARIUS: But are not some whole that we must make sick?
BRUTUS: That must we also.
(*Julius Caesar*, II.i.328–330. You are both plotting an assassination.)

2.   CLOWN: I think his soul is in hell, madonna.
OLIVIA: I know his soul is in heaven, fool.
CLOWN: The more fool, madonna, to mourn for your brother's soul being in heaven. Take away the fool, gentlemen!
(*Twelfth Night*, I.v.73–76. You are talking about Olivia's brother, who has died. The clown is trying to bring Olivia out of her extended mourning. "Madonna" is gently satiric, chiding Olivia out of her "Pietà" mode.)

3.   HERMIA: I frown upon him, yet he loves me still.
HELENA: O that your frowns would teach my smiles such skill.
HERMIA: I give him curses, yet he gives me love.
HELENA: O that my prayers could such affection move!
HERMIA: The more I hate, the more he follows me!
HELENA: The more I love, the more he hateth me.
HERMIA: His folly, Helena, is no fault of mine.
HELENA: None but your beauty; would that fault were mine!
[*A Midsummer Night's Dream*, I.i.193ff. You are talking about Demetrius, whom Helena loves, but who is pursuing Hermia (who is pursuing Lysander). This is also in a comic framework, and the antitheses are also wordplay, calculated to entertain each other as much as to address serious romantic concerns.]

EXERCISE 5-6

This one is perhaps a little over your head at this point (you might not agree), but try it anyway.

Read aloud these famous opening lines of *Richard III*, paying attention to the running antitheses, which are numbered in parentheses for your convenience:

GLOUCESTER:

(1)   Now is the winter of our discontent
       Made glorious summer by this sun of York;

(2)   And all the clouds that lowered upon our house
       In the deep bosom of the ocean buried.

(3)   Now are our brows bound with victorious wreaths;

(4)   Our bruised arms hung up for monuments;

(5)   Our stern alarums changed to merry meetings,

(6)   Our dreadful marches to delightful measures.

(7)   Grim-visaged war hath smooth'd his wrinkled front;

(8)   And now — instead of mounting barbed steeds
       To fright the souls of fearful adversaries —
       He capers nimbly in a lady's chamber
       To the lascivious pleasing of a lute.

Word notes: The "sun of York" is Edward IV, son of the Duke of York, with the pun intended. "Alarums" are military trumpets, "measures" here means dance music, and "front" means forehead.

This speech concerns change. Gloucester, who will soon become King Richard III, is explaining that the war is over; victory has been achieved; psychological "winter" has become "summer"; clouds of anxiety have, as it were, sunk beneath the water; soldiers' brows have unfurrowed; their battered swords have been mounted on the walls as souvenirs; their war cries have turned into happy greetings; martial marches have been superseded by dances; and war has turned pixie-ish: The struggles of armies have been replaced by the playful battle of the sexes.

Look at the structure of the speech: Gloucester begins with two two-line antitheses (1 and 2), then gives five one-line antitheses (3–7), concluding with one four-line antithesis (8).

At each level, Gloucester's antitheses become more complex. Indeed, antitheses (7) and (8) are somewhat intermixed; the subject of (7), war, is carried over to be the subject of (8); so that it is war — its front, or forehead, now smoothed — that has dispensed with armored horses in order to caper nimbly in the boudoir.

Now "play" this speech. In the actual play, it is addressed directly to the audience, and as such it may properly be seen as something you have prepared and rehearsed. Gloucester himself has certainly "rehearsed" it.

Let the first antithesis stand as a prologue, setting up the series to follow.

Play the second antithesis as a variation of the first, but build it up a little bit, confident that you have already seized our attention.

Play the five one-line antitheses as a steadily escalating series of variations — and take more and more pleasure in your ability to come up with these clever paradoxical insights.

Play (8) as your ultimate *action* — this is to move us into the present tense ("and now"), drawing us from the war we have been thinking about, into the bedroom you want us to inhabit.

This speech of Gloucester's, which involves both antitheses and building, may well be too advanced to memorize and try to work on at this time. It's also particularly difficult because of the competition: Many Shakespearean acting teachers and directors will have the cadences of the late Laurence Olivier very much in mind when they hear you do this one since Olivier's filmed Richard is quite well known. Work on it as an exercise only, and come back to it later in your work.

SUMMARY OF LESSON 5

Antithesis is a powerful speaking tool because it makes points through oppositions and contrasts, demonstrating what "is" by clearing away what "is not." Playing antithesis involves a calibration of speaking stress: Contrasting words must carry both a defined stress — with the "preferred" alternate usually carrying a higher stress, such as a higher pitch, volume, and/ or level of articulation — and often a physical gesture or action. Often the escalation can be lighthearted and entertaining, as in wordplay. Often the antitheses are built on top of each other, in a complex escalation of oxymorons, paradoxes, contradictions, and variations.

The Demands of Shakespeare

The demands facing a Shakespearean actor are multiple since they are occasioned both by the nature of Shakespearean texts and the specific conditions of the Shakespearean stage for which the texts were written. To a certain degree, you will find parallel (although quite different) demands in performing the text of all dramatic authors, including modern ones. Before working on any more practical exercises, take a little time out to consider the breadth of these demands. Most of them will be studied more comprehensively, and through practical applications, in later lessons.

THE DEMANDS OF THE TEXT

The first thing we notice about the Shakespearean text is that most of it is in **verse**. In this, Shakespeare is no different from the vast majority of playwrights who preceded him. Most classical theatre, both Greek and Roman, was written wholly in verse, as was the theatre of the Middle Ages. Indeed, one of the growing movements of the Elizabethan age is **prose** drama, which accounts for about a quarter of Shakespeare's actual dramatic dialogue (as much as 90 percent in one play, *The Merry Wives of Windsor*), and some Elizabethan plays—for example, George Gascoigne's *The Supposes* (1566)—are written entirely in prose.

Still, it is verse that most characterizes Shakespeare's dramatic language structure and differentiates it from the modern drama with which we are more familiar. The analysis of verse for emphasis is sometimes called **scansion,** and lessons will be devoted to this subject later on. But some introductory words are useful here.

The main form of Shakespearean verse is **blank verse,** which was introduced to the theatre by Thomas Norton and Thomas Sackville in what is considered the first English tragedy, *Gorboduc,* written in 1561. Blank verse is unrhymed **iambic pentameter,** which means that each line of verse has five "feet," each foot being two syllables long, with the second stressed. Thus, from *Gorboduc*:

> I take your faithful hearts in thankful part.
> But sith I see no cause to draw my mind
> To fear the nature of my loving sons,
> Or to misdeem that envy or disdain
> Can there work hate, where nature planteth love;
> In one self purpose do I still abide.
> My love extendeth equally to both,
> My land sufficeth for them both also.

You will look in vain in *Gorboduc* for a line that is nine or eleven syllables long, and you will rarely find a stress that is on an odd-numbered syllable; the blank verse of this earliest of blank verse plays is almost numbingly *regular* — a regularity not practiced, thankfully, by Shakespeare or later playwrights.

But blank verse is not the only verse form the Elizabethans, or Shakespeare, used. Even *Gorboduc* includes some rhyming iambic pentameters in its choruses:

> When youth, not bridled with a guiding stay,
> Is left to random of their own delight,
> And wields whole realms by force of sovereign sway,
> Great is the danger of unmastered might,
> Lest skilless rage throw down, with headlong fall,
> Their lands, their states, their lives, themselves and all.

Shakespeare, a master poet and sonneteer when not writing plays, uses dozens of verse and speech forms, with varying degrees of regularity. He mixes iambs with trochees, pentameters with trimeters, blank verse with prose, lyrical songs with doggerel rhymes, sonnets with epithets, and bawdy puns with rhyming couplets. A full appreciation of Shakespeare's expression through language — since language is the primary expressive medium of Shakespeare's plays — is essential for every Shakespearean actor. We will discuss Shakespearean language in greater detail, including identifying the terms above, in the concluding chapters of this book.

A second demand of the Shakespearean text is its **imagery,** in which the dialogue may on occasion be densely saturated. There is no question but that this provides enormous challenges — and problems — for modern actors. Look, for example, at the messenger's speech when he comes in to warn King Claudius of the imminent arrival of the revengeful Laertes in *Hamlet*:

> MESSENGER: Save yourself, my lord:
> The ocean, overpeering of his list,
> Eats not the flats with more impetuous haste
> Than young Laertes, in a riotous head,
> O'erbears your officers.

The military situation at that moment is utterly urgent: Laertes and his followers, armed and threatening vengeance, are right outside the door, battering their way in. Yet the poor messenger who informs the King does so by way of an extended and complicated metaphor: comparing Laertes' advance to the swells of the ocean beating upon the shore. The problem for the actor is not merely to make sense of the image, which is difficult enough, but to make sense of a messenger who would, at a moment of life-or-death crisis, compose an extended literary nicety.

A third demand of Shakespeare's language is a **rhetoric** that is no longer fashionable in private discourse, and which contemporary actors are often ill prepared to deliver forcefully and effectively. Shakespeare's London audience was raised not on comic strips and television shows but on fiery sermons from the pulpit of St. Paul's, great debates at the inns of court, and grand pronouncements at public coronations and executions. Rhetorical precision and a level of triumphant grandiloquence characterized formal Elizabethan speech in a way we can only admire today. Many of the lessons in this book will be devoted to raising ourselves to the level of rhetorical brilliance so perfectly captured, and transcended, by Shakespeare in his dramatic works.

THE DEMANDS OF THE THEATRE

We don't know everything about the Shakespearean playhouses, but we do know that most of them (including Shakespeare's own Globe Theatre, whose foundations were unearthed in 1989) were large, open to the elements above, and basically unadorned with what we think of as realistic stage scenery. Essentially, the Shakespearean playhouse was built around a large platform stage. In one theatre (the Fortune) whose dimensions are known, the stage was 43 feet by 27 feet, or roughly the dimensions of one side of a modern tennis court. (The Rose Theatre, whose foundations were also uncovered in 1989, was a bit smaller.) The platform was surrounded by the audience on at least three of its four sides. Some spectators stood around the platform, while others sat on benches in the three tiers of surrounding galleries. Thus an actor in the center of the platform could look straight out and see spectators in every corner of his field of vision—from left to right and from top to bottom—a phenomenon all but unknown in the theatre today.

The Shakespearean platform stage was reached by at least two doors leading from the back wall of the theatre—which held the "tiring room," in which actors put on their costumes ("attires," or "'tires"). The back wall could be assumed to represent a palace or a house or even a part of the forest; no scenery decorated it, however. The platform was surmounted by some sort of balcony level, possibly part of a structure erected on the platform proper, or possibly an inset in the back wall. The staging featured a good number of props, including large set pieces such as walls, thrones, banquet tables, and cauldrons. However, the scenic elements were, in general, architectural and practical rather than pictorial or representational. Little or no scenery existed simply to indicate locale. In addition, no front curtain masked whole-stage scene changes, and, obviously, there was no stage lighting, at least not in the outdoor theatres.

So it is clear that the "magic" of Shakespearean staging—in Shakespeare's time—was created not by technological wizardry or painterly verisimilitude, but by the precision and sublimity of the language and by the virtuosity of the acting. For example, this is how Shakespeare shows us—outdoors on a London afternoon—that it is dawn in Verona:

> ROMEO: . . . look, love, what envious streaks
> Do lace the severing clouds in yonder east:
> Night's candles are burnt out, and jocund day
> Stands tiptoe on the misty mountain tops.
> (*Romeo and Juliet*, III.v.10)

or dawn in Denmark:

> HORATIO: But look, the morn in russet mantle clad,
> Walks o'er the dew of yon high eastward hill.
> (*Hamlet*, I.i.165–166)

And here two characters jointly describe the gathering storm on a Bohemian beach:

> MARINER: The skies look grimly,
> And threaten present blusters . . .
>
> ANTIGONUS: The day frowns more and more . . .
> I never saw
> The heavens so dim by day . . .
> (*The Winter's Tale*, III.iii.3–4, 54–55)

It was words, expression, tone of voice, and an attention to the character-to-character communication—the speech act—of every line that created environment as well as story, "setting" as well as events.

Costumes in Shakespeare's theatre were given elaborate attention, and the evidence indicates they were quite grand. It was the custom of the day for "eminent Lords or Knights at their decease to bequeath and leave almost the best of their clothes to their serving men, which it is unseemly for the latter to wear, so they offer them for sale for a small sum to the actors."[5] Thus there was considerable finery at the playhouse's disposal, which is confirmed by the wardrobe lists that have come down to us.

Shakespearean costuming had both a symbolic and representational nature. Abstract characters, such as "Rumor, painted full of tongues" in *2 Henry IV*, the winged Time in *The Winter's Tale*, and conventionally costumed

---

[5]Thomas Platter, writing in 1599. In David Bevington, *Action Is Eloquence* (Cambridge: Harvard University Press, 1984), p. 36.

ghosts, witches, and "invisible" fairies were intermixed with characters dressed according to historical realism (in a sketch of the period, Titus Andronicus is shown wearing a toga) or simply dressed in contemporary clothing (in the same sketch Titus's Roman sons appear in ordinary Elizabethan doublet and hose). Costumes were also crucial in suggesting appropriate "time of day" wear for specified scenes (Julius Caesar and Brabantio both appear in nightgowns, according to the original stage directions of *Julius Caesar* and *Othello*). They were often fundamental as well to the play's plot, as in the cross-dressing scenes involving female characters playing men. In addition, Shakespeare employed "meta-costumes" for characters who themselves play characters, such as Player King in *Hamlet,* who plays "Gonzago" in a play within the play, and Bottom the Weaver in *A Midsummer Night's Dream,* who similarly plays the role of "Pyramus." Costumes also indicate the rising or falling fortunes of characters: Macbeth dons royal robes during the play while King Lear doffs them ("Off, off, you lendings," Lear cries). Costumes then become both realistic clothing for the characters, as well as symbols for the characters' changing function and prestige.

Just as with language, then, the Shakespearean actor must develop a special rapport with costume, both historical/realistic and symbolic/theatrical. Exercises later in this book will get you started in this direction.

The Shakespearean stage also demanded certain abilities in movement and performance that our own stage rarely does. Shakespeare's actors created their characters amid a huge crowd of spectators crammed about them: above, below, and farther left and right than the eye could possibly see. And they projected their characters, as well as action, feeling, situation, locale, and time of day using only the very basics of acting: language, costume, and movement on a basically bare stage.

They were not student actors, of course; they were pros — perhaps the finest actors who ever lived. Most had been acting all their lives, beginning as boys (first playing children and then women), and then growing into adult male roles. They acted to survive: They acted at court, in the streets, on tour in the country, in rural innyards and university commons, and, when they could, in playhouses, which they often built and maintained themselves. They played comedies, tragedies, histories, verse dramas, and prose dramas, and they played them in rotating repertory, learning thirty to fifty roles a year. Most of them could sing, dance, clown, and hold the stage on their own when things went wrong.

It was by rising to the specific and multivaried demands of the Shakespearean theatre that these first Shakespearean actors became extraordinary, and this is why, even today, Shakespearean training is the broadest, deepest performance background any English-speaking actor can have. The following lessons in this book approach, in somewhat more detail, the actor's response to these individual demands.

L E S S O N   7

The Straight Build

Speeches in the theatre, and coherent statements in daily life, are built. They are not simply good ideas randomly thrown together. They are structured arguments, based on solid foundations and put together in a persuasive order, with logic and a sense of building excitement, of *momentum*. Building a speech is just like building a building; you need a solid footing to begin with, sound engineering principles to guide you, and a stable architectural substructure in place before you add the decorative touches.

EXERCISE 7-1

This is the resounding conclusion of a speech from *Hamlet*:

KING: Give me the cups;
And let the kettle to the trumpet speak,
The trumpet to the cannoneer without,
The cannons to the heavens, the heaven to earth,
"Now the king drinks to Hamlet." Come, begin.

1.   Speak the words aloud, and become familiar with them without yet committing them to memory.
     The King is Claudius, Hamlet's uncle and the usurping King of Denmark. Claudius is here proposing a formal toast to Hamlet before Hamlet's duel with Laertes, which concludes the play. In the speech, Claudius commands imaginary instruments — the kettle (drum), the trumpet, the cannons, and the "heaven" — to "speak," and to celebrate, as it were, his drinking a toast to Hamlet.
     There is much more to this toast than meets the eye, however. Claudius has rigged the duel so that Hamlet will lose (and die — Laertes' foil has been secretly sharpened and poisoned), and he is also about to poison a drink to give Hamlet in the event that the poisoned sword plan doesn't work.

Through the speech, therefore, you are trying to encourage a spirit of blind and *reckless* revelry, in which your murderous plots can unfold unnoticed.

Give the speech, then, trying to incite recklessness in your hearers. Try to stimulate them to drink deeply.

Memorize the speech before working on it further.

Now look at the structure of the speech. It begins with a little prologue, setting the framework of the action:

Give me the cups,

And then it elides into a four-part command:

And let the kettle to the trumpet speak,
The trumpet to the cannoneer without,
The cannons to the heavens, the heaven to earth,
"Now the King drinks to Hamlet."

It concludes with an implementing directive:

Come, begin.

The prologue sets the stage for the rest: Claudius calls for a physical prop that he will use to illustrate, or gesture with, in his ensuing (well-rehearsed) incitement to carousal.

The four-part command is more complexly structured. Study it closely.

Essentially, it is an *ordering* of these four imaginary sounds that Claudius demands, and the specific order is significant. First, a drum will "speak" to a trumpet, then a trumpet will sound to a cannon operator, then the cannon will sound to the heavens, and then, finally, heaven (now singular) will sound to "the earth." What is heaven's sound? Thunder, we might suppose, or more metaphorically, Gabriel's trumpet, or a choir of angels, or God's voice—or a composite of all of these.

Structurally, these sounds represent an *ascendancy* of intensity and power. A drum is loud, but a trumpet is louder (in penetration, if not in actual decibels), and the cannon louder yet. Thunder (not to mention God's voice) is louder still. Thus the words imply a building of sound intensity; we can even number the steps of this build, as:

And
(1) let the kettle to the trumpet speak,
(2) the trumpet to the cannoneer without,
(3) the cannons to the heavens,
(4) the heaven to earth:
"Now the King drinks to Hamlet."

Imagine these sounds in sequence. They comprise a musical crescendo some-what like that in Tchaikovsky's "1812 Overture"—a drum roll, followed by a trumpet blast, followed by the firing of massed cannons, followed by a chorus of heavenly thunder and demonic/angelic voices crying (Claudius would have us believe) "Now the King drinks to Hamlet!"

2.   Since the sounds build in volume and intensity, speak this four-part command aloud, building its sounds the same way. Make each numbered directive a little louder than the one preceding; in other words, raise your overall volume level a little bit at each comma in the text.

Make your increases in volume regular. That is, try to increase your volume by the same amount each time. Think of yourself as going up a volume "ladder" — a ladder that has equally spaced treads.

3.   Have a partner speak aloud the numbers in parentheses at the points indicated, as though they were part of the speech, and use these spoken numbers to stimulate and order your steady, regular build of the speech. It will help the build if you complete all but the last numbered phrase or clause with a *rising pitch inflection* on the final syllable or syllables. Thus the words "speak," "without," and "heaven" should be given an upward glide, and should be higher in pitch than the word or syllable preceding. (For "without," the "out" should be higher than the "with.") This may seem mechanical at first, but rising pitch inflections work to sustain a build. They are *natural* in speaking when the speaker is sustaining a complete thought, or a multipart statement such as this one.

This is what we will call a *straight volume build*. It is not, by any means, the only way to perform this or any other speech, but it is the basis of building a rousing speech.

Caution: Let me interrupt the exercise with a cautionary comment. This straight build is simply an exercise. It does not presume to give you a definitive "reading" of this or any speech; it is aimed to help you understand certain rather technical aspects of dramatic writing and stage speaking. Do not try to "improve" the exercise at this point by developing "creative variations." There will be ample time for that later on. Also, do not now concern yourself with the intricacies of Claudius's feelings or his character. At this moment you are asked only to study certain structural foundations of language and rhetoric, not role interpretation or dramatic or psychological nuance. These can be approached later, when your structural foundation is solidly built.

4.   The sounds described by Claudius also seem to build in respect to the *distance* they must travel. The kettledrummer is apparently nearby, the trumpeter farther off, and the cannoneer is completely outside the castle walls ("without"). The heavens are, of course, farther off still.

"Build" the speech, then, by addressing these individual "musicians" at increasing distances: The kettledrummer is 20 feet to your left, the trumpeter is atop the wall to your right, the cannoneer is on the roof of a nearby building, and the heavens are way into the sky above. Project further and further as you "throw" each numbered command a greater distance than the last. Remember to connect the steps with rising pitch inflections at the ends of each step.

5.   Begin again, but this time start at the prologue. Imagine that the person with the cups is immediately over your right shoulder. Take the cups from him or her before going on with the rest of the build, which is now a five-part escalating series of commands, each louder than the last, and each addressed to a more distant "hearer."

6.   Now note that when this escalating series of imagined sounds returns to earth, the sounds have become words, specifically the words: "Now the King drinks to Hamlet." The words are now (retroactively) revealed as the "text" that the kettle was initially told to "speak" to the trumpet, and the trumpet to the cannons. Thus, as your build rises in volume and projected intensity, it also develops a semantic content: A "speech" grows out of it. Your overall build, we now see, is not merely toward greater volume and projection, but also toward intellectual complexity. Its culmination involves suggestions of divinity (God's voice) and ritualized language. From a simple percussive sound (the kettle), your speech grows into a thundering chorus, divinely sanctioning your behavior.

Although the words can be played in any number of ways, play Claudius's "Now the King drinks to Hamlet" as a thundering chorus, a sound that has built up on this five-part escalating series and has now reached heroic proportions.

Since "Now the King drinks to Hamlet" *tops* the build prior, give a rising inflection to the word "earth," which sets it up.

Use these heroic proportions and building, rising intensities to incite reckless revelry among all your hearers, as you did at the very beginning of this lesson.

IMAGE: A straight build is like a ladder, with each step equidistant from the ones around it. Imagine, with this speech, that you are going up a five-step ladder, one step at a time, saying "Give me the cups" on the first step, and going a step farther up the ladder with each of your directives. Then, imagine you ascend to the top platform (the "sixth step") on "Now the King drinks to Hamlet."

Give the speech with this image in mind. Let the image replace your partner's speaking the numbers aloud if he or she has continued doing so.

7.   Complete the speech with "Come, begin." This is not part of the build, however. Now you may speak quietly, gently: not to cannoneers without or to the heavens high above, but to Hamlet and Laertes, who are right at hand. Make the line intimate, confidential, welcoming — as if you were now nursing these very creatures you have just incited into a drunken recklessness.

In the ladder image, imagine that you have now returned to the first step for this last line. Give the whole speech.

8.   Try it again, and this time imagine that, on the last line, you magically appear not on the first step but on the floor — below the first step.

Take the last syllable of the speech (the "gin" of "Come, begin") as *low* on the pitch range as you can manage.

Go up and then down the ladder, "by the numbers." Remember to use rising inflections, particularly at the ends of the straight building lines (2) through (5):

> (6) "Now, the King drinks to Hamlet!"
>   (5) The heaven to earth: ↗
>   (4) The cannon to the heavens, ↗
>   (3) The trumpet to the cannoneer without, ↗
> (2) And let the kettle to the trumpet speak, ↗
(1) Give me the cups.

>   (7) Come, begin. ↘

9.   Do the speech once more, taking cups (you can mime this) in each hand after "Give me the cups," and drinking deeply from one of them after ". . . drinks to Hamlet."

Remember to play to the varying locales (with their varying distances) as you address the cupbearer, the separate (imaginary) musicians and cannoneers and heavenly voices, and the nearby Hamlet and Laertes. And remember to link your building lines with rising inflections until you come to the last line, which you may conclude with a falling inflection.

Practice the speech several times in varying situations. Begin it seated, then stand, then stroll. Play it while wearing a (real or imaginary) heavy cape. A tuxedo. A dress. Make the "cups" (real or imaginary) beer steins. Champagne glasses. Bowls. Carry a walking stick or scepter (and accept only one cup).

In every case, deliver a straight build of the numbered lines (1) through (6), with each line developing a higher intensity than the last. Drop line (7) out of the build altogether.

Remember that this is just an exercise, not a mandatory (or even suggested) reading for Claudius's speech. But it should make clear some fundamental principles.

A straight build — when the words support it and the actor is using it to play toward a goal, such as to stimulate blind revelry — creates a steadily rising interest, an excitement, in the hearers. This means it is an effective tactic in arousing other characters — and in transporting an audience. Momentum, the steady escalation of intensity, is always moving and exciting: frightening, thrilling, enwrapping. In a word, it is *momentous*.

Builds encapsulate action. A speech that is simply laid out on a table or a canvas is merely passive language, decorative. A speech that is built, on the other hand, is a speech that acts; it is a speech act, propelling other characters into action, and conveying the dramatic force of the dialogue right to the audience through empathy and vicarious experiencing.

All good dramatic dialogue, and certainly all Shakespearean dialogue, must be built from the ground up, not just recited off the page.

SUMMARY OF LESSON 7

All dramatic dialogue is built, often quite carefully. Speeches are not individual lines just strung together in random order. They are constructed in logical order so as to establish a strong foundation, and to achieve active, often thrilling, momentum. A "straight build" within a speech is a series of ideas (words, phrases, or clauses) that develops an increasing importance as it goes along, and that requires a steadily escalating intensity of delivery. The ability to build such a speech in a straightforward manner is a very basic acting skill (particularly in Shakespeare) that should be practiced and learned; all sorts of variations can be developed subsequently.

The Nature and Structure of Builds

Henry V concludes his "Once more into the breach" speech (Exercise 3-4) with this rallying cry:

> The game's afoot:
> Follow your spirit, and upon this charge
> Cry God for Harry, England, and Saint George!

With that charge his army plunges into the breach of the French castle wall — to their honor or their death.

Why are Henry's words — "Harry" (meaning himself; Harry is Henry's nickname), "England," and "St. George" — given in that particular order? Try them another way:

> Follow your spirit, and upon this charge
> Cry God for England, Saint George, and Harry!

There's a metrical and an assonance problem, of course, so let's change that to:

> Follow your spirit, and on this command
> Cry God for Harry, Saint George, and England!

or

> Cry God for Saint George, Harry, and England!

It still doesn't work. Shakespeare's arrangement is (naturally) the best, because it is a logical *ascension:* Harry is but a man, England is a country, and Saint George is a patron saint. The man is under the protection of the country, the country under the protection of the saint. Harry, England, and St. George describe an ascending list of powers, each greater than the last.

Also, "George" sounds a lot like "Charge!" and by ending the speech with this name, the language evolves to action; the speech act becomes literal.

In simpler language, this ascension is a build. And builds are what the theatre is made of. The build, in other words, is not merely an acting technique, it is a fundamental structure of drama.

AN ASCENDING SERIES OF ACTIONS

Basically, a build is an ascending series of actions. Ascending in what way? Ordinarily, ascending in intensity of one form or another. This is a life-truth, not just a theatre-truth.

Consider a quarrel between two persons. Generally, whether we're talking about a quarrel on the playground, or in the boardroom, or in the divorce court, the quarrel's individual arguments, no matter how repetitive in content, are not repetitive in expression or intensity: They escalate, and the quarrel grows in fury:

JACK: You will.

JILL: I won't.

JACK: You will!

JILL: I won't!

JACK: YOU WILL!

JILL: I WON'T!!

Every time Jill repeats "I won't," she is tacitly admitting that her earlier speech didn't stop Jack from insisting, so she has to try "harder" this time. The escalation, particularly when the content is unvarying, is simply a matter of each character "trying harder" each time.

Shakespeare rather whimsically describes seven discrete steps of such "trying harder" in *As You Like It*:

TOUCHSTONE: I did dislike the cut of a certain courtier's beard. He sent me word, if I said his beard was not cut well, he was in the mind it was: this is called the Retort Courteous. If I sent him word again it was not well cut, he would send me word he cut it to please himself: this is called the Quip Modest. If again, it was not well cut, he disabled my judgment: this is called the Reply Churlish. If again, it was not well cut, he would answer I spake not true: this is called the Reproof Valiant. If again, it was not well cut, he would say I lie: this is called the Countercheck Quarrelsome: and so to the Lie Circumstantial and the Lie Direct."

Touchstone's line reflects a natural escalation of intensity that the actor might well echo in the speech. Try reading the speech aloud, and see if your natural reading doesn't escalate with the seven steps of the quarrel.

Touchstone follows his speech with a snappy condensation of its main steps, simply naming and numbering the degrees he has already described. The mere escalating and enumerated list, when built naturally by the actor, packs a terrific dramaturgical punch, which is then capped by a whimsical observation:

> TOUCHSTONE: I will name you the degrees. The first, the Retort Courteous; the second, the Quip Modest; the third, the Reply Churlish; the fourth, the Reproof Valiant; the fifth, the Countercheck Quarrelsome; the sixth, the Lie with Circumstance; the seventh, the Lie Direct. All these you may avoid but the Lie Direct, and you may avoid that too, with an If. Your If is your only peacemaker. Much virtue in If.

Notice the structure of this speech; read it aloud also. The speech builds quite steadily up to "the seventh, the Lie Direct"; the use of the seven ordinal numbers intensifies the measured regularity of the escalation. It's a direct mathematical progression (remember your partner's "numbering" of Claudius's commands in the previous lesson).

And then the speech turns on an observation: that you can avoid the Lie Direct, and the whole seven-step quarrel for that matter, with the "peacemaker" word "If." *The observation is not itself part of the build, but it is set up by the build.* As in the previous lesson, we might again think of the build as a ladder, with the ladder leading to a platform. When you climb the ladder (when you go up the seven steps), you get to stand on the platform and deliver your observation. The observation then does not need to build in intensity; indeed, while standing on your platform, you have the luxury of whispering, of pausing, of wrinkling your nose. You have achieved your platform; now you can *use* it. You can also enjoy it.

Builds call attention to your right to speak. They establish that you're not rambling about, but that you're going somewhere; that you have focused and forward-thinking energy. As such, they set up the speeches that follow.

Why? Because builds convey purpose and intention. Builds make clear that you care, that you are "trying harder." Builds make clear that you want to succeed, that you are pursuing victories, and that you will keep building until you get what you came for — whether that's someone's attention or someone's support or someone's defeat — or until you crack. Builds are simply the *structure of action,* for anyone seriously committed to pursuing an action.

BUILDS IN DRAMA

Builds are essential to drama as a whole. Plays themselves build. In a tragedy, the author builds toward what Aristotle identified as developing terror (of menacing events) and pity (for the characters caught in a tragic conflict). In a comedy, the author builds an awkward situation to hilarious conclusions. Rarely is a tragedy deeply moving, or a comedy wickedly funny, in the first scenes; the peak impact of every great play is invariably in its last half, or even its last scene. Witness the devastating climaxes of *Hamlet* and *King Lear,* and the side-splitting hysterics of the "Pyramus and Thisby" and "Mammamouchi" playlets that conclude, respectively, *A Midsummer Night's*

Dream and Molière's *The Bourgeois Gentleman*.[6] And, as a play must build, so must the individual moments and performances in the play.

Plays tend to move from quiet exposition, where the characters are introduced, often in a reasonably unperturbed state, to an incitement of conflict, then to intensified struggle, and then, just at or near the breaking point, to crisis and climax. This is the normal structure of drama, and it is both lifelike and theatrical; that is to say, (1) life's conflicts tend to escalate until someone (or something) breaks, and (2) *we tend to want to watch* situations that are intensifying more than situations that are winding down. As to the theatricality of escalation, understand that we are fascinated with a volcano about to blow, a fire threatening to engulf a town, a political candidate being grilled at a press conference, a bank robbery in process, a little girl who has fallen down a well shaft. We have little interest in the mop-up operations that follow these "dramatic" events. Call this morbid curiosity or human nature, it is the basis for news programs and dramatic writing. We like the vicarious flirtation with danger; we like the rising excitement of watching—from a safe distance—approaching unnamables.

The quickening heartbeats that greeted the masterful development of Sophocles's *Oedipus Tyrannos,* in which Oedipus comes closer and closer to his horrific truth, is a universal model for the enormous emotional force of carefully escalated dramatic events. So even in plays that seem so chary of escalation and climax as Chekhov's *Three Sisters,* a play that treats an apparently hopeless situation for all of its characters, one must sense underneath the accelerated pulse of "trying harder" from everyone on stage. Indeed, it's that rising pulse, against the stolidly unyielding social situation, that gives *Three Sisters* its legendary poignancy.

Thus plays build because life does—purposeful life, anyway—and because it is more exciting to watch ascending actions than descending ones.

THE ACTOR AND THE BUILD

The actor, as we saw, must learn to build parts, not merely to spill them out as a series of lines, movements, actions, and expressions. Nevertheless, there's a tendency for actors to distrust builds; they may seem mechanical or forced when imposed by a director, and they may seem contrived techniques, applicable only to the theatre.

I hope the preceding discussion has ameliorated some of these concerns, particularly the concern that builds are contrived. They are natural—but then again, drama is, at bottom, contrived: It is contrived by a playwright.

---

[6]There are, of course, exceptions. The "gulling scene" in *Much Ado About Nothing,* usually the production's most comic episode, occurs less than halfway through—but then that play becomes more of a tragedy than a comedy for the next two acts. When a play "peaks too early," and this is sometimes argued about Shakespeare's *The Merchant of Venice* and *The Winter's Tale,* the directors and actors must work to avoid a premature climax to the audience's involvement.

The late actor Laurence Olivier (1907–1989), whose mastery of dramatic builds has been unparalleled in our century, has wonderfully described his own frustration at the builds seemingly demanded by the title role of *Henry V,* one of the most rhetorically controlled plays ever written:

> Rehearsals began, and . . . I started by completely undercutting Henry. . . . I fought against the heroism by flattening and getting underneath the lines; no banner waving for me. "God for Harry! England and Saint George!" was not going to ring out across the footlights as on a poor night at a third-division *Gang Show.* . . . The night scene really was a night scene; my fellow actors were going to have no difficulty sleeping—and if I had played it that way, the audience, I'm sure, would have joined them.

> One morning [director] Tyrone Guthrie spoke. . . . "Larry . . . let's have it properly."
> "Properly?"
> "Properly."
> "Tony, I am doing it properly."
> "Like this . . . this is how I want it."

> He went into "This day is called the Feast of Crispian. . . ," and as he built up toward the end, he vocally began to climb a ladder. Heroics, bloody heroics. . . . He stopped and looked at me.

> "That's the way to do it."
> "Like that?"
> "Like that."
> "Tony. . . ?"
> "If you don't do it like that and enjoy doing it like that, you just won't carry the audience with you."

> He was right. He knew. . . . He was no actor, but he pointed me in the direction I had fought against, and he was right.

> I worked on the great arias, molded and fashioned them to me, and then from Guthrie's launch pad, took off. I was heroic—no one could have been more so—but I was truthful, I was not showing off; I played the man like a trumpet as clearly and truthfully as I knew how.[7]

Olivier's Build

Here is Olivier's description, with his own self-directions, of the build that went into his ensuing "Once more unto the breach" speech from *Henry V,* with which this chapter begins:

> Once more unto the breach, dear friends, once more:
> Or close the wall up with our English dead!
> [*Confident, encouraging, steady; lead them and prepare them.*]

---

[7]Laurence Olivier, *On Acting,* Copyright © 1986 by Wheelshare, Ltd. Reprinted by permission of Simon and Schuster, Inc. pp. 95–96.

In peace there's nothing so becomes a man
As modest stillness and humility;
[*Hold them; let the words work.*]

But when the blast of war blows in our ears,
Then imitate the action of the tiger;
[*Begin to feel that tingle in the base of the stomach; prepare, get ready for a change of gear.*]

Stiffen the sinews, summon up the blood,
Disguise fair nature with hard-favour'd rage;
[*Stay in control but begin to feel the excitement. Then change the intonation.*]

Then lend the eye a terrible aspect;
Let it pry through the portage of the head
Like the brass cannon; let the brow o'erwhelm it
As fearfully as doth a galled rock
O'erhang and jutty his confounded base,
[*Up a gear and beginning to move, the words blazing in front of you.*]

Swill'd with the wild and wasteful ocean.
[*"Swill'd"*]

Now set the teeth and stretch the nostril wide,
Hold hard the breath and bend up every spirit
To his full height! . . .
[*Now we're really motoring, climbing vocally but in complete control. The politician and the hero.*]

. . . On, on, you noble English,
[*Patriotism*]

Whose blood is fet from fathers of war-proof!
Fathers that like so many Alexanders
[*Change the tune to as natural a one as is humanly possible.*]

Have in these parts from morn till even fought,
And sheath'd their swords for lack of argument.
Dishonor not your mothers; now attest,
That those whom you called fathers did beget you!
[*Now take them with you; they want to come; climb the ladder.*]

Be copy now to men of grosser blood
And teach them how to war! . . .
[*Now, like any good politician, speak to them collectively in such a way that they think you are speaking to them individually.*]

. . . And you, good yeomen,
Whose limbs were made in England, show us here
The mettle of your pasture. Let us swear
That you are worth your breeding; which I doubt not,
[*Got them . . . now hold them. Remember, never give them everything.*]

For there is none of you so mean and base
That hath not noble lustre in your eyes.
I see you stand like greyhounds in the slips,
[*Moving up the ladder, pace, excitement, almost flying.*]
Straining upon the start. The game's afoot!
[*NOW LET GO.*]
Follow your spirit; and upon this charge
Cry . . .
[*We're there.*]
. . . God for Harry! England and Saint George!
[*Take off.*][8]

Of course, this is one of the most famous single speeches of twentieth-century performance. When Olivier gave it on tour in England during the darker days of World War II, it (and he) became a national treasure. Olivier is not boasting when he says "I don't think we could have won the war without 'Once more into the breach . . .' somewhere in our soldier's hearts."[9]

We are none of us Oliviers, of course, and Olivier's builds were his own, not Guthries, and not ours. Many theatregoers have their own favorite actors in this part, and Kenneth Branagh was seen by many to have surpassed Lord Larry in his 1989 film of the same play. We will all find our own ways to play this and other speeches, but the understanding that a speech (and role) must be built from exposition to excitement, not merely assembled as a sum of separate and equal parts, should be the clear and present understanding of Lesson 8.

SUMMARY OF LESSON 8

The build is not merely an acting technique, it is a fundamental structure of drama — fundamental to speeches and to entire plays. Because it is so naturally and so obviously "dramatic," actors — including some of the greatest actors — are often shy of its power and embarrassed by its potent theatricality. They mustn't be. A build is nothing more than an ascending series of actions, each more focused and intense than the last. It is true to life, as it is brilliantly theatrical. Actors should learn to master builds in performance, as Laurence Olivier did in *Henry V*.

[8] Olivier, *On Acting*, pp. 98–100.
[9] Olivier, *On Acting*, pp. 102–103.

L E S S O N   9

Platforms, Cutbacks, and Interpretation

In my beginning textbook, *Acting One*,[10] there is an exercise on building the days of the week. It goes: "I detest Monday, Tuesday, Wednesday, Thursday, Friday, Saturday, and Sunday." This is an easy build to practice, since the memorization is simple and the build straight and direct. The goal is to make every day sound a little worse than the one before, but to keep the build from being completely predictable. There is also a companion exercise: "I adore Monday, Tuesday, . . ." and so on. Both of these make good warm-ups for Lesson 8, but they are too simple themselves to be fully dramatic.

In *Othello,* Shakespeare creates a more complex days-of-the-week build. This is Desdemona's plea to Othello, asking him to meet with and forgive his erring lieutenant, Cassio. Desdemona tries to suggest a date and time for this meeting.

▗▚▞▚▞▚▖ EXERCISE 9-1

> DESDEMONA: Why then, tomorrow night, on Tuesday morn,
> On Tuesday noon, or night, on Wednesday morn,
> I prithee name the time, but let it not
> Exceed three days.

Memorize and deliver this speech to someone who will be playing Othello.

Build each of the five proposed "appointment times," making each more attractive than its predecessors. Then make a sixth step with your final plea to "name the time."

---

[10] (Mountain View, Ca.: Mayfield: 1984), p. 196. This is Exercise 24-4 in that book.

It may help to have a coach call out at appropriate moments imaginary numbers for each step, such as those given below in parentheses. This will help the build escalate in a steady fashion.

Why then . . .
("one") tomorrow night . . .
("two") on Tuesday morn . . . ?
("three") on Tuesday noon!
("four") or NIGHT!
("five") on *Wednesday morn*!
I prithee . . .
("six") *NAME THE TIME* . . .
but let it not exceed three days.

Make clear, as you do this, that Othello rejects tomorrow night, and Tuesday morn, and Tuesday noon, and Tuesday night, and even Wednesday morn. *But you keep trying anyway*. Try to make Othello agree at *each* step, including the first, and make each step more attractive to him than the last. In your mind, make up the subtext for each separate step of the ladder:

("one") Come on, meet him tomorrow night, OK?

("two") Well, tomorrow's probably too early, but then on Tuesday morning, after breakfast, OK? when you're rested . . .

("three") Hey, better yet! . . . later in the day, after lunch, that would be better, OK?

("four") No? Well, at *night* then; of course, that's the best time for reconciliations; listen, we'll have a drink together and . . .

("five") Oh hell, sure! Take another day on it, but *Wednesday* for certain! Yes?

("six") All right, honey, *YOU* decide . . .

(then . . .)   but . . .

It's important, in playing a build, not to play "I'm playing a build." Desdemona doesn't want to build, she wants to *win*. So you want to win at step one. You don't, so you go on to step two. Then step three, and so forth. You don't *want* to go to steps two, three, four, and five, but you *have* to because you want to get the appointment fixed, and there's no other way to do it.

PLATFORMS

With Desdemona's speech, your build is not as absolutely straight as in the "I detest Monday, Tuesday, . . ." exercise because it reaches a climax on step six ("name the time") and seems to go into another key altogether on the following step ("but let it not exceed . . .").

We may call that climax a **platform**. Like the platform at the top of a ladder, it's level ground and you can't go any higher, but from it you have a commanding view. Claudius reaches a platform on "King drinks to Hamlet," and from there he can look benignly around (at his shivering courtiers) and say quite calmly, "Come, begin."

A platform enables you to *cut back*. Obviously, you cannot escalate your intensity indefinitely; after a short time this would both overtax your ability and exhaust the audience. Nor can you simply sustain high-energy dramatics at a peak level without engaging in monotonous shouting. So the cutback is an essential feature of a build. It gives you a second start. It's somewhat like the momentary slowing you experience as you shift from second to third gear. If you look back at the Olivier "Once more into the breach" speech, you can define numerous cutbacks.

Reaching a platform, then, allows you both to conclude your build, and to shift ground and start a *new* ladder. And you can start at the bottom rung—the quietest step—of that new ladder.

As Desdemona, reach a peak intensity on "name the time." With this line—your top step—you are no longer asking for a fixed date but a general understanding: "Just agree to meet with Cassio, and you can name the time yourself!" It's an offer to compromise, and it also says "I quit, I'm giving up climbing this ladder, I'm through proposing appointment times." This step tops the first five, but it also puts a cap on the build; it announces that the build is over.

Now, on your platform atop this ladder you've climbed, you have Othello's full attention. You've softened his resistance and, although you haven't yet won, you've sensed the possibility of compromise. Now, from the safety of your platform, you can afford to tease him a little.

but . . . let it not exceed three days.

This is the first step of a *new* ladder, erected on the platform you've already built. You can use your newfound "height" to try something different.

Play this speech several times, and try the last line, the cutback line, many different ways. Use it to win (to get a nod of agreement from your Othello) with any tactic you can think of. Coax him. Charm him. Seduce him. Taunt him. Have *fun* up there. The play is a tragedy, but Desdemona doesn't know that yet, so neither should you. Indeed, one of the most tragic things about *Othello* is that the more innocently seductive Desdemona becomes, the more Othello (falsely) believes she is evil.

▚▞▚▞ EXERCISE 9-2

Here's a pleasant variation:

CAPULET: Well, Wednesday is too soon,
O' Thursday let it be: o' Thursday, tell her,
She shall be married to this noble earl.

(*Romeo and Juliet*, III.iv.19–21)

This is just a three-step platform, with a repetition ("Thursday") that gets you to the top, where you announce your daughter's marriage to the man you've chosen. Since the marriage is against her will (your daughter is Juliet and you're marrying her to Count Paris), you need all the platform you can get! So take it and use it.

Make the top step of this speech "She shall be married," and, secure on that platform, cut back severely for an admiring and reverential ". . . this noble earl."

EXERCISE 9-3

HAMLET: Bloody, bawdy villain!
Remorseless, treacherous, lecherous, kindless villain!
O, vengeance!
Why, what an ass am I!

This build is so famous and so theatrical that some critics believe "O vengeance" was not written by Shakespeare, but was added to the text during rehearsal by some scenery-chewing actor! (There is, in fact, evidence supporting this conjecture.[11])

The situation here is meta-theatrical; that is, it's a dramatization of a dramatization. Hamlet has just watched a professional actor demonstrate his skill by delivering a fiery monologue from what we suppose is an Elizabethan revenge play. Now, left alone, Hamlet tries to "act" in the manner of the professional actor. Hamlet, therefore, is aware of his own histrionics. In expressing his rage at Claudius (the "kindless villain"), Hamlet tries to do so in the fashion of a professional actor. Hamlet then accounts himself a failure ("what an ass am I"), not because he's a bad actor but because he's acting, not doing. He's speaking the words of revenge — but not "revenging." The entire speech (it's the "Hecuba soliloquy," beginning "Now I am alone/O, what a rogue and peasant slave am I") bears detailed study, but this acting exercise can be approached through the given excerpt.

Try the exercise. Give it a three-part build, with each of the first three lines being a step apiece, with the mighty "O vengeance" at the top.

Build also *within* each step, particularly concentrating on the lists of negative adjectives in the first two lines. First, build the two alliterative adjectives of line one (that is, make "bawdy" more disgusting than "bloody"); then, going beyond this level, build up the four assonant adjectives of line

---

[11]"O Vengeance" is in the Folio version, but not in the earlier Second ("Good") Quarto, and the current editor of the Arden Shakespeare version of the play (English professor Harold Jenkins) deletes it from the text as having "all the marks of an actor's addition." My own opinion is that it was indeed added by an actor — an actor named William Shakespeare.

two: (remorseless! treacherous!! lecherous!!! KINDLESS!!!!). Now, on top of these builds, cut loose with your final self-call to action: "O vengeance!"

"Kindless" might seem a rather weak word to be used as the top step here. Did Shakespeare make a mistake? When you suspect Shakespeare erred, look again; chances are pretty good Shakespeare knows something you don't. In this case, "kindless" means "unkind," of course, but it also means "childless" or "kinless" — "without a family," even "unnatural." Claudius is "kinless" because he has killed his only brother and alienated his only nephew; he has no kin. He can also no longer claim Hamlet is "my cousin and my son," which claim Hamlet had earlier only answered enigmatically: "A little more than kin, and less than kind."[12] Now Hamlet knows that Claudius is fully "kindless," which is, we see, several levels more wretched than merely "treacherous."

The audience won't, on its own, follow the close etymological reasoning here (although a reading audience may), but if the actor makes "kindless" build on top of "treacherous," the audience will think — for a split second at least, which is all the time they will have — about these other meanings of "kindless." The reading that builds these words will deepen the speech (and the play) that the audience ultimately perceives.

Go all out on this build; build your ladder to the sky. Since Hamlet is trying to imitate a melodramatic actor anyway, do what he does: Imitate a melodramatic actor! Go ahead, tear the scenery on "O vengeance"; after all, Hamlet's point, soon to be made, is something on the order that "no amount of hammy hollering or empty posturing is going to earn me my revenge." The more you can carry on here, the better you can repudiate the act of carrying on in the next lines.

Now, on the platform you have built with the first three lines, recognize its shaky legs, its hollow (melodramatic) foundation. In this spirit, tell us (or yourself): "Why, what an ass am I." This is one of the most famous cutbacks in drama.

As with Desdemona's line, have fun with it. Make it a ridiculous joke. Laugh your head off. Whisper. Use a clown voice. Back the line into the end of "vengeance" so the build tops halfway through the last syllable of that word and it sounds something like:

VENNNNNN . . . GENNNNSSSWhy what an ass am I?

This is a build that pokes fun at building. As you can see, it's very difficult to parody Shakespeare — he got there first.

---

[12] The syntax indicates, and most critical opinion argues, that Hamlet is referring to himself in this line. I, however, along with several other critics, believe Shakespeare means Hamlet to refer to Claudius. This is not the place to argue the point except to say that interpretation is always a matter of informed opinion. *You* the actor have every right (indeed, I feel you have the obligation) to study the actual text, examine previously considered opinions and interpretations, and come up with your own analysis and decision.

▚▞▚▞ EXERCISE 9-4

Lists are ordinarily built upward, which is to say as escalations. Look at this one:

PETRUCHIO: Nay, look not big, nor stamp, nor stare, nor fret;
I will be master of what is mine own.
She is my goods, my chattels; she is my house,
My household stuff, my field, my barn,
My horse, my ox, my ass, my anything.

Memorize it.

In this speech from *The Taming of the Shrew*, Petruchio is telling Katherine, and the crowd around her, that he intends to treat her as property. Whether he's a hero or a villain might depend on what century you live in and what your gender is, but let's look at the technical aspects of the speech first. Later in the exercise we can decide just how to play the character.

There are two lists here. The first is a list of verbs, delivered to Katherine ("look not big," and so on) and reaching to a conclusion ("I will be master of what is mine own"). Then there is a list of nouns, by which Petruchio tells the household what he considers a wife to be ("my household stuff, . . . my horse, my ox," and so on).

Actually, the second list is subdivided; there is a sublist of plural nouns (goods, chattels) and one of singular nouns (house, stuff, ox). There's a useful cutback opportunity between these sublists, signified by this change in number (from plural to singular).

Shakespeare helps you out in many ways to build these lists and sublists. "Fret" is clearly the best word to cap the first list; it has an uncluttered consonant ending (it's also a wonderfully *unusual* word that's used elsewhere in the play to refer to violin frets smashed over somebody's head), and it can be given a ringing percussive force—with an abrupt terminal *t* to end the first build.

The ten nouns by which Petruchio metaphorically defines Katherine could be a bit daunting to build without a cutback, so Shakespeare divides them into the two sublists.

The two plural nouns build as "chattels" tops "goods" by virtue of its curiously comic sound (a cross between "rattles" and "chatter").

The eight single nouns build in their abusiveness. Each is (in some sense) shabbier than the last, so as to degrade Katherine by degrees, using progressive steps toward her "taming." One's "house" is ordinarily one's most valuable possession, the household "stuff" somewhat less so. Then Petruchio takes us out to the "field," then to the "barn," and then into the barn to see the barn animals, from the smartest ("horse") to the dumbest ("ass"). Of course, "ass" also has a sexual connotation. Katherine's worth is estimated at the level of the grossest animal in the barnyard, and she is a crude sexual object as well. Petruchio concludes the downward build with the all-inclusive "my anything," which tops the previous steps by encompassing them—and everything else. The three syllables of "anything" puts a fulsome cap on a list that has been, since "stuff," single-syllabled.

There are technical names for the rhetorical devices employed here. The sequence of phrases beginning with "my" constitute **anaphora,** which are adjacent phrases beginning identically. Those phrases that are the same length ("my horse, my ox, my ass") are called **isocolon,** adjacent phrases of the same length. These writing schemes, which can also be found in natural speech, intensify the build by giving it a structural regularity; ladders are easier to climb when the steps are evenly spaced and all the same size. When the three-syllable "my anything" bursts out of the preceding two-syllable isocolons, it caps a steady build still held together by anaphoras. The terms are not important, however; what *is* important is capturing the rhythmic, structural energy of the text. A fuller discussion of these rhetorical devices is given in Lesson 18.

INTERPRETATION

Now try Petruchio's speech, but try it *two ways,* each yielding a different interpretation of his character.

1.   Play it joyously: "I am going to make this woman mine, and she will love me for it; enthusiasm and sexual energy are such life-giving forces that they outweigh considerations of sexual fairness and shared relationships." Build the speech *up,* so as to infect your hearers with your unstoppable excitement.

2.   Play it viciously: "I will destroy this person; I will annihilate her will; I will make her my slave forever." Build the speech *down,* so as to make oppressively clear to all comers that there is no way you can be stopped.

The first (joyous) interpretation is, more or less, the conventional one of our midcentury. It is in this general spectrum that we are likely to see the play today, and it is almost certainly the basic interpretation of Shakespeare's own time (although we can never be absolutely certain). However, the second (vicious) interpretation is sometimes broached in the current theatre. Author/director Charles Marowitz has produced a shortened adaptation of the play (called simply *Shrew*) that approaches the scenes in an absolutely terrifying manner. Katherine leaves the stage virtually dehumanized. Marowitz's production makes the play a scathing attack on sexism. When Petruchio sodomizes Katherine in this production's intense climax, we nervously remember his earlier boast that she is "my ass, my anything."

SUMMARY OF LESSON 9

Builds do not go on forever; they are punctuated by cutbacks and topped off by platforms. The goal of this lesson is to move fluidly through a build, recognizing (and using) the cutbacks, and reaching (and exploiting) the platforms.

L E S S O N   1 0

Shared Builds

In *Acting One,* there is a simple building exercise where two actors exchange repetitive but contradictory commands:

A: Be quiet.

B: You be quiet.

A: No, you be quiet!

B: No, you be quiet!

A: YOU BE QUIET!

B: YOU BE QUIET! . . . and so on

or:

A: Yes.

B: No.

A: Yes!

B: No! . . . and so on

Let's look at the same sort of exchange, Shakespeare-style.

■■■■■ EXERCISE 10-1 THE ARGUMENTATIVE BUILD

LEAR: No.

KENT: Yes.

LEAR: No, I say.

KENT: I say yea.

LEAR: No, no, they would not.

KENT: Yes, they have.

LEAR: By Jupiter, I swear no!

KENT: By Juno, I swear ay!   ["ay" = "aye," meaning "yes."]

With a partner, read this exchange aloud, escalating the argument as you go. Notice how each line contradicts the line previous; try to persuade your partner of the rightness of *your* "yes" or "no" position. Try to end the argument with every line. Try to win the argument.

Notice how you must "top" the previous line in order to win, or to try to win, the argument. How do you top your predecessor? Forcefulness, intensity, and sheer volume are clearly important, but there are also subtler techniques, some of which Shakespeare has built into the text. First, let's look at the scene in context.

King Lear, having suffered ill treatment from Goneril, his eldest daughter, decides to visit his next eldest daughter, Regan. He sends his servant Kent ahead to inform Regan of his impending visit, but when Lear finally arrives, he is astonished to find Kent in the front yard, his legs imprisoned in wooden stocks. Lear asks Kent who has so mistreated him: Kent replies that it was Regan — and Regan's husband, Cornwall. Lear doesn't want to believe this, and questions his servant further.

The expanded dialogue is:

LEAR: What's he that . . . set thee here?

KENT: It is both he and she, your son and daughter.

LEAR: No.

KENT: Yes.

LEAR: No, I say.

KENT: I say yea.

LEAR: No, no, they would not.

KENT: Yes, they have.

LEAR: By Jupiter, I swear no!

KENT: By Juno, I swear ay!

LEAR: They durst not do't!
They could not, would not do't! 'Tis worse than murder
To do upon respect such violent outrage!

Look at the four contradictory paired exchanges, with an eye to how Shakespeare creates the "topping" escalation.

   I. LEAR: No.
       KENT: Yes.

This is a simple contradiction: a basic statement of opposition.

   II. LEAR: No, I say.
       KENT: I say yea.

A restatement and elaboration of the opposition, one notch up. Both speakers have moved from one syllable to three, both have added a level of self-consciousness of intention: instead of saying "yes" or "no," they are saying *that they are saying* "yes" or "no." They are "meta-stating" their positions.

Kent's meta-stating is more powerful than (and therefore tops) Lear's. While Lear's "No, I say" implies something like "I, the King in all his dignity and wisdom, say no," Kent's "I say yea" implies "I, the one person here who actually saw what happened, say yes!" Royal authority may have been on Lear's side a few weeks ago, but Kent's eye-witness factual testimony now rules the day.

Kent tops Lear in three other ways as well:

1. by choosing a synonym for yes ("yea"), whereas Lear has merely repeated his "no"

2. by employing rhyme ("say" and "yea"), where Lear has remained unversed

3. by moving the stress from the first to the last (and most contradictory) syllable

The synonym shows that Kent is cleverer than Lear; the rhyme shows that he is cuter, funnier, more confident (as one can be when one has the facts on his side, as Kent does), and the emphasis on the last syllable gives him the stronger "parting" shot. Lear will have to try harder!

III.   LEAR: No, no, they would not.
       KENT: Yes, they have.

Lear repeats his claim with emphasis, but his repetition of "no" is only redundant; an empty **epizeuxis,** or simple repetition of a word or phrase.

Lear provides no elaboration or development because he has none. Kent undercuts Lear by demonstrating the *physical* fact: by simply pointing to the reality of the stocks at the moment he says "have." Whereas Lear has escalated his argument from a one-syllable line to a three-syllable, and now a five-syllable one, Kent can hold to the three-syllable retort this time: It is as if to say, "No number of words can refute the reality of these stocks." If Kent takes the same amount of time for his three syllables as Lear does for his five (taking, for example, a double beat on both "yes" and "have"), the "top" will be very clearly established.

LEAR: No, no, they would not.
KENT: *Yessss,* they *haaaave*!.

IV.   LEAR: By Jupiter, I swear no.
      KENT: By Juno, I swear aye.

Lear has again added two syllables, but still little elaboration, to his build (although he has added the implication of divine support, and moved to a final syllable stress). Kent matches his calling on divinity and stressing the final syllable, and surpasses Lear's rhetoric by cutting out a syllable (and thereby simplifying his argument). Kent now uses yet another synonym for "yes" ("aye") and another rhyme (or, technically, identity, with the homonyms "I" and "aye"), with which he concludes his appeal. And while Jupiter may be the king of the Gods, Juno—Jupiter's queen—is certainly more than a match for her husband, and the storminess of their marriage is an apt indication of the violence of this argument. Kent's "Juno" also tops Lear's "Jupiter" by incorporating and co-opting the syllables "Ju" of Lear's "Jupiter" and the "no" of Lear's conclusion, making Lear's line simply a point of departure. Thus Kent's retort essentially mocks Lear's swearing by rearranging and condensing Lear's own syllables:

LEAR: By Ju-piter, I swear no.
KENT: By Ju-no, I swear I!

("Ju-no" also sounds enough like "you know" to imply the notion to Lear: "You know I'm telling the truth," which in fact Lear does know, in his heart of hearts.)

Finally, Kent's line completes an image, for by bringing Juno into the argument, Kent forces Lear to see not just a king, but a tyrannical king and queen—that is, Cornwall and Regan, the very subjects of this current inquiry!

Using these understandings, play the dialogue between Lear and Kent, seeking to make each character build an argument until it explodes in Lear's outburst:

LEAR: They durst not do't!
Would not, could not do't!

Trade parts; both partners should play each role. Make no effort to create the "characters" of a king or messenger (Kent, an Earl, is actually in disguise during this scene), and, in this exercise, do not be concerned with either character's age or sex. Pay attention only to each character's drive to "win" the debate, the rhetorical tactics and builds that each employs, and the overall escalation of the dialogue.

This scene is a **shared build**. The building of individual speeches, with which we have mainly been concerned up to this point, is now expanded to the notion of building stage dialogue—dialogue that builds to an explosion. Most scenes, in and out of Shakespeare, require such shared builds—simply because most dramatic scenes build in intensity during the course of a play.

But builds are not only argumentative. Builds can be constructed in a complementary way just as easily.

◄▨◢▨◣▨► EXERCISE 10-2 THE COMPLEMENTARY BUILD

LYSANDER: Ay me! for aught I that ever I could read,
Could ever hear by tale or history,
The course of true love never did run smooth;
But, either it was different in blood—
HERMIA: O cross! Too high to be enthralled to low.
LYSANDER: Or else misgraffed in respect of years,—

HERMIA: O spite! too old to be engaged to young.

LYSANDER: Or else it stood upon the choice of friends, —

HERMIA: O hell! to choose love by another's eyes.

LYSANDER: Or, if there were a sympathy in choice,
War, death, or sickness did lay siege to it . . .

Read this with a partner; conventionally (but not necessarily) with a man reading Lysander and a woman Hermia.

The situation takes a little understanding. This is the opening private dialogue between two lovers in *A Midsummer Night's Dream*. Their love is endangered by Hermia's father's disapproval, which prompts Lysander to complain that throughout history "the course of true love never did run smooth," and that lovers always seem to run into obstacles. Then he and Hermia share examples of such obstacles to true love: racial differences ("different in blood"), social class ("too high to be enthralled to low"), age differences, the opinions of others, and, lacking these, war, death, and sickness.

The literal, superficial point of this dialogue is that true love is virtually impossible to find, but Shakespeare's more fundamental point is just the opposite for we see that Lysander and Hermia fall more deeply in love, precisely while they exchange these sentiments! The fact that they finish each other's sentences, agree with each other's conclusions, and harmonize with each other's syntax and imagery, *totally overrides the literal meaning of what they are saying*.

Were this dialogue rewritten as a single speech for one character, it would prove a rather bitter statement. As a dialogue for two persons, however, it is an interweaving of language that suggests a meaning quite opposite to its literal sense. The joint statement of inevitable discord "says" discord but "shows" agreement; and the fact that the characters agree (on the inevitability of discord) is far more important than (it even disproves) the point of discord they are so energetically trying to make. Here is a dramatic excerpt where the "sound" of the text is far more important than the literal semantic meaning of the individual lines. Here is also an example of the brilliance of dramaturgy — of dramatic structure — in which the audience's conclusion proves the exact opposite of what is being said to them.

The build of this dialogue, then, is toward the effusion of love rather than the disagreement in the previous exercise. Lear and Kent are trying to win a win-lose game (a "zero-sum" game, social scientists call it), where victory can be obtained only at the capitulation of the other. Lysander and Hermia are seeking to be victors in a win-win game — the game of mutual love — where either both win or neither does. Thus their goal is to top each other's speeches both by way of supporting them in fierce agreement and by stimulating their lover to even greater expressions of passion.

LYSANDER: Ay me! for aught I that ever I could read,
Could ever hear by tale or history,
The course of true love never did run smooth;

This is a prologue. It establishes the grounds for a responsive reading on the theme of "the course of true love never did run smooth."

LYSANDER: But, either it was different in blood—

Lysander's opening gambit. He has no intention of finishing this sentence, but is seeing if Hermia will prove (1) to be in agreement with him and (2) to be up to his level of improvising (in blank verse) on a romantic theme. The use of "either" makes clear this is only the first line of what will be an extended inquiry.

HERMIA: O cross! Too high to be enthralled to low.

She is up to it! Her first two words show Lysander that she will commit passion and energy to this game; her use of "enthralled" shows off a level of vocabulary commensurate to the task. She matches him syllable by syllable; and she is also holding something back in reserve.

In responding to Lysander's single line of verse with a single line of verse of her own (a special case of *isocolon*), Hermia is also broaching a dramatic form known as **stichomythia**. Invented by the ancient Greek playwrights, this is an extended interchange of single lines—no more and no less—of verse dialogue between two characters. Lysander proves up to the gambit.

LYSANDER: Or else misgraffed in respect of years,—

Lysander raises the stakes with "misgraffed," which he pronounces with three syllables to beat out his ten syllables of verse.

HERMIA: O spite! too old to be engaged to young.

Hermia maintains her syntax, raising "cross" to the more potent "spite," and replacing her high/low dichotomy with old/young. She is warming to the game.

LYSANDER: Or else it stood upon the choice of friends,—

Lysander moves into the area of choosing, as his next task is to have Hermia choose him.

HERMIA: O hell! to choose love by another's eyes.

Raising "spite" now to "hell," and taking Lysander's noun, "choice," to the present tense verb, "choose," and bringing "love" back into it—as if to urge Lysander, "Don't choose love by another's eyes, choose me with your own eyes!"

LYSANDER: Or, if there were a sympathy in choice,
War, death, or sickness did lay siege to it . . .

Lysander boils over, unable to contain himself within the ten syllables or the stichomythic pattern. He brings in the great catastrophes, "war, death, or sickness," to lend a violent "siege" of power to his romantic quest.

Play this dialogue with a partner, aiming (quite beneath the literal meaning of the lines) to support your partner's gambits, to entice and stimulate your partner toward mutual excitement, and to stimulate him or her toward a paroxysm of mutual abandon — signalled by an enthusiastic coming together and embrace immediately following "siege to it." The results will be powerful — both romantic and comic in the right situations.

PLAYING SHARED BUILDS

Playing a shared build obviously requires teamwork. If you or your partner should "drop" the build at any point, there's nothing the other person can do to restore it. For example,

LEAR: No.

KENT: Yes!

LEAR: No, I say!!

KENT: I say yea!!!

LEAR: NO, NO, THEY WOULD NOT!!!!

KENT: Uh . . . yes, . . . uh . . . they . . . have . . .

There's simply no way for Lear to continue this build without seeming absolutely pompous and ridiculous. The climax is eliminated. In the same way, if either Lysander or Hermia let down their escalating enthusiasm midway in their exchange, if they indulge in a stagy moment of introspective reflection, the build is shot, and there can be no credibly ecstatic embrace at the appropriate moment. Actors must *feed* each others feelings — each others' ire (in *Lear*) or rapture (in *Dream*) — and that takes both discipline (in preparation) and teamwork (in execution). Some actors, particularly in the British theatre, have made the "feeding" of lines into something of a religion. "What's Horatio's function in *Hamlet*?" a young actor is supposed to have asked Sir John Gielgud. "To feed Hamlet," answered Sir John, "so that next year he can *play* Hamlet." Well, feeding isn't yet a religion, but plays are *built,* not just spun out like so many yards of yarn, and an actor has to learn to be part of the collective building process — in order to perform in the theatre.

That means teamwork. Sharing builds by feeding lines and energy to others, and thus *collectively* building the shape of your scenes.

SUMMARY OF LESSON 10

Shared builds are fundamental to the architecture of plays, to characters rising to emotional climaxes together. There are essentially two kinds of shared builds: (1) *argumentative builds,* in which characters disagree and try to thwart each other's reasoning (win-lose situations); and (2) *complementary builds,* where characters stimulate each other to higher and higher levels of excitement through agreement (win-win situations). Playing shared builds requires teamwork — "feeding" your partner's energy and emotions rather than privately indulging in your own feelings.

Physical Shakespeare

So far, we have been looking at acting Shakespeare primarily as a verbal, or speaking, activity.

This should not be too surprising since Shakespeare is generally considered the greatest master of our (or any) language, and his works are masterpieces of written literature. Speaking the text effectively is always central to any Shakespearean performance.

Also, actors usually begin working on a role through the words of the text — often by reading and memorizing those words — sometimes long before putting those words together with any physical movement or activity. Often directors begin rehearsing a play (or scene) with a read-through of the text, or a period of read-throughs that may last for several days — often while the actors remain seated around a table.

Still, we must remember that Shakespeare's plays are also intensely *physical* works. The plays are composed of *actions,* and the scripts contain, in addition to their celebrated words, equally celebrated physical actions: duels, streetfights, full-stage battles, dances, chases, suicides, beatings, pratfalls; eating, drinking, marching, running, kneeling; persons climbing balconies, lugging corpses, assassinating dictators, picking pockets, stocking servants, piling logs, murdering children, delivering letters, throwing dishes, changing clothes, kissing (jack)asses, fleeing bears, falling into trances, leaping over walls and into graves, and hiding in laundry baskets, under gaberdines, and behind box trees — all while conveying complex ideas in iambic pentameters!

It is no wonder that directors often cite the basic problem of acting as being able to "speak and move at the same time." What is so hard about that, you say? It turns out to be one of the actor's most difficult tasks — at the higher levels of performance. The deeper you get into Shakespeare, or into any well-structured dramatic work, the more profoundly you can see into this serious — albeit seemingly trivial — problem.

Hamlet's advice to the player is sounded here: "Suit the action to the word, the word to the action." But Hamlet does not simply mean that you must echo the literal meaning of the text with a physical gesture — clenching your fist on "Peace, Kent!" for example, or raising your arms heavenward on

65

"Come, thick night." Hamlet means that *both the words and movements of a role seem to emanate from the action of the play,* and that they must flow together in a coordinated, mutually supportive fashion.

This is what directors mean when they ask actors to speak and move at the same time: that *they speak and move as a total action,* as a total response to the situation in which they (their characters) find themselves. And since most actors learn their lines and their moves at different times and from different sources (getting the former from the text and the latter from the director), the job of integration is particularly difficult.

In the following seven exercises, you are invited to use speeches you have already learned in earlier exercises so you can concentrate on working new moves into previously memorized words.

◤◣◤◢◤ EXERCISE 11-1   HIGH AND LOW

Take Lear's line from Exercises 2-1 and 2-2:

LEAR: Peace, Kent!
Come not between the dragon and his wrath.

Say the line to a group while standing on a chair or high platform. Or say it standing while they (and Kent) kneel.

Say it seated on a "throne" while they (and Kent) crawl on the floor beneath you.

Are you a smaller than average person? You might find amazing things happening with your voice in this simple exercise.

Now take Lady Macbeth's line from Exercises 2-3 and 2-4:

LADY MACBETH: Come thick night,
And pall thee in the dunnest smoke of Hell.

Say the line to the "night" while lying on your back, either on the floor or on a comfortable mat or couch.

Roll from side to side while saying it; address the night above and around you. Sway suggestively, and wrinkle up your body. Curl into a fetal position. Try to bring the "night" close around your body, and even into you. Try to bring "Hell" around and into you.

These two exercises will show you the impact of sheer stature—how high or low you are off the ground, how much above or below other people—on your acting, and even on your feeling about yourself. We are all somewhat conditioned in life by our height. The shorter-than-average person may be consistently compliant due to the fact that he or she physically looks up at others all the time; or, conversely, the shorter person may develop a rigid defensive pugnacity (viz. Napoleon and Al Capone). The larger-than-average person may similarly develop a complex of unwarranted feelings of bullish awkwardness, and may overcompensate by taciturn remoteness. Acting can be a liberation from, among other things, the social conditioning generated by our size. Try it and see—just with this exercise.

▖▚▞▚▞▙ EXERCISE 11-2 MOVING HIGHER, MOVING LOWER

Take these same two speeches and move to the directed positions during the speech itself. Actually climb the chair on "Peace, Kent!" making your move on "Kent," or "not" or "dragon." And settle into the ground on "Come, thick night," slithering onto the floor on "night" or "pall" or "Hell."

Understand carefully: The point is not to "coordinate" your line with your movement. The point is *to make both the line and the movement emanate from your purpose and desire*—which is to intimidate Kent, or to attract night (or to what? You decide). No move is actually necessary on either of these lines; quite often they are delivered without moving. But playing around with possible moves, and with varying stature, will give you a sense of the dramatic potential in physicalizing Shakespearean (or any) language.

▖▞▚▞▚▙ EXERCISE 11-3 WALK THE CIRCLE

Take the line from Exercise 3-1:

GLOUCESTER: They do me wrong, and I will not endure it!

Say this line *three times* in succession, each time a little louder than the last.

Arrange most of the "court" in a loose circle around you—about 15 to 20 feet away—except for a few persons who can sit closer to you at the center. Walk casually around the persons near the center; the rest of the court will be an outer ring around you.

Now, while walking, play Gloucester's triple line to the "court," addressing both those in the center and those in the outside ring. Play with the stature variations—with those standing around you and those seated within your circle.

Don't walk mechanically, and don't look down at your feet! Look at the court, and connect with the individuals comprising it. Vary your pace and focus, gesture emphatically when you feel like it, and *single out* members of the court to "zero in on" for certain key words.

Now *spin* in the contrary direction for an occasional key word; that is, if you are walking clockwise, spin suddenly counterclockwise on a word you want to emphasize to someone in the outside ring. (The spin will keep you pointed in the same direction for an extended moment, like a dancer "pointing" during a series of pirouettes. You will be walking backward during that moment.) Practice this movement until you can do it fluidly, expressively, and without falling over your feet. (Aren't you glad you don't have to learn new lines for this exercise? This is the "speak and move at the same time" problem you're dealing with, and it's easier to start off with words you don't have to struggle for.)

You might like to know that "walking the circle" is a classic exercise in British actor training. They can spend months on it, and so can you. The point is not that Shakespearean speeches should be done while walking in circles; the point is to begin connecting the words of the author with free, fluid, expressive, continuous, and dynamic *movement*. The circle, because of its continuous arc (and consequently its continuously shifting focus) is a starting point for dramatic movement. Think of it not as a stage direction, but as an alternative to standing still and reciting.

◼︎❧◼︎❧◼︎ EXERCISE 11-4   LIMP THE CIRCLE

Let's add some character. From Exercise 3-2, remember that Gloucester has a deformity that he can either try to hide from the court or parade in front of them. Try making your Gloucester circle with a *limp* — first trying to hide it, then trying to exploit it.

◼︎❧◼︎❧◼︎ EXERCISE 11-5   ASCEND THE LADDER

Again, you can work with either of two speeches already memorized: Claudius's "Give me the cups" speech (Exercise 7-1) or Desdemona's "Why then tomorrow night" (Exercise 9-1). Find a solid staircase or stair unit (a ladder won't do), and give your memorized speech, going up one step each time you escalate the build. As:

CLAUDIUS: Give me the cups!
[*Step up*] And let the kettle to the trumpet speak,
[*Step up*] The trumpet to the cannoneer without,
[*Step up*] The cannon to the heavens,
[*Step up and together*] the heaven to earth.
[*No step*] Now the King drinks to Hamlet!

Note you are directed to step "up and together" on the last step, planting yourself squarely on your (imaginary) "platform" for "Now the King. . . ."

Try this several times. Can you find the places in each line where it feels most "right" to shift your weight upward? Is it on the last syllable? Or on the "instrument"? Try making your upward movement on "without," "heavens," and "earth." Then try on "kettle," "trumpet," "cannon," and "heaven."

Don't look at the stairs! They're there, and your lines are there, too. Look at the (imaginary?) courtiers around you. Look at the (imaginary) trumpeter, cannoneer, and thunderer in heaven. Look at Hamlet.

◼︎❧◼︎❧◼︎ EXERCISE 11-6   DESCEND THE LADDER

Try going *down* the staircase in reverse fashion. Look at Hamlet all the while. Don't look at the stairs!

Try both this exercise and Exercise 11-5 again, this time as Desdemona. Assume Othello is above you at the top of the steps, and try approaching him with your request:

DESDEMONA: Why then,
[*Step up*] tomorrow night,
[*Step up*] on Tuesday morn,
[*Step up*] on Tuesday noon,
[*Step up*] or night,
[*Two quick steps up and together*] or Wednesday morn.
[*No step*] I prithee name the time
[*Run down the steps to Othello, as if he had moved down ahead of you*]
   but let it not exceed three days.

Notice here you are directed to make a more complex physical ascent (and descent): four regular steps, then two quick ones, then quickly running down. Try this speech several times, playing around with the "stepping" possibilities.

Now try going *down,* step by step, for the whole build, and crossing the room on the last line to approach your Othello.

Don't look at the stairs! Why not? Because it calls too much attention to you, the actor. It's like seeing a fire marshal in the wings when Lady Macbeth enters with her lighted candle. Claudius and Desdemona *know* where the stairs are — and if they don't, it makes no relevant dramatic point to show that they don't. Be brave (though not foolhardy). Learn how to exclude, from your acting, behavior that calls attention to your own insecurity.

◼️ ▧▨▧▨ ◼️   EXERCISE 11-7   THE SPIRAL

We are now at the exercise that will separate the could-be actors from the couldn't-be actors — except that it may take you months to find out.

Take Petruchio's speech in Exercise 9-4, which you have already learned (or learn it now).

PETRUCHIO: Nay, look not big, nor stamp, nor stare, nor fret;
I will be master of what is mine own.
She is my goods, my chattels; she is my house,
My household stuff, my field, my barn,
My horse, my ox, my ass, my anything.

Petruchio is, you remember, explaining his view of Katherine, his future bride, to Katherine's friends and family — while Katherine remains on stage.

Place "Katherine" in the center of the room, and the "friends and family" in a large circle around her — say about 15 feet away at the closest. Start to walk around the *outside* of this outer circle, and begin speaking after you have taken a few steps.

Continue walking and speaking. At "I will be master . . .", stroll *inside* the outer circle, while continuing to walk around Katherine. Continue your speech, and as you do so, continue to circle Katherine, spiralling in closer and closer to her with each pass. But though you close in on her, continue to speak both to her and to the family. As you spiral around her, spin around in the opposite direction from time to time, addressing the outer ("family") ring. Play with this move, *trying to bring everybody in the room around to your point of view.*

On the very last line, spiral all the way in to your Katherine. On "my ass," take her hand; on "my anything," pull her to you. On a second go round, you can rehearse something specific here: an embrace, a spank, a "dip," a kneel at her feet (serious? ironic?), or a kiss of her hand (gentle? snarling?). Let this moment of physical contact, joined to the word "anything," become the climax of the speech.

◢◤◥◣◢◤◥◣ EXERCISE 11-8   THE SPIRAL II

Do the same exercise, but with a female character. The Duke of Gloucester (Richard III) is in the middle here, the court in the outer circle, and you are (Mad) Queen Margaret, spiralling in, and trying to publicly humiliate your vicious nephew:

QUEEN MARGARET: Thou elvish-marked, abortive, rooting hog!
Thou that wast sealed in thy nativity
The slave of nature and the son of hell!
Thou slander of thy mother's heavy womb!
Thou loathed issue of thy father's loins!
Thou rag of honor!   thou detested —

And Gloucester interrupts:

GLOUCESTER: Margaret!

MARGARET: Richard!!

Word Note: Pronounce "loathed" as "loath-ed," with two syllables, and the "th" as in "then," so as to get the full ten syllables into the pentameter line. There will be a fuller discussion of accented "èds" — and when you might use them — later, but for now just do it![13]

Spiral in, as in the last exercise, and rehearse a physical action at very close proximity (or even touching) from when you speak the word "detested" onward. Speak for the benefit of the court, as well as to Richard. *Try to get them on your side.*

If you have a real Gloucester (Richard) to play this with, let him (or her) learn his (her) line and cue so that in the final exchange — "Margaret!"/ "Richard!!" — you can top Gloucester's energy both vocally and physically, matching *and surpassing* (if you can) whatever he (she) does. Let spiralling "wind you up" for this final escalation of name-calling.

---

[13] If you want to look ahead, it's on page 156.

■⚡⚡■ EXERCISE 11-9   THE SPIRAL III

You've mastered these two spirals? Then try one more: Touchstone's "I did dislike the cut of a certain courtier's beard" speech from *As You Like It* (and Lesson 8).

The character of Jacques is in the middle here, and you're replying to his question ("How did you find the quarrel on the seventh cause?"), but that's really just an excuse. Your main target here is the surrounding "court" of the good duke and his band, residing in the Forest of Arden. Show off—and to all of them equally—your brilliant intelligence, your creative imagination, and your dashing linguistic accomplishment. "Illustrate," by your escalating spiral, your advancing twirls and spins, and your progressively charged vocal delivery, each discrete level of attack, from the Retort Courteous to the Lie Direct.

You could spend *months* working on these three spiral exercises, and shaping these speeches to rousing climaxes.

SUMMARY OF LESSON 11

Actors must speak and move at the same time, which means both speech and movement must seem to emanate, in an integrated fashion, from the character's drive to achieve specific victories and objectives. Speech and movement, in other words, must seem to be the same thing, though they may be learned separately. Exercises in speaking while ascending, descending, circling, and spiralling are useful practice pieces and warm-ups toward this integration of speech and movement.

LESSON 12

Costume and Character

When does the notion of "acting" first come into our lives? For many of us, it all began when we put on our first Halloween disguise, or rummaged through a parent's closet, and "dressed up" in that borrowed finery.

Since the beginning of the theatre, costume — which is to say the clothing of the characters — has played a crucial role in acting. It also plays a crucial role in the drama.

Shakespeare's plays, as far as we know, were produced with rather sparse scenery but with sumptuous costuming. The kings, queens, and emperors of Shakespearean drama did not roam the stage in an Elizabethan equivalent of jeans, sneakers, and tee-shirts, but in the handed-down robes and gowns of aristocratic royalty. And at least some attention was given to what could be found of historical authenticity. The sole surviving Shakespearean costume illustration from Shakespeare's own time (from a production of *Titus Andronicus*) shows a mixture of Roman togas and Elizabethan court dress — not an accurate rendition of ancient Rome, to be sure, but a clear attempt to create a Romanesque atmosphere for actors and audience alike. Contemporary reports of stage wear described impressive, lavish attention to actor apparel.

Costume is embedded in the *meaning* of Shakespeare's plays as well. "Apparel oft proclaims the man," says Polonius (in *Hamlet*); "Robes and furred gowns hide all," says King Lear. In many plays certain costumes are fundamental to both plot and character: Hamlet's "inky cloak," his (ghostly) father's "complete steel," Coriolanus's "gown of humility," and Edgar's "blanket[ed] loins." Lear moves from furred gowns to near-nakedness to an entrance "fantastically dressed with wild flowers." In several of Shakespeare's plays, women dress as (and pretend to be) men (Rosalind and Celia in *As You Like It*, Viola in *Twelfth Night*, Julia in *Two Gentlemen of Verona*, Imogen in *Cymbeline*). These amusing cross-dressings also convey several distinct levels of meaning: social, psychological, and sometimes philosophical. In other plays characters use costume to convey, or to disguise, social class: In

The Winter's Tale, royalty, aristocrats, shepherds, and thieves all change costumes with each other in a near pandemonium of hilarious (and revealing) clothing contrasts.

Costume, being intrinsic to acting, helps the actor enter the role by helping the actor "feel" himself or herself in the character's situation (which may include a historical period). Just as you feel more "regal" when you stand amidst a group of seated (or grovelling) "subjects," so you will feel more regal sitting on an elevated throne, wearing a grand cape and a crown, and carrying a "scepter." This is the same "dressing up" you may have done as a young child. Even delivering a simple line such as

They do me wrong and I will not endure it

will probably "feel" better to you, and will also have a stronger impact to your hearers, if you give yourself a royal cape and a hunchback's crutch. Or do as British actor Anthony Sher did—give yourself *two* crutches.

What happens when you don a costume is that you don a host of associations that go with it. By putting on a cape, you put yourself in a world where people wear capes. By wearing doublet and hose (standard male gear in the Renaissance), you find yourself back in the 17th century. By picking up a scepter, you enter a world where people bow to scepters. By taking a crutch, you give yourself a hunched back or a deformity that makes you need a crutch.

In other words, you *respond* to your costume and props. They propel you—even without your thinking about it much—into a world quite different from your own. *Costumes and props are not mere "decor."* They don't just decorate a play; they are not simply devices to "dress" a production or to create an illusion for the audience. Costumes and props help you create your situation. They are part of that situation: as much a part, indeed, as the words of the text. Hamlet's inky cloak is as much a part of *Hamlet* as is "To be or not to be."[14] All your acting exercises from now on can be explored with the aid of a costume and props.

But you can't, of course, give yourself a costume every time you work on a speech or a scene, for a good period costume can cost up to a thousand dollars or more, not to mention the time involved in construction, fittings, and so on. Even in a full academic or professional production of Shakespeare, you will not get a costume until the dress rehearsal, which is usually just a couple of days before the first performance. How can the student actor work with costume—without a costume? In the next exercise a simple blanket can come to the rescue.

---

[14]That doesn't mean, however, that the director or designer need *use* the inky cloak. There are limitless possibilities in interpreting a line and in creating a production: The inky cloak might turn out to be a white tuxedo or a pair of boxer shorts if the artistic team can make it work. The point is not that any specific costume is crucial, but that the actor's clothes are as much a part of the play as the actor's words.

◼◿▨◿▨◺ EXERCISE 12-1   THE BLANKET

Get a plain green or gray woolen blanket, twin-sized, as from an army surplus store. This will become your all-purpose, do-anything-with costume.[15]

Also get a 5-foot piece of ordinary rope, and a 3-foot dowel or yardstick. These will become your all-purpose accessories and props.

The blanket is a cape, a gown, a monk's robe, a headdress, a toga, a loincloth, a nightdress, a witch's dress, a wraparound — or anything else you want it to be. Some practice, and perhaps a few safety pins, can make it almost anything at all.

Experiment by draping it in various ways: over one and then the other arm, and then both arms; folded and unfolded. Try it over the head and shoulders. Move around with the garment, and gesture with your free hand (or hands).

Watch it float behind you as you move. Make *it* move. *Maneuver* the blanket like a matador's cape, a queen's train, a lord's mantle, a thief's cloak, a beggar's shawl; like Lear's robe of state, Gloucester's deformity-disguising wrap, Henry V's battle cape, Lady Macbeth's blanket of "thick night," palling her in "the dunnest smoke of Hell."

The rope is a belt, headband, sash, sling, tie, or strap. You can use it to tie the blanket around you at various points, or to make a crown or a noose.

The dowel or yardstick is your sword, staff, scepter, crutch, club, or walking stick.

Experiment by walking around in various "costumes," produced by different arrangements of these components, and see what sorts of lines (from previous exercises, perhaps) spring to your lips. How do you think you appear to other "characters"? To other persons in the room, also wearing blanket costumes? To King Henry? To Mark Antony? To Cleopatra?

Improvise. Take some of the speeches you've worked on already — King Lear's "Peace, Kent"; Lady Macbeth's "Come, thick Night"; Cleopatra's "O happy horse"; Henry V's "Once more into the breach"; Bernardo's "Who's there?"; Desdemona's "Why then, tomorrow night"; Claudius's "Give me the cups" — and dress yourself in your blanket as you imagine such a character might wear a garment. Move, and say your lines, linking the garment to the speech — the fabric to the word — in any way that seems possible or useful.

How can you move your costume and props to make points? To win goals? To intimidate? To seduce? To gain an advantage over other characters? How can you *use* your costume and props?

In Lesson 13 you will find many specific opportunities to do this.

---

[15] In my own Shakespearean acting classes, I provide this, checking out a blanket to each student for the term.

SUMMARY OF LESSON 12

Clothes "proclaim the man," Polonius says, and costume in acting plays a prominent role in creating your character. But donning an appropriate costume not only shows others what kind of character you are, it helps you, the actor, begin to "feel your way" into a character's specific situation — which may include a historical period. Putting on a costume means responding to a set of new associations. By dressing up in a simple piece of fabric, such as a blanket, you can experiment with a wide variety of "costumes" — perhaps those suggesting historical periods or perhaps something wholly fanciful — that will invite you to explore the associations of character these may provoke.

A Gallery of Shakespearean Characters

What follows is not so much a series of exercises as a gallery of Shakespearean characters for you to explore, using the blanket, rope, and stick we discussed in the previous lesson. There are thirty-two characters in all, about half of them men, half women. You can work on one, two, ten, sixteen, or all of them as you wish (or as you are assigned). But you must *work on only one at a time*. Each character can be a minor (or major) masterpiece; each can be explored far more fully than in the few notes you will be given here. Allow yourself plenty of time for each.

In each case, you are given a small speech (some six to fourteen lines) and explanatory word notes, where necessary, to explain unfamiliar terms or references in the text.

A photograph shows how your blanket—and in some cases your yard-stick and rope—may serve as costume and props for the speech. These photographs are posed, but each costume was created in an actual exercise with student actors.[16] Your costume may not come out quite this way, but with a little experimenting and adjusting, and maybe the judicious use of safety pins, you can achieve wonderfully exciting results. Feel free to combine your blanket with apparel and accessories of your own (scarves, shoes, hats) to create a variety of usable costumes.

You are given the basic situation in which you (as the character) find yourself. You are not told exactly what kind of character you are—that will be fairly evident from the situation and your speech. You are also given suggestions of what your *goal* (victory, objective) might be, and what sort of tactics you might consider to win it.

Finally, you are given suggestions as to how you might use the language and your costume to help create the character. These suggestions will come

---

[16]The actors in the photos are Philip Thompson and Sarah Salisbury. Both are now professional actors and university acting instructors.

to you as directives; they are exactly the sort of things a director might ask you to do in a production — kneel here, take off your cape here, build to a climax here, whisper here. Try to do the speeches precisely as instructed, and *then* try to improve on them. Following the instructions may seem limiting at first, but doing so will give you a good start, help you develop a larger repertoire of performance skills, train your instrument, and, eventually, build your confidence. In other words, learn and master these speeches according to the directions — then *transcend* those directions. Make your *own* directions. But master those given here first. OK? (Here you say: "Yes, OK!")

It isn't necessary to know the whole play to work on this exercise, which is a beginning exploration of Shakespearean characters. For now you are creating only character *fragments,* but some day these may lead to more complete character development. (Of course, since the act, scene, and verse are given, you can locate the speech in the play, and, if you wish, work on the entire speech or scene.)

You can also leave until later most considerations of versification, pronunciation, and style. Right now, just know that you are working on speaking and moving at the same time. Feel free to bluff your way through the other problems as best you can. This is just for experiment!

As you play with your costume, text, and props (if any), start to ask yourself some of the fundamental elements of characterization:

How might I (my character) try to control people?

How might I try to get what I want?

Until you read the play, you can only guess at the answers, but *do* make an informed guess, based on the words you speak and on how you wear your costume and handle your props.

CASSIUS

CASSIUS: Why man, he doth bestride the narrow world
Like a Colossus, and we petty men
Walk under his huge legs and peep about
To find ourselves dishonorable graves.
The fault, dear Brutus, is not in our stars,
But in ourselves, that we are underlings.
(*Julius Caesar,* I.ii.134ff.)

Word notes: "Bestride" here means stand over.

You are a Roman senator, with a "lean and hungry" look, complaining to your friend Brutus of the growing power of Julius Caesar, the recently honored Roman general and ruler, who is at this very moment being cheered by the crowds a little way off. You are seeking to embitter Brutus against Caesar, his former friend, and are hoping to plot, with Brutus, Caesar's assassination.

Use the words to make Caesar unattractive in Brutus's eyes. Chew on the word "petty." You don't mean that you and Brutus *are* petty, but that Caesar's new strength has made you *seem* petty in Roman eyes. Make Brutus painfully aware of his loss of significance in the shadow of Caesar's new, "huge" public stature (the Colossus was a giant statue that stood near the harbor of the island of Rhodes during ancient times). The word "graves" has a double meaning: You are implying that you and Brutus will be politically dead without honor (in our "dishonorable graves") if Caesar continues to rise, and that you will also be seen as colorless, noncharismatic, "grave" bureaucrats if the exciting Julius Caesar assumes greater powers of state.

The Roman toga is a garment that you must hold with one arm, giving you only one free arm with which to gesture. You will at first find this limiting—but why, do you think, did the Romans (at least the Roman senators) choose this garment? What *advantages* does it have? Try to find how the toga helps you attain a greater stature in the eyes of your friend Brutus. Find an effective way to gesture with your free hand, as by pointing to the "stars" and then to our "selves" at the appropriate moments.

DOLL TEARSHEET

Your friend has just called Pistol, a rogue whom you detest, by the elevated title of "Captain." You respond directly to Pistol:

DOLL: Captain! thou abominable damned cheater, art thou not ashamed to be called captain? An captains were of my mind, they would truncheon you out, for taking their names upon you before you have earned them. You a captain! you slave, for what? for tearing a poor whore's ruff in a bawdy-house? He a captain! hang him, rogue! he lives upon mouldy stewed prunes and dried cakes. A captain! God's light, these villains will make the word as odious as the word 'occupy;' which was an excellent good word before it was ill sorted: therefore captains had need to look to it.

(*2 Henry IV*, II.iv.151ff.)

Word notes: "An" was commonly used in Elizabethan English for "if." A "ruff" was an article of clothing worn about the neck, and a "bawdy house" was a whorehouse. "Occupy" seems to have been a contemporary euphemism — a polite term — for fornication.

You, Doll, are a lady of the taverns, a high-spirited member of London's lowlife, quite used to barroom brawls, good times, and bad language. You, Pistol, and several of your friends are drinking in the Boar's Head Inn, a 15th-century London tavern. Use your colorful insults both to intimidate Pistol and to impress the tavern crowd. Out-"man" him; beat him at his own game, in front of his own friends. Try to make him leave the room.

By standing up for the rights of "captains," you are trying to assume for yourself their social rank while shaming Pistol's. Try to *publicly* humiliate him in his friend's eyes. Make the tavern spectators associate Pistol with cheaters, slaves, villains, third-rate whores, and eaters of mouldy leftovers — while associating *you* only with might and eloquence: the captains' truncheons (a kind of billy club), and "excellent good words." *Build* your insults; *build* your repetitions of the word "captain."

Use your exaggerated bosom and your broad-beamed hips (you've stuffed extra blankets into each) to comically "outswagger" this "swaggering rogue." Kick the hem of your dress, if you wish, on "He a captain!" and raise it, flauntingly and provocatively, on "occupy."

RICHARD II

KING RICHARD: What must the king do now? Must he submit?
The king shall do it: must he be deposed?
The king shall be contented: must he lose
The name of king? O' God's name, let it go:
I'll give my jewels for a set of beads,
My gorgeous palace for a hermitage,
My gay apparel for an almsman's gown
My figured goblets for a dish of wood,
My scepter for a palmer's walking staff,
My subjects for a pair of carved saints
And my large kingdom for a little grave,
A little grave, an obscure grave;
Or I'll be buried in the king's highway,
Some way of common trade, where subject's feet
May hourly trample on their sovereign's head;
For on my heart they tread now whilst I live
And buried once, why not upon my head?
(*Richard II*, III.ii.143ff.)

Word notes: An "almsman" was a recipient of charity, and a "palmer" a religious pilgrim, in Richard's times, and a "hermitage" was a house of religious retreat. By "their sovereign" Richard means "their king;" or, in other words, himself.

You are King of England, but you have made foolish mistakes, and you know you will soon be forced to abdicate in favor of your cousin, Bolinbroke. Speaking here to your supporters, raise their spirits by making clear that you are fully in control of your demise (even though you're not). Try to *revel* in your tragic end, so that you don't have to wallow in public despair. Make the court see that you become greater in defeat — through your command of language you command your own emotions. As a king, you commanded only armies.

Notice that the last 13½ lines of the speech contain just one sentence; study its structure. *Build* the repeated "gifts," making each one more precious than the last; present your court with a veritable litany of your generosity. *Milk* the court's emotion with the pathetic, down-building repetitions: "little grave, a little grave, an obscure grave. . . ." Use your garment and props as you strip yourself of outward glory. Cast aside your crown at "jewels," flutter your royal robes at "gay apparel," and toss down your scepter when the line suggests. At the same time, you can caress your royal robes, perhaps on "hourly trample on their sovereign's head," thus evoking sympathy for your state as a fallen noble; a regal, lyrical sensualist.

Make the court both *sorry for you* in your downfall, and at the same time *envious* of your charismatic, regal skill at painting your own end in such vivid colors.

HERMIONE

HERMIONE: Verily!
You put me off with limber vows; but I,
Though you would seek t'unsphere the stars with oaths,
Should yet say "Sir, no going." Verily,
You shall not go: a lady's Verily's
As potent as a lord's. Will you go yet?
Force me to keep you as a prisoner,
Not like a guest: How say you?
My prisoner? or my guest? By your dread 'Verily,'
One of them you shall be.
(*The Winter's Tale*, I.ii.46ff.)

Word notes: "Limber" here means "bending," or, metaphorically, "untrustworthy." "T'unsphere the stars" means, metaphorically, to knock the stars out of their orbits (stars at that time were thought to rest on great revolving crystal spheres). "Verily" means "truthfully," but is here spoken ironically, as explained below.

You are the Queen of Sicilia, eight months pregnant; you are the hostess of a state visit from your husband's childhood friend, Polixenes, now King of Bohemia. Polixenes has decided to leave, however, and, at your husband's request, you are begging him to stay. "I may not, verily," Polixenes has responded to your initial request, and your speech is an effort to embarrass him by turning his own language on him in front of the court.

Make fun of Polixenes's verbal stiffness, the artificiality of his language. Publicly tease him; make it seem *fun* to stay here in Sicilia; shame him into staying. Contrast the directness of your "Sir, no going!" with the stuffiness of his "Verily."

Take advantage of your feminine (and pregnant) state. Make your feminist point ("a lady's 'verily' [is] as potent as a lord's") with a little sexiness as well (your husband will later use this speech to accuse you of adultery). Sashay your gown playfully at the stiff Polixenes. Use your pregnancy as well—caress your tummy on "Force me to keep you as a prisoner. . . ." Is your infant-to-be a prisoner, or a guest? (Indeed, your baby soon *will* be a prisoner!) It is harder for Polixenes to turn down a pregnant woman than a king, so make your pregnancy and your lady's gown tactics in pursuit of your goal.

Build your repetitions: "verily," "prisoner," and "guest." Try to make Polixenes blush!

GREMIO

GREMIO: Tut, she's a lamb, a dove, a fool to him!
I'll tell you, Sir Lucentio: when the priest
Should ask, if Katherine should be his wife,
'Ay, by gog's-wouns,' quoth he; and swore so loud,
That, all-amazed, the priest let fall the book
And, as he stopped again to take it up
This mad-brained bridegroom took him such a cuff
That down fell priest and book and book and priest;
'Now take them up,' quoth he, 'if any list!
(*The Taming of the Shrew*, III.ii.159ff.)

You have just come in breathless from the wedding of Katherine (the "shrew") and Petruchio, the groom (you think him a "devil") who "tames" and marries her, and you hastily describe the events to your friend, Lucentio. ("Lucentio" is actually Tranio in disguise, but you don't know that.)

Word note: "Gog's wouns" is Elizabethan shorthand for "God's (that is, Christ's) wounds," and was a mild oath.

Although you are exasperated by what you've seen in church, you also know that it makes an amusing story, and since you want "Lucentio" to like and admire you, get as much comic mileage out of the story as you can. *Entertain*

Lucentio with your comic juxtapositions and *illustrate* your story by acting it out.

Use your ridiculous headpiece to let Lucentio know just how aristocratic and "upright" you are, and how *you* would never put up with Petruchio's infantile behavior. Try to contrast your upright and dignified costume with the roughhouse behavior (swearing, cuffing the priest, challenging the congregation) that you act out.

CALPURNIA

CALPURNIA: Alas, my lord
Your wisdom is consumed in confidence.
Do not go forth today: call it my fear
That keeps you in the house, and not your own.
We'll send Mark Antony to the senate house;
And he shall say you are not well today:
Let me, upon my knee, prevail in this.
(*Julius Caesar*, II.ii.48ff.)

You are the wife of Julius Caesar, ruler of Rome, and you suspect he will meet with foul play at the Senate this morning; you beg him to stay home.

The female version of the toga is a bit freer, and belted. It will permit you to kneel, so try to make your kneeling and your words "prevail" with your husband, and persuade him to throw off his (false) confidence and stay with you.

Notice that your speech is broken up. It has several separate thrusts, as though you are thinking on your feet, one idea at a time: "call it my fear," "send Mark Antony," "he shall say you are not well." Starting with the despairing cry "alas," build a suppressed hysteria so as to *break your husband's false self-confidence*.

Then, unable to "think on your feet" further, sink gracefully to your knees to plead with a Roman wife's ultimate weapon — pity — and a combined physical and verbal appeal to your husband's instinct to protect you.

Let your toga "float" down onto the ground at your feet. Let your toga, so spread on the floor, become an abject statement of humility — and a particularly forceful statement because of the beauty, the *magnificence,* of that humility!

TROILUS

TROILUS: Call here my varlet; I'll unarm again:
Why should I war without the walls of Troy,
That find such cruel battle here within?
Each Trojan that is master of his heart
Let him to field; Troilus, alas! hath none.
The Greeks are strong and skillful to their strength,
Fierce to their skill and to their fierceness valiant;
But I am weaker than a woman's tear,
Tamer than sleep, fonder than ignorance,
Less valiant than the virgin in the night
And skilless as unpracticed infancy.

(*Troilus and Cressida*, I.i.1ff.; actually a compilation of two adjacent speeches of Troilus.)

Word notes: "Varlet" in this case means a servant or slave acting as your valet; you are calling your varlet to help you unarm, *or take off your armor. "Without" means "outside" (remember Claudius's "trumpeter without"? Shakespearean language gets easier to understand the more you work with it).*

And "fonder" means "more foolish." The sense of the whole speech is: Why should I fight outside the Trojan walls when I am fighting a battle inside my own heart? Let stouthearted Trojans and skillful Greeks fight the war; I am just a weak, unskilled boy.

You are an armed young soldier in the Trojan War; you are also the son of Priam, King of Troy. The Greeks are attacking your country, but, though you are armed for battle, you are desperately in love with Cressida, and you are now trying to find a way out of the war, and into Cressida's arms. You are speaking with her uncle, Pandarus, in the hopes that he will "pander" to your desires and bring Cressida to you.

Show Pandarus that you are *crazed* with love. Use the alliteration — "war without the walls" — and the deliberate oppositions — "without/within," "strong/weak," "skillful/skilless," "valiant/less valiant" — to make a "mad aria" of your passion. Show that in your overwrought state you would make a terrible soldier, and thus should be released from duty.

The speech is not grammatical; "hath none" replaces "is not," and "fierce to their skill" is substituted for "fierce in their skill." But this, of course, is not an author's mistake. The bad grammar is intentional, on your (Troilus's) part, to show Pandarus your desperation: "Better do what I ask — I am so out of control I am capable of anything!"

And *don't* remove your blanket costume, representing armor, despite your words; rather *flaunt* it to show that, though you might be "weaker than a woman's tear," you could also run your sword through Pandarus if he failed to comply with your request. Nothing is more frightening than a crazed, reckless, *armed* man, fighting for his self-esteem. You're not *really* tamer than sleep, and Pandarus should be made aware of this.

If you're up to it, remove your shirt before putting on the armor. Show Pandarus some flesh, emphasizing the sensuality of the "cruel battle here within," as well as some real muscle on "fierceness valiant." If you are "weaker than a woman's tear," show that this is from choice, from love, rather than from mere physical frailty.

QUEEN ELIZABETH

ELIZABETH: Ay me, I see the downfall of our house!
The tiger now hath seized the gentle hind;
Insulting tyranny begins to jet
Upon the innocent and aweless throne:
Welcome, destruction, death, and massacre!
I see, as in a map, the end of all.
(*Richard III*, II.iv.49ff.)

Word notes: By "our house" the queen refers to her royal family, and the line of succession after her. A "hind" is a deer. And "jet" means, in this instance, to "strut"; it also connotes the idea of "blackening." "Aweless," which is a made-up word, simply means the opposite of "awesome."

You are the queen in her palace, but your husband (King Edward) has just died, and you have just found that your chief lords have been arrested by the tyrannical Duke of Gloucester, your sworn enemy. You believe that your reign is quickly ending, and the speech, which is a lament, is an effort to gain sanctuary. You are speaking to the Duchess of York and the Archbishop of York (he will take you into sanctuary), but you are also speaking to God.

Build the speech downward, echoing the "downfall" you are describing, ending ("the end of all") in a profound despair that will evoke the archbishop's sympathy and God's protection. Notice this last line has no word longer than three letters. This is the simplest possible verbal expression, stripped of all complexity and ornamentation.

Use the dignity of your gown to present the archbishop — and God — with a vision of Elizabeth, the "gentle hind." Present your case for sanctuary and heaven. Show, with your words and your clothes, your absolute innocence. (And, by the way, she is *not* at all innocent!) Caress your gown — this may be the last time you get to run your fingers over its luxurious folds, its delicate embroidery. Give yourself memories of queenliness that you can carry off to your cloistered sanctuary, and perhaps to prison (or heaven, or the other place . . .).

Question: Why did Shakespeare invent the word "aweless" here? There are plenty of existing words, such as "feeble" and "vacant," which fit the meter and work into the sense. Why did he have to create "aweless"? What does it *do* that the other words don't?

GRUMIO

GRUMIO: Why, therefore fire; for I have caught extreme cold. Where's the cook? Is supper ready, the house trimmed, rushes strewed, cobwebs swept; the serving men in their new fustian, their white stockings, and every officer his wedding garment on? Be the jacks fair within, the jills fair without, the carpets laid, and everything in order?

(*The Taming of the Shrew*, IV.i.44–51)

Word notes: "Rushes" are wheat sheaves laid about on floors (in country houses particularly) to pick up dirt and absorb grease. "Fustian" is a kind of cloth; "jacks" and "jills" are men and women servants, but also refer to drinking goblets. "Carpets" actually referred to tablecloths.

Petruchio has just married Kate and is headed to his home. You are his servant, and are preceding him to his house. Your goal—after warming yourself following your cold journey — is to shape up the household staff in preparation for the master's arrival. Know that you will be beaten if you fail! You are talking to Curtis, whom you left in charge during your absence, but you are probably hoping to be overheard by all the jacks and jills scattered about the house in Petruchio's service.

Build the list of things that must be attended to, continuously increasing the pressure on Curtis — and the servants who must be overhearing this — as you go. Reestablish your authority over the staff; Curtis has probably been taking your role in your absence, and you should try to take it back. *Take charge,* then, with your voice and physical presence.

Yes, this is the same costume worn in the Troilus sketch. But it's not armor now; it's a foreman's vest, with impressively padded shoulders and bare arms, giving an impression of brawny power, yet leaving your arms free to whip the horses (and the servants). Impose your authority over Curtis and the other servants with your rambunctious physicality, your energetic animation, your bare-armed hyperactivity, your football-y shoulder pads.

ISABELLA

ISABELLA: Most strange, but yet most truly, will I speak:
That Angelo's forsworn; is it not strange?
That Angelo's a murderer; is't not strange?
That Angelo is an adulterous thief,
An hypocrite, a virgin-violator;
Is it not strange and strange?
(*Measure for Measure*, V.i.37)

Word notes: "Forsworn" here means "lied."

You are a novice in a nunnery. Earlier, you had gone to Angelo, the deputy duke, to plead mercy for your condemned brother, Claudio. Angelo offered to intervene — if you would first go to bed with him! After much anguish ("I had rather give my body than my soul!"), you finally complied with his request (actually you managed to sneak in a substitute), but Angelo apparently has had your brother killed anyway. Now you seek justice from the royal duke, recently returned. Angelo, present at this session, tries to stop you, telling the Duke "she will speak most bitterly and strange." This speech is your reply.

The speech is a fairly straight build on the word "strange," which becomes more and more powerfully ironic as the accusations build. The doubling of "strange and strange" at the end reaches meaning beyond semantics. The sheer sound of the word, as it reverberates in multiple repetitions, creates an even deeper "strangeness" than mere semantic meaning can create.

Try to build the accusations, too. Notice that they are built in the reverse of how they might be built in today's world: "adulterous thief" is worse than "murderer"; "hypocrite" is worse yet; and "virgin-violator" is worst of all,

the apogee of evil. To a 16th-century novitiate, however, this is an ascending order of wickedness, and by building it this way, you enter the world of the Renaissance nunnery — the world of your character.

Here's where your costume, your novitiate's habit, comes in. Find a way to move it, and to move with it, that demonstrates to the duke your holy purity and the truth, despite the strangeness, of your accusations. Use it as a demonstration of your modesty, as a cover for all that is fleshy or sensual in your body; use it, and your rope, as a religious icon. (All this, of course, may make you *more* sensual to some observers, such as Angelo; such are the ironies of drama, and of life.)

Remember, you are a person unknown to the duke; to him you are simply a young novice in his kingdom. You must fight for his attention, and win his approval. Use your words, your build, and your costume to do this.

RICHARD III

GLOUCESTER: They do me wrong and I will not endure it!
Who are they that complain unto the king,
That I, forsooth, am stern and love them not?

By holy Paul, they love his grace but lightly
That fill his ears with such dissentious rumors.
Because I cannot flatter and speak fair,
Smile in men's faces, smooth, deceive and cog,
Duck with French nods and apish courtesy,
I must be held a rancorous enemy!
Cannot a plain man live and think no harm,
But thus, his simple truth must be abused
By silken, sly, insinuating Jacks?
(*Richard III*, I.iii.42ff.)

Word notes: "Forsooth" means "truly," "cog" means "cheat," "apish" here means "slavish," and "Jacks" means common men ("Jacks" and "Jills"). Gloucester is the duke who, later in the play, becomes King Richard III.

This is, of course, the rest of the soliloquy from Exercise 5-1. Having already sent your brother to his death, murdered the Prince of Wales, and seduced his widow, you are now trying to head off attacks by the court by accusing them of ill will toward you! The best defense being a good offense, charge into the court (you are speaking to the queen and six of her lords) and assume complete control. Use irony ("that I, forsooth, am stern . . ."); religious invocation ("by holy Paul"); self-deprecation ("I cannot flatter and speak fair") that subtly turns to self-praise ("[or] Duck with . . . apish courtesy"); mocking imitation of affected court talk ("rancorous enemy," which can be delivered "in quotation marks"); taking the high road ("Cannot a plain man live?"); asking for pity ("his simple truth must be abused?"); and finally, rapidly building insults of your own ("silken, sly, insinuating Jacks?"). The rapid and escalating succession of s's in the last two lines brings the speech to a triumphal climax, with the oddly thrilling and single-syllable put-down "Jacks?" (set up by the five-syllable adjective "insinuating") forcing an answer from the court that will be in your favor.

Practice, apart from the entire speech, just the words "insinuating Jacks?" — and then work backward to "silken, sly, insinuating Jacks?" before working on the beginning of the speech.

Begin the speech with a bold entrance. Limp briskly, turn rapidly and frequently as you speak; circle and spiral jerkily around the court, and let your cape virtually fly around the room as you talk. Take up space! This is an entrance speech, so make an entrance: Take the stage; make your flowing costume seem to triple your apparent size. Indeed, boldly taking the stage is how Richard will get the crown. (It's also how he will lose it.)

Although your body is deformed, your cape is glorious; let its supple grandeur stand in contrast to your misshapen limbs.

Use the two-crutch prop made famous by British actor Anthony Sher for the speech. And use both prop and costume, and your limp and hunch(back), to make the court quail at your efforts to show what ducking with a French nod might be like, and to demonstrate, by way of contrast, how a "plain man" should appear.

Try using your cape to cover your deformed hand, deliberately throwing the cape aside on "apish courtesy." Gross 'em out! Let them know what an *unashamed* creature they're dealing with.

ABBESS

ABBESS: Whoever bound him, I will loose his bonds
And gain a husband by his liberty.
Speak, old Egeon, if thou be'st the man
That hadst a wife once called Emilia,
That bore thee at a burden two fair sons:
O, if thou be'st the same Egeon, speak,
And speak unto the same Emilia.
(*Comedy of Errors*, V.i.339ff.)

Word notes: "Be'st" is the second person singular conjugation of "to be" in certain older English uses; it is pronounced "be-ist," and "thou be'st" simply means (singular) "you are." "Burden" here means "birthing."

The play is one of Shakespeare's first; it is a farce about mistaken identity, adapted from the Roman author Plautus. You are the abbess, the administrator of a priory in which one member of each of two sets of twins has taken

refuge. You bring them out at the duke's command, and the twins meet for the first time. At the same time you see your husband, Egeon, currently bound in chains, whom you have not seen in thirty-three years. Your goal is to find if this man is indeed your Egeon, to have the duke recognize this and unchain him, and to induce and excite Egeon with your love, to take up with you again, and to do all this without causing old Egeon to have a heart attack!

Build the three "speaks," particularly the doubled "speak, And speak . . ." at the end. Also build the names Egeon and Emilia, which are intentionally paralleled by the author. The "two fair sons" are one set of the twins that you have also discovered. They are now again part of your and Egeon's family, so include them (with a gesture) when you refer to them, by way of rebonding with Egeon.

The robe represents sexual denial, but underneath is a vibrant, still-lusty woman. Let the woman's sensuality grow beneath the garment on "loose his bonds," and let your own sensuality struggle to break free.

Remove your abbess's robe during the speech, perhaps at "the same Egeon, speak," casting it dramatically on the floor with your final "the same Emilia," as if to say "the pre-abbess Emilia." As you do so, "liberate" the lusty young wife of thirty-three years ago from the devout older abbess you have been playing up to now.

MERCUTIO

MERCUTIO: Nay, I'll conjure too. —
Romeo! humours! madman! passion! lover!
Appear thou in the likeness of a sigh:
Speak but one rhyme, and I am satisfied;
Cry but "Ay me!" pronounce but "love" and "dove";
Speak to my gossip Venus one fair word,
One nickname for her purblind son and heir,
Young Adam Cupid, he that shot so trim,
When King Cophetua loved the beggar-maid! —
He heareth not, he stirreth not, he moveth not;
The ape is dead, and I must conjure him. —
I conjure thee by Rosaline's bright eyes,
By her high forehead and her scarlet lip,
By her fine foot, straight leg, and quivering thigh,
And the demesnes that there adjacent lie,
That in thy likeness thou appear to us!
(*Romeo and Juliet*, II.i.6ff.)

Word notes: "Purblind" means "blind"; Shakespeare probably used the two-syllable word instead of its more common synonym to fill out the meter. King Cophetua and the beggar maid was a popular ballad of the time. "Demesnes" is a fancy word, even in Shakespeare's time, for "domains."

You are a friend of Romeo's, and, in the company of Benvolio, another friend, you are in the orchard trying to call Romeo from hiding. Knowing him to be in love, *tease* him with romantic thoughts of love and love poetry. Then, commenting to Benvolio that Romeo "moveth not," conjure (tease) him with the body parts of Rosaline, Romeo's supposed love object, moving down from the top (eyes, forehead, lip) and up from the bottom (foot, leg, thigh) to the most delicate "demesnes" right in the middle — between Rosaline's "quivering thighs." Build the eroticism of this "conjuring" list. "Conjure" implies a devilish spell, so invoke the black magic — spellbinding to the romantically inclined young Romeo — of sexual excitement to draw him from his hiding place. (What you don't know is that Romeo has by this time fallen in love with Juliet, so your appeal won't work!)

Play with "King Cophetua" and "Adam Cupid" (and build the *k* sounds beginning these words), emphasizing your wit and the fact that you are summoning Romeo to good times and sexy merriment.

Toss your cape and sword about dashingly, making it a "costume" for you to enact Romeo appearing "in the likeness of a sigh," or to play the roles of "Adam Cupid" and "King Cophetua." (If you are speedy enough, whip the costume around to be the gown of the "beggar-maid" as well.

Make your cape and sword manly to make clear to Romeo that if he were truly a man, he'd come and join you.

Make Rosaline's "quivering thigh" erotically stimulating, and her "demesnes" mysteriously compelling. Pretend Rosaline is on stage with you, and point to her presumed body parts with your sword as you name them, allowing your sword to take on metaphoric (phallic) proportions as you get closer and closer to the sacred "demesnes."

Question: Why did Shakespeare use this obscure (even to an Elizabethan) word, rather than a more common (or grosser) slang one?

KATHERINE

KATHERINE: Nay, then,
Do what thou canst, I will not go to-day;
No, nor to-morrow, not till I please myself.
The door is open, sir; there lies your way;
You may be jogging whiles your boots are green;
For me, I'll not be gone till I please myself:
'Tis like you'll prove a jolly surly groom,
That take it on you at the first so roundly.

(Taming of the Shrew, III.ii.221ff.)

Word notes: "You may be jogging whiles your boots are green" probably means something like "Run along now before your boots get stiff." "Jolly" simply intensifies the word it precedes, as in "jolly well." "Take it on you" means something like "take it on yourself to be so arrogant."

You are an unmarried elder sister, and you are aware that some people consider you a "shrew" that must be "tamed" before you can find a husband. On the other hand, you know yourself to be attractive, competent, and highly intelligent, and you see no reason to put up with the foolishness that surrounds you. A short time ago, Petruchio, a rude—but handsome and rich—young man arrived at your household. He proposed to you in a rather crude but undeniably dashing manner, and, while giving it many second thoughts, you have just now married him. But at this moment he is refusing to attend the wedding banquet prepared by your family, and is demanding instead to take you back to his country home immediately, as your family and guests are waiting to eat. You decide you have to assert your authority and independence—for if you give in now, you will be a slave to him for the rest of your marriage.

Make your first two lines build to an absolutely incontrovertible statement of defiance. Then, in the repetition of "till I please myself," solidify your bottom line; make *myself* the last word in how this marriage will be directed.

With your last two lines, try to entertain your family and your friends by mocking and shaming your husband. "Jolly surly groom" takes a deliberately superior tone; so should the way you swirl your splendid wedding gown. Let him know that you and your family are aristocrats, and he's just a country bumpkin in green boots. Stride about the room, letting your train fill up with air and surround him with flowing fabric, the fabric of aristocratic finery. Impress your family with your own mature magnificence. You, the eldest daughter, are upholding the family's honor by the way your gown fills the air. You are, as it were, flying your family's heraldic flag!

"Groom," you should know, means "bridegroom," but also means the servant who takes care of the horses. Try to make him understand this second meaning, and put him in his place. (Of course, you will fail. In a moment, Petruchio will reply with his "she is my good, my chattels . . . my horse" speech seen in Lesson 8 [so much for his being the groom] and will cart you away.)

SIR ANDREW AGUECHEEK

SIR ANDREW AGUECHEEK: By my troth, the fool has an excellent breast. I had rather than forty shillings I had such a leg, and so sweet a breath to sing, as the fool has. In sooth, thou wast in very gracious fooling last night, when thou spokest of Pigrogromitus, of the Vapians passing the equinoctial of Queubus: 'twas very good, i' faith. I sent thee sixpence for thy leman: hadst it?

(*Twelfth Night*, II.iii.18ff.)

Word notes: "Leman" means "sweetheart." The "fool" is a character called by that name; his job is to entertain the court and to sing, dance, and mock-philosophize. "Fooling" refers to the latter. You don't have to be concerned with the meaning of Pigrogromitus, Vapians, equinoctial, or Queubus—they are meaningless, and you can pronounce them any way you wish—as the fool was only "fooling" with Sir Andrew. The fool's "leg" refers to his dancing ability, his "breath" and "breast" are in reference to his singing. "By my troth," "in sooth," and "i' faith" are all common Elizabethan expressions for "truly."

You are a minor lord, certainly through inheritance rather than accomplishment, and you hang around the court of Lady Olivia with your friend Toby Belch, to whom you loan large sums of money. Your goal is to make everybody happy with your infectious charm and wisdom, so they will keep you around longer. You *adore* Olivia, and hope some day she will notice you.

Show off your intelligence by your pronunciation of these wonderfully intellectual and clever terms—indeed, pronounce them *better* than the fool did when he told them to you. Also show your familiarity with courtly niceties by peppering your conversation with the (utterly meaningless) phrases "by my troth," and "in sooth," and "i' faith." Show that you *belong* in

this rarefied court atmosphere, and appeal to your hearers (the Fool and Sir Toby) to keep you around longer — and to bear your petition to Olivia. Build your speech publicly (that is, for Toby's overhearing) until ". . . very good, i' faith," and then drop to a confidential tone as you speak to the fool, to whom you are also giving money, but without Toby's knowledge.

Flaunt your costume, which is like a diaper with a codpiece. Use it in an effort to emphasize your (lacking) maturity and masculinity. Flop one of the loose ends of your diaper about wildly to show off your male phallicity (cockiness), and hang on to it for security when you get nervous (Linus Gloriosus!). Put your well-formed fist boldly on your hip as if to draw a sword upon the least provocation (if you only knew how).

OLIVIA

OLIVIA: Your lord does know my mind; I cannot love him:
Yet I suppose him virtuous, know him noble,
Of great estate, of fresh and stainless youth;

In voices well divulged, free, learned, and valiant;
And, in dimension and the shape of nature,
A gracious person: but yet I cannot love him;
He might have took his answer long ago.
(*Twelfth Night*, I.v.276ff.)

Word notes: "In voices well divulged" means "well spoken of"; "dimension"
means "physically"; "of great estate" refers to his wealth.

You are a recent widow being wooed by the local count Orsino through an
intermediary whom you know as the young man Cesario. (This Cesario is
actually a young woman, Viola, in disguise, and the play is a romantic
comedy.) You are rejecting Orsino's suit through this Cesario, but you find
yourself falling in love with Cesario at the same time. As you tick off Orsino's
positive qualities (he's virtuous, noble, and so on), *find* the same qualities in
the young "man" you're looking at—and speaking to. *Gush* your approval,
so that this Cesario might fall in love with you, while at the same time taking
back a message of "no go" to the count.

Build these positive qualities sensually as you say them, and get more infatuated with Cesario as you praise his/Orsino's moral character (virtuous), economic standing ("of great estate"), intelligence (learned), bravery (valiant), and sexual attractiveness (dimension and "shape") — culminating in a summary judgment ("a gracious person") that makes you shudder with held-back excitement.

Use your dress and figure as provocatively and seductively as your voice. The more your words say no (to Orsino), let your tone of voice, the movements of your body, and the sashaying of your gown say yes (to Cesario). Playfully finger your garment at its tie-points, as to make clear that, at a word from Cesario, you could disrobe yourself in an instant.

THERSITES

THERSITES: Here's Agamemnon, an honest fellow enough, and one that loves quails; but he has not so much brain as earwax: and the goodly transformation of Jupiter there, his brother, the bull — the primitive statue, and oblique memorial of cuckolds; a thrifty shoeing-horn in a chain, hanging at his brother's leg — to what form but that he is, should wit larded with malice and malice forced with wit turn him to? To an ass, were nothing; he is both ass and ox; to an ox, were nothing; he is both ox and ass. To be a dog, a mule, a cat, a fitchew, a toad, a lizard, an owl, a puttock, or a herring without a roe, I would not care: but to be Menelaus! I would conspire against destiny. Ask me not what I would be, if I were not Thersites; for I care not to be the louse of a lazar, so I were not Menelaus.

(*Troilus and Cressida*, V.i.54ff.)

Word notes: "Quails" are prostitutes. Agamemnon's brother is Menelaus, a cuckold — his wife, Helen, has been abducted by Paris — and therefore someone wearing a cuckold's "horns," like a bull. A "fitchew" is a polecat, a "puttock" is a bird, "louse" is the singular of "lice," and a "lazar" is a leper.

You are speaking to the audience of the sorry lot of generals running the war. Let us know your contempt of, and superiority to, the stupid Agamemnon and the pathetic Menelaus. It's a complicated speech: In the first part, you describe Menelaus's fall from king/general/god to cuckold bull, and explain that even with all your wit and malice you couldn't transform him into anything lower than he already is: ass and ox. In the second part, you list all the things you would rather be than Menelaus, ending with a leper's louse.

Build downward, from the god Jupiter to the eggless herring, so that you take Menelaus down (in our eyes) along with you. *Disgust* us further and further as you go through the speech; impress us with the utter depths of your contempt (and your brilliant word choices along the way!). Make each animal and insect more putrid than the last, until the leper's louse hits rock bottom, turning our stomachs. (Notice that while the list is of single

words, the final two items have four words each, to give you the possibility of climaxing with them.)

Use your own sagging belly (stuffed with your blanket, of course) and unkempt appearance to show us how you are dragged down by living and working for such vile people — when you are so eloquent with language and critical ideas.

Use your (gross) body, your movements, and your facial expressions to "portray" for us the animals you find "superior" to Menelaus — the Meneleus you wish us to see. *Be* the ass, the ox, the toad, the puttock, and the "herring without a roe." This last line literally means "fish without an egg," but you can play (with) it to suggest "fish-flesh without a penis."

At the word "louse," pluck an imaginary louse off your costume, (out of your armpit, maybe?) as you play the role of the lazar/leper, and say "so were I not Menelaus" right to the louse!

CASSANDRA

CASSANDRA: Cry, Trojans, cry! Lend me ten thousand eyes,
And I will fill them with prophetic tears.
Virgins and boys, mid-age and wrinkled eld,
Soft infancy, that nothing canst but cry,
Add to my clamors! Let us pay betimes
A moiety of that mass of moan to come.
Cry, Trojans, cry! Practice your eyes with tears!
Troy must not be, nor goodly Ilion stand;
Our firebrand brother, Paris, burns us all.
Cry, Trojans, cry! a Helen and a woe:
Cry, cry! Troy burns, or else let Helen go.
(*Troilus and Cressida,* II.ii.101ff.)

*Word notes: "Eld" means "elders"; "betimes" in this instance means "now";
a "moiety" is a portion. "Ilion" is another name for Troy, and Paris is the
Trojan warrior-prince who abducted Helen, causing the Trojan War.*

You are a princess and prophetess in Troy, and you clearly foresee your fellow Trojans defeated in the war with Greece. Although the Trojans consider you mad, you urge them to reckon with their fate — that if they don't give Helen back to the Greeks, their city will be burned and their country destroyed.

Since you offer prophecy, not provable facts, you must impress your countrymen with your powers of religious incantation. Don't appeal to their reason so much as try and make them have faith in your prophetic vision. *Sing* the "cry, Trojans, cry" refrain, and build the "cry" motif. "Receive" your speech from divine sources, and pass it through your body to your hearers (the Trojan court: Hector, Priam, Troilus, Paris, and Helenus). *Shiver* with religious fervor at the alliterative *m*'s in your "moiety of that mass of moan." Build up to a platform at the end, and then make your final rhyming couplet the last word: the divine truth. Give it the strength of a commandment.

Since the Trojans account you mad, make no effort to preserve your dignity or rational "good taste"; take advantage of your eccentric reputation. Find new sounds in your voice — sounds resounding from the bottom of your belly and the top of your scalp.

Your robe is pure fantasy; use it in any way that inspires religious awe and convinces your hearers that you are transmitting messages from the gods. Make it a tent for a thousand eyes, a basket for a thousand tears, an acoustical shell for your voiced "clamors." Whirl your robe in enveloping cascades of swirling fabric. Show them that you are possessed — with the truth!

"Mad" characters are liberating to play, and to play with. Enjoy this one!

LAUNCELOT

LAUNCELOT GOBBO: Nay, indeed, if you had your eyes, you might fail of the knowing me: it is a wise father that knows his own child. Well, old man, I will tell you news of your son: give me your blessing. Truth will come to light; murder cannot be hid long, — a man's son may; but, in the end, truth will out. Pray you, let's have no more fooling about it, but give me your blessing: I am Launcelot, your boy that was, your son that is, your child that shall be. I am Launcelot, the Jew's man; and I am sure Margery your wife is my mother.

(*The Merchant of Venice*, II.ii.80ff; this is a slightly edited combination of two successive speeches.)

Word notes: "The Jew" is Shylock, a Jewish moneylender.

You have just met your nearly blind father, Gobbo, (see the next character sketch) on the street, and he has failed to recognize you. At first you tease him, telling him his son is dead, but now you want to tell him the truth. You clinch it by naming his wife, your mother.

Try to entertain yourself, and any passersby that happen upon this scene, by teasing your old man. Show your father, and the passersby, how intelligent you've become — how clever, how wise to the ways of the world. Show

him that now *you're* the father. As he once dominated you in the world, now you dominate him: Tell him the truth, lead him to wisdom and safety. Show off your new adult powers of verbal construction: "boy that was, . . . son that is, . . . child that will be." Give your eloquent, sententious thoughts — "murder cannot be hid," "truth will out," and "it is a wise father that knows his own child" — with newly bestowed paternal authority. *You* are the expert now, the fount of pithy, eternal wisdom. (You even get to be the bore your father was!) Let your father see how grand you have become.

Rearrange your costume to disguise yourself at the beginning; cover one side of your face; make your cloak more mysterious, dashing, manly. Parade around for him so that he, near-blind, can be dazzled by your super-hip, big-city sophistication. As he dominated you as a child, now you can dominate him as a dotard. Then (at "let's have no more fooling") drop the pretense, return your cloak to its proper position, and (at "I am Launcelot") use the garment to identify yourself. Then, realizing that this won't do (your father doesn't recognize these new clothes), further the identification process by removing the cloak at "your son that is, your child that shall be." Show him the real (that is, unadorned) you. You might then use the rope (around your neck), showing it as your new emblem of servitude, in demonstrating that you are now "the Jew's man."

OLD GOBBO

OLD GOBBO: Her name is Margery, indeed: I'll be sworn, if thou be Launcelot, thou art mine own flesh and blood. Lord worshipped might he be! what a beard hast thou got! thou hast got more hair on thy chin than Dobbin my fill-horse has on his tail. Lord, how thou art changed!

(*The Merchant of Venice*, II.ii.94; this is a slightly edited combination of two successive speeches.)

Word note: A "fill-horse" is a working horse.

You are an old and nearly blind man, failing to recognize your son, Launcelot, in a chance street encounter after a period of separation. Launcelot (the preceding character sketch) insists that he is your son and confirms it by saying "I am sure Margery your wife is my mother." This speech is your reply.

Show your son that you love him, by expressing your joy at finding him, your embarrassment at not recognizing him, and your astonishment at how much he has changed (thereby excusing your not recognizing him).

Use your costume and prop to show how increasingly blind you have become. *Feel* his flesh all over with your hands, suggesting that you cannot see it; fail to find the beard on his face, and first find something else instead. Point to Dobbin with your stick, and, twirling back to Launcelot, let the stick whack him on the buttocks before exclaiming "Lord, how thou art changed."

Keep from getting cold; wrap the costume (it's a shawl, here) around you to protect your fragile, too-sensitive bones.

LAUNCE

LAUNCE: O, 'tis a foul thing when a cur cannot keep himself in all companies! I would have, as one should say, one that takes upon him to be a dog indeed, to be, as it were, a dog at all things. If I had not had more wit than he, to take a fault upon me that he did, I think verily he had been hanged for't; sure as I live, he had suffered for't: you shall judge. He thrusts me himself into the company of three or four gentlemanlike dogs, under the duke's table: he had not been there—bless the mark!—a pissing while, but all the chamber smelt him. 'Out with the dog!' says one: 'What cur is that?' says another: 'Whip him out' says the third: 'Hang him up' says the duke. I, having been acquainted with the smell before, knew it was Crab, and goes me to the fellow that whips the dogs: 'Friend,' quoth I, 'you mean to whip the dog?' 'Ay, marry, do I,' quoth he. 'You do him the more wrong,' quoth I;   'twas I did the thing you wot of.' He makes me no more ado, but whips me out of the chamber.

(*Two Gentlemen of Verona*, IV.iv.1ff.)

Word notes: "Keep himself" means restrain himself; "verily" means "truly"; and "wot" means "know." "Crab" is the name of Launce's dog, who is the subject of this story. This is only the middle of a longer speech; you might want to work on the entire piece after starting with this section.

You are a servant who loves your dog, which is standing next to you as you speak. You have been ordered to give it away, and are telling us—the Globe Theatre audience—how much you love the dog, no matter how bad his behavior. Perhaps you have an unconscious hope that we will somehow prevent your losing your faithful Crab; in any event, try to endear us to your dog, and to you as a loyal dog-master.

First, *show* your good sense of discipline by chastising Crab. *Insult* him: that he cannot keep himself, that he hasn't as much wit as you do. This will build your credibility with us.

Then *tell the story* to us so that we "shall judge." Make the story clear, and *entertain* us with the recounting of Crab's misdemeanor and the public reaction against it. *Build* the four quoted attacks against Crab to show the powers you are forced to confront in protecting your dog.

And reach for a level of rustic eloquence when you conclude with your canine rescue. Deliberately choose to use the fancy "you wot of" instead of

the commonplace "you know of" so as to dignify your sacrifice. Say these ceremonial last words before your whipping, implying "I regret that I have but one life to give to my Crab."

Your costume is a giant scarf that, as you narrate the story, can help you demonstrate a leash ("a dog indeed"), a noose ("he had been hanged for't," "hang him up") and a whip ("whip him out," "whip the dog," "whips me out of the chamber").

It can also be your wringing garment, for squeezing in despair at the beginning of the tale, and your dashing scarf (think of the Red Baron) that you whip triumphantly over your shoulder on "'twas I did the thing you wot of." The juxtaposition of that swashbuckling gesture and the pathetic absurdity of your claim (that it was you who pee'd beneath the table) together with the silliness (even to an Elizabethan audience) of the medieval word "wot," all makes this a wonderfully comic finish to the speech — as well as gives us insight into the kindly character of Launce.

LUCIANA

LUCIANA: A man is master of his liberty . . .
There's nothing situate under heaven's eye
But hath his bound, in earth, in sea, in sky:
The beasts, the fishes, and the winged fowls,
Are their males' subjects and at their controls:
Men, more divine, the masters of all these,
Lords of the wide world and wild watery seas,
Indued with intellectual sense and souls,
Of more pre-eminence than fish and fowls,
Are masters to their females and their lords:
Then let your will attend on their accords.
(*Two Gentlemen of Verona*, II.i.6 and 15ff.)

Word notes: "Situate" is short for "situated"; "indued" means, essentially, "imbued," or "such is in their due." "Accords" means "agreements," or in this case perhaps "orders." The first line of this speech actually comes from a slightly earlier speech of Luciana's in the scene, and has been edited in here to provide context.

Your older sister is complaining that her husband hasn't come home; with this speech you urge your sister simply to "dine and never fret."

The speech asks you to take an utterly unfeminist position: to argue total subjugation to men (we are "males' subjects," you tell your sister). So make a virtue out of wide-eyed innocence.

Make your ideas pretty, but make them also *eternal truths*. How? By rapturizing over the "earth and sea and sky." *Don't* build these; get lost in them, and get lost also in the "beasts, the fishes, and the winged fowls." These words do not create structured arguments so much as pretty pictures for you and your sister to look at and admire.

Draw out the vowels in "wide world" and "wild, watery seas," so your sister will succumb to the admiration of Men who can tame such grand forces of nature.

And play the rhymes in your speech to create a feeling of *holy verities,* as though this were a church hymn (and you a one-woman church choir) praising the glory and honor of the divine Man.

With your costume, flaunt your innocence; show how pretty and happy a totally submissive woman can be, and try to induce such subjugation in your too-aggressive elder sister.

Toss your hair, play with the folds of your dress, and emphasize the femininity of your figure and gown on "masters to their females." Make a delicate curtsey, as to your "man," and stay down on the next phrase of that line, ". . . and their lords." Then, from a lowered position, look up shyly at your man on the "their" in "Then let your will attend on their accords." Don't let your own political feelings get in your way! You wouldn't do so if you were playing Iago or Lady Macbeth, would you? Don't here; this is *acting*!

MARK ANTONY

ANTONY: O mighty Caesar! dost thou lie so low?
Are all thy conquests, glories, triumphs, spoils,
Shrunk to this little measure? Fare thee well. —
I know not, gentlemen, what you intend,
Who else must be let blood, who else is rank:
If I myself, there is no hour so fit
As Caesar's death's hour: nor no instrument
Of half that worth as those your swords, made rich
With the most noble blood of all this world.
I do beseech ye, if you bear me hard,
Now, whilst your purpled hands do reek and smoke,
Fulfil your pleasure. Live a thousand years,
I shall not find myself so apt to die:
No place will please me so, no mean of death

As here by Caesar, and by you cut off,
The choice and master spirits of this age.
(*Julius Caesar*, III.i.148)

Word notes: "Mean" means "means."

Your friend Julius Caesar has just been assassinated, and you have come to the site. Now, over Caesar's corpse, you are speaking with the assassins. Your goal is to both persuade the assassins of your loyalty, offering them your life, and at the same time start sowing the discord you plan to exploit in revenging Caesar's death.

Build "conquests, glories, triumphs, spoils" just enough to fire up any potential counterrevolutionaries that may exist among the assassins. Burn into their minds the magnificence of the man they just killed.

Fiercely pretend to honor the assassins by pretending to submit to their will. *Trust* in your knowledge of human nature, which tells you that Brutus, the leader of the assassins, will never accept your offer of mortal sacrifice. Show your great Roman courage in making the offer (you know will be refused).

Now put these together with your gruesome reading of "purpled hands" and an unctuous "fulfil your pleasure." *Make them squirm* with guilt—as contrasted to your self-sacrificial purity.

Use your costume and movement here, making them terribly aware of the unspoken contrast: that you are in a clean, white, unspotted toga — and they are drenched in Caesar's blood. Stand tall, unashamed, unafraid. Open your arms as far as you can on "Now, whilst your purpled hands do reek and smoke," to show the whiteness of your toga, your guileless innocence, the reach of your (public) appeal, and your sacrificial, saintly purity — all against their vile and bloodstained palms.

At your conclusion, play viciously on Brutus's Roman conscience, intensifying your hearers' sense of shame with your empty, ironic flattery, calling them "choice and master spirits of this age." You don't have to be sarcastic. Their own guilt and shame will make your point only too painful to hear.

VIOLA

VIOLA: Most radiant, exquisite, and unmatchable beauty, — I pray you, tell me if this be the lady of the house, for I never saw her: I would be loath to cast away my speech; for, besides that it is excellently well penned, I have taken great pains to con it. Good beauties, let me sustain no scorn; I am very comptible, even to the least sinister usage.
(*Twelfth Night*, I.v.147ff.)

Word notes: "Con" means to "memorize," and "comptible" means "accountable."

This is one of Shakespeare's "pants" roles. You are a young woman in a strange foreign country, and for safety you have disguised yourself as a man. You are employed by a count to deliver a love letter to a countess, and you are trying to do this now, speaking to a group of women and unsure which of them is the countess and which are the ladies-in-waiting.

Your goal here is to appear manly and romantic, and to woo the countess for your master, the count. Many things confuse you, however: the unfamiliarity of your male costume, the strange flowery language of the speech you have "conned," and the odd reception you are receiving from this group of women, none of whom you know. Moreover, you are yourself falling in love with the count and have mixed feelings about your mission. You aren't too eager for it to succeed, but can't afford to have it fail, either. Work to conquer your confusion. Start to *build* your opening "rehearsed" adjectives: "radiant, exquisite, and unmatchable beauty." Then let your "conned" speech fall apart when you realize you're quite possibly talking to the wrong person.

Make your "I have taken great pains to con it" a show of brute masculine authority (play "con it" as though it were a slangy, locker-room male expression); and make your "sustain no scorn . . . very comptible . . . sinister usage" as brawny as you can — somewhat like an embattled brigadier-general testifying before a congressional committee.

Make your costume *tough,* super-manly. Put a sword (yardstick) in it if you wish. Wear a man's boots, and swagger. Take big strides. Make fists. Spit in a spittoon. Take liberties.

BENVOLIO

BENVOLIO: Madam, an hour before the worshipped sun
Peered forth the golden window of the east,
A troubled mind drave me to walk abroad;
Where — underneath the grove of sycamore
That westward rooteth from the city's side —
So early walking did I see your son:
Towards him I made; but he was 'ware of me,
And stole into the covert of the wood . . .
(*Romeo and Juliet,* I.i.125ff.)

Word notes: As you probably guessed, Shakespeare's "drave" is another word for "drove," and "'ware" is short for "aware." By this time, you probably need the word notes less and less, no?

A bitter street brawl involving servants of the Montague family has just ended, and the fighters have departed. You are a worthy friend of Romeo, a Montague; and his mother has just asked you if you have seen her son. This is your reply.

Your goal is, first, to assure her of Romeo's noninvolvement in the street fight. Thus, use the poetic, descriptive imagery of the speech to take Lady

Montague's mind away from the current events, and back to the predawn scene of Romeo wandering in the woods outside of town. Use the (quite self-consciously) lovely imagery to show Lady Montague that Romeo is interested in loving, not fighting.

The poetic language — "worshipped sun," "golden window," "westward rooteth," "covert of the wood" — is your tool with which you try to ease Lady Montague's anxiety. Caress her with these words and images; float them gently but firmly into her mind, as tranquilizers to her troubled mind.

Use your open, flowing cape to show that you have opened up entirely to her (show her that you have nothing up your sleeve). Calm Lady Montague (even try to hypnotize her a little) with the broad, sweeping arcs of your cloak, choreographed to your poetic images. Physically assume your highest stature, your most believable worthiness, your most gracious cordiality to your best friend's nervous mother. Calm her nerves; give her the strength she needs.

"Drave" and "ware," which are listed in the word notes, are words that were uncommon even in Shakespeare's day; use them to make her think a bit more, and to distract her from her current concerns. Remember: Shakespeare could easily have written "drove" and "aware" (a little rewriting would save the meter); that he did not indicates he wanted you to play with the more obscure words, so as to increase the hypnotic effect of the speech.

Remember also: It is not important to the play that Romeo walked in a sycamore grove instead of, say, an elm grove. What is important is that you make Lady Montague think thoughts of love instead of battle.

JOAN OF ARC

> JOAN: First, let me tell you whom you have condemned.
> Not me begotten of a shepherd swain,
> But issued from the progeny of kings;
> Virtuous and holy; chosen from above,
> By inspiration of celestial grace,
> To work exceeding miracles on earth.
> I never had to do with wicked spirits:
> But you, that are polluted with your lusts,
> Stained with the guiltless blood of innocents,
> Corrupt and tainted with a thousand vices,
> Because you want the grace that others have,
> You judge it straight a thing impossible
> To compass wonders but by help of devils.
> No, misconceived! Joan of Arc hath been
> A virgin from her tender infancy,
> Chaste and immaculate in very thought;
> Whose maiden blood, thus rigorously effused,
> Will cry for vengeance at the gates of heaven.
> (*1 Henry VI*, V.iv.36ff.)

Word notes: "Want" is in the sense of "lack"; "rigorously effused" means "forced from my body."

You want the world to think you are a virgin saint, descended from kings, parallel to the Virgin Mary ("chosen from above"). You have been accused of consorting with devils, but here taunt your accusers, suggesting that they, "polluted" with lust and "stained" with blood, lack the grace to understand your saintliness.

You should understand that, in this play, all these claims are lies. You are, in fact, a shepherd's daughter, a promiscuous woman, and a willing consort with evil fiends. This is *not* the St. Joan of French historians, the Catholic Church, or George Bernard Shaw!

Because it's a lie, and because you are pretty sure they know it's a lie, work all the harder: You have only rhetoric to save your life. *Build* your holiness directly. You are, or want them to think you are: (1) royal, (2) virtuous, and (3) divine; they are (1) lusty, (2) bloody, (3) corrupt, and

(4) tainted with a thousand vices. In your coda, play the Mark Antony role: Eloquently offer your maiden blood; *reach* for the sophisticated phrase "rigorously effused," which clearly tops the otherwise simple language of the speech. Then, having taken the high intellectual ground, promise the fiercest vengeance from God, your (!) father.

Play this speech right to the audience—your "court." Use your bare costume at the start to display your purity and innocence: "virtuous and holy," "chaste and immaculate," "a virgin from her tender infancy." But then use it, and the freedom of movement it provides, to show them your strength—particularly at the speech-turning words, "No, misconceived!" and at the "cry for vengeance at the gates of heaven" conclusion.

PETRUCHIO

PETRUCHIO: Signior Hortensio, 'twixt such friends as we
Few words suffice; and therefore, if thou know
One rich enough to be Petruchio's wife, —

As wealth is burden of my wooing dance, —
Be she as foul as was Florentius' love,
As old as Sibyl, and as curst and shrewd
As Socrates' Xanthippe, or a worse,
She moves me not, or not removes, at least,
Affection's edge in me, were she as rough
As are the swelling Adriatic seas:
I come to wive it wealthily in Padua;
If wealthily, then happily in Padua.

(*Taming of the Shrew*, I.ii.60ff.)

Word notes: "Signior," pronounced in Elizabethan English as "seen-your," is the Italian "Mr." "Burden" here means "the most important part of," technically in a musical scoring (the "obligato"). "Curst" means "cursed with shrewishness," as does, to some extent, "shrewd." Most of Shakespeare's audience, and today's as well, would neither know nor need to know that Florentius marries a hag in Confessio Amantis, *that Sybil was a prophetess blessed by Apollo with long life, or that Xanthippe was Socrates's shrewish wife. These references are clear from the context in which they are presented, however. The "a" in "or a worse" indicates a contraction for "or even worse," but really is primarily added for the meter. Padua is the Italian town where the play takes place.*

You are seeking to find and marry a rich woman, no matter how shrewish she might prove to be (you plan to "tame" her), and you want to make clear to your friend Hortensio how "immovable" you are in this determination.

Your goal is to surround your hearers with rhetoric so they won't argue against you. Your speech is *rehearsed* — for you have known all along you would be giving it when you got to Padua. So build it precisely: Your "few words" will indeed suffice if you build your argument into an impregnable position.

Your classical allusions (Florentius, Sybil, and Xanthippe — drawn, respectively, from Renaissance novels, Greek mythology, and Greek history) and your geographical references (Adriatic seas, Padua), and even your referring to yourself in the third person ("to be Petruchio's wife") are your means of establishing the *solid and fixed context* of your determination. Use them to indicate the sense that "it is not only my will, but the force of history, mythology, and geography that fixes my determintion on this quest."

Build the adjectives "old," "foul," "curst and shrewd," and "a worse" so that "foul" is worse than "old," "curst and shrewd" worse than "foul," and "a worse" is worst of all. Similarly, make Florentius's wife bad, Sybil much worse, and Xanthippe horrible beyond belief. (Note that Shakespeare helps with the progression of their names: "Xanthippe" is even ugly to look at.)

Use your rhetoric and literary figures in the same way: the antithesis ("moves . . . not"/"not removes"); alliteration and grandiloquence ("swelling Adriatic seas"; "wive it wealthily"); parallel construction ("if wealthily, then

happily"); and your concluding lines ending with identical words (". . . in Padua"/". . . in Padua"). This latter rhetorical device is called, by the way, *epistrophe,* and here puts a stunning "cap" on the speech.

Make your ending refrain (from "were she as rough") all but musical in its cadences, and sing out your final lines as an invitation to some sort of victory dance (indeed, these last two lines were set to music by Cole Porter in *Kiss Me Kate*).

Get your hips into this victory dance — your hips which, in this case, will be extended by the flying fabric at your waist. Let your body move and your costume fill the air, surrounding your hearers, and Hortensio particularly, with your loin-centered masculine presence and your extraordinary energy. You may only be offering "few words," but you are also giving thousands of signals with your physical presence.

CHARMIAN

CHARMIAN: . . . So, fare thee well. —
Now boast thee, death; in thy possession lies
A lass unparalleled. — Downy windows, close;
And golden Phoebus never be beheld
Of eyes again so royal! — Your crown's awry;
I'll mend it, and then play.
(*Antony and Cleopatra*, V.ii.317)

Word notes: "Golden Phoebus" refers to the sun — technically, to Apollo, god of sunlight. By "downy windows" Charmian refers to Cleopatra's eyes.

Cleopatra has just committed suicide. You were her faithful lady-in-waiting; you were both captured by the Romans, and she has been the first to "escape" by placing the poisonous snake to her breast. You are about to do the same (that's what you mean by "play").

Your speech, technically, consists of a series of "apostrophes," which are speeches directed to nonpresent persons or abstractions. You speak both to the dead Cleopatra and to the personified figure of "death."

But you are also speaking, in your mind at least, to the Roman guards outside the door who have imprisoned you, and who have caused this tragic ending of your queen (one of the guards enters after this speech). You are speaking as well to your Eastern (Egyptian) gods, and to the figure of "death" you soon shall greet.

Use this strange, apostrophic format: your classical allusion and poetic, literary expressions ("downy windows," "golden Phoebus"), and even your graceful and beautifully ironic sense of humor in the face of death ("your crown's awry; I'll mend it and then play") to proclaim to the world your cultural superiority to the crude Romans, as well as to prepare your imminent meeting with death and your gods. So don't just speak these words, *proclaim* them, and *pray* with them.

Make yourself physically presentable to your (Egyptian, Eastern) gods. With your posture and costume, as well as your tone of voice, transform your prison to a religious temple, and you the high priestess of it. Cleopatra represents, in Shakespeare's play, the mysterious East ("all the East . . . shall call her mistress," Alexas says), so *contrast* your Eastern gown, your poetic and refined manner of expression, your classical allusions, and your ability to speak directly with "death" and with the dead, against the boorishness of your Roman military captors.

Make your best "case" to your gods—you might be on the losing side in the political arena, but you are more sensitive, more beautiful, more spiritual, more dignified, and more eloquent than the Romans. In adjusting Cleopatra's crown, adjust your own attire. Make the two of you fit companions for divinities.

GLOUCESTER

EARL OF GLOUCESTER: I' the last night's storm I such a fellow saw;
Which made me think a man a worm: my son
Came then into my mind; and yet my mind
Was then scarce friends with him. I have heard more since.
As flies to wanton boys, are we to the gods,—
They kill us for their sport.
(*King Lear,* IV.i.31)

You are an earl. Earlier today your eyes were gouged out by a rival duke, who has also thrown you out of your home; warrants are now out for your death. You are led on by your son, Edgar, but he's in disguise, and, blinded, you don't recognize him. (Edgar was also the "madman" you saw last night, before your blinding, but you didn't recognize him then, either. At that time you thought he was allied with your enemies, though you "have heard more since.") Now you are planning suicide—to be led to the cliffs of Dover, where you will jump off to your death.

In these late tragedies, Shakespeare often uses simpler language and less formal rhetoric than in the earlier plays. There are no unfamiliar words here, and no building lists of adjectives, but the speech does build from the specific (a narration of the fellow in the storm) to the general (an aphorism concerning the relations of gods and man); and from metaphor (". . . think a man a worm") to simile ("as flies to wanton boys are we . . ."). Try to make this a build toward *profundity,* toward a summing up of your life-philosophy — given moments before your expected death.

Show the gods what they have reduced you to — in the paucity of your language; the raggedness of your costume; and the affliction of your blinding, which you can emphasize to the gods by your grappling with your walking stick.

But also use your blindness to show that you *can* see — if not superficial reality, then deeply into the relationships between gods and man. ("I want [lack] no eyes, I stumbled when I saw," you said a moment earlier.) Use your walking stick to probe your chief subjects: man, worms, and gods. "Look at" and point to the gods on the last line; although you are speaking to Edgar, what do you want the gods to hear? Or what can you make them hear? *Try*

to make them hear, though you fear they will not. Build the speech emotionally, so as to demand a reckoning with brutal gods who have treated you so abominably.

Notice the enormous difference between your presuicide speech and that of Charmian in the previous exercise: Charmian will "play" at her approaching death, whereas you find yourself *played upon* by the gods, toyed with as part of "their sport." Your speech, therefore, is not a prayer to the gods, but a challenge to them. So *challenge* them. *Change* them.

MARGARET

QUEEN MARGARET: Stay, dog, for thou shalt hear me.
If heaven have any grievous plague in store
Exceeding those that I can wish upon thee,
O, let them keep it till thy sins be ripe,
And then hurl down their indignation

On thee, the troubler of the poor world's peace!
The worm of conscience still begnaw thy soul!
Thy friends suspect for traitors while thou livest,
And take deep traitors for thy dearest friends!
No sleep close up that deadly eye of thine,
Unless it be while some tormenting dream
Affrights thee with a hell of ugly devils!
Thou elvish-marked, abortive, rooting hog!
Thou that wast sealed in thy nativity
The slave of nature and the son of hell!
Thou slander of thy mother's heavy womb!
Thou loathed issue of thy father's loins!
Thou rag of honor! thou detested—
(GLOUCESTER: Margaret!
MARGARET: Richard!)

(*Richard III*, I.iii.216ff.) (This is a fuller version of the speech from Exercise 11-8, and you may wish to refer back to that exercise before proceeding.)

Word notes: "Loathed" should be pronounced with two syllables, as "loathe-ed."

You can see that this is a building exercise par excellence. Margaret's curses are legendary, awesome, and incendiary; they escalate directly to the end, where Gloucester interrupts her at the last minute, inserting her name where she was about to say his. If you have a partner, include the last two lines, given here in parentheses.

You are the old queen, widow of Henry VI, no longer in power; you serve as a chorus or prophetess in this play, often speaking directly to the audience. You are here speaking in the court to your nephew, the Duke of Gloucester, soon to be Richard III.

Your goal is to make Gloucester hated at court and revealed to heaven—as a traitor, plotter, hellion, and "slave of nature" (that is, not a follower of Christian law). You seek for heaven's wrath to come down on him, and you believe you have a direct line to heaven.

This will test your building powers, for there are well over a dozen curses structured into an accelerating pattern.

Use your mysterious, otherworldly gown to create a larger-than-life character who "speaks in tongues," and who, more than inventing these curses, is drawing them from deep spiritual sources and passing them on. Try to make as grand a figure in the court as possible, and as tight a structure of curses as you can, so that nobody will interrupt you. After all, you're onstage with the active queen of England, the future king, and at least two royal lords, none of whom have to keep listening to you.

Circle around Richard, and find a moment (perhaps "hell of ugly devils!") to spin all the way around, dervishlike, letting your cloak fill with air and thus vastly enlarging your presence and your demonic power. Make your costume a witch's cloak, with black magic of its own. Margaret ("Mad

Margaret" she is usually called) is a seer and a prophetess, and has witchlike characteristics, so play them for all they're worth. They will, if anything will, force the court's attention to Richard's evil.

SOOTHSAYER

SOOTHSAYER: O Antony, stay not by his side:
Thy demon, that's thy spirit which keeps thee, is
Noble, courageous, high, unmatchable,
Where Caesar's is not; but, near him, thy angel
Becomes a fear, as being o'erpowered: therefore
Make space enough between you.
(*Antony and Cleopatra*, II.iii.18ff.)

Word notes: Soothsayer" means "truth-sayer;" "keeps" here means "protects" and "a fear" here means "afraid." "Demon," "spirit," and "angel," in this case, all refer to the same thing: Antony's guiding spirit. The gist of the soothsayer's "sooth" is that Antony's guiding spirit is noble, except when [Octavius] Caesar is near, so Antony should stay away from Caesar.

You are an Egyptian prophet of truth, accompanying Mark Antony to Rome; your goal is to convince Antony to return to Egypt (and Cleopatra), and to leave Rome (and Octavius Caesar).

You have to convince Antony that you speak *divine truth* — that is, truth from other than normal sources. This is why you use the poetic words "O" and "o'erpowered," and why you refer to Antony's demon, spirit, and angel — all otherworldly guideposts to his future as you propose it.

You then must *be* otherworldly to show you have these otherworld connections. Don't worry about seeming "hokey." Yes, a soothsayer communing with spirits certainly may seem hokey in a modern setting, such as a contemporary acting studio, but if you *commit* to the goal of convincing your Mark Antony of your otherworldliness, you will not seem hokey at all. You will, in fact, transport to a (fictional?) world where soothsayers and spirits exist.

Use the cloaking of your costume to do this. *Imitate* the angel becoming "a fear." Since nobody knows what a frightened angel would look like, you can give your imagination free play. Use your costume to alternately hide and reveal yourself, or parts of yourself; make your cloak rise and fall like waves of the ocean; make it reflect the physics (the gravity, aerodynamics, and so on) of the otherworld that you, the soothsayer, inhabit.

Boom out "make a space between you" in a quavery, awestruck (and awestriking) voice, as though you were delivering the eleventh commandment from the mountain. Be "spooky" — not to entertain the audience but *to make Antony afraid*. If he's afraid and if he believes you commune with truthful spirits, he may take your advice. (You do, by the way, tell the truth: Caesar will destroy Antony. But Antony doesn't take your advice, and the play is a tragedy because of that.)

TOBY BELCH

SIR TOBY BELCH: Wherefore are these things hid? Wherefore have these gifts a curtain before 'em? are they like to take dust, like Mistress Mall's picture? why dost thou not go to church in a galliard, and come home in a coranto? My very walk should be a jig; I would not so much as make water but in a sink-a-pace. What dost thou mean? is it a world to hide virtues in? I did think, by the excellent constitution of thy leg, it was formed under the star of a galliard.

(*Twelfth Night*, I.iii.105ff.)

Word notes: By now you probably can see that when a character has many words you don't know, he or she is probably "showing off" a false intellectuality. That is certainly the case here. No one knows who Mistress Mall was, but pictures were often kept behind dust curtains in Elizabethan times. "Galliard," "coranto," "jig," and "sink-a-pace" are all dances or dance steps. "Make water" means to "urinate."

You are a minor lord in the house of Olivia, your niece. You keep as a guest there Sir Andrew Aguecheek, an odd fellow whom you flatter, and from

whom you take regular payments. (Andrew is hoping you will fix him up with Olivia; you have no intention of doing so, but you lead him on shamelessly.) Right now, Andrew is showing off his dancing ability, and you are praising him (in jest, although Andrew doesn't know it) to Maria, Olivia's woman-in-waiting.

What you are after, now and always, is a good time, which you create by stimulating a party atmosphere from one moment to the next. Impress Sir Andrew with your wit and knowledge, encourage him to dance for you, and entertain Maria by making her laugh at Andrew's foolishness — and then make her stifle her laughs so that Andrew doesn't hear.

Build your initial four questions, making each one more aggressive than the one previous. Make Andrew increasingly proud of himself and stimulated to keep dancing, and drive Maria crazy with amusement (you will marry her at play's end). Speak the names of dances with great authority — to indicate that you know them, too — and improvise steps for them by way of illustration. Dance in and with your costume, to your own version of galliards and corontos, whatever they are, and do something quite ridiculous on "make water in a sink-a-pace" (that is, peeing while dancing).

Revel publicly in the pronunciation (which you can make up) of the French and Italian dance names. Exaggerate their Frenchness and Italianness so as to stimulate Sir Andrew into a paroxysm of hilarious dancing, and to make Maria all but explode in stifled giggles.

SUMMARY OF LESSON 13

This lesson, the longest in the book, is really a sampling of Shakespearean work that you can develop over many months and years. Each of these thirty-two character fragments is part of a wonderful Shakespearean role that would prove the talent and ability of any actor, beginning amateur or veteran professional. You can use these fragments as a nucleus from which to develop a longer speech or scene of the character, or to prepare the role as part of a play production.

Remember, you aren't expected to work on but one of these speeches at a time. You could take years just to develop the repertory of characters of your own sex.

In each case, you should learn from this exercise how a role's lines and costumes are linked to the character's goals and tactics, and how people (characters, in this case) adopt voices, select clothing, make word choices, arrange sentences, and move their bodies in order to achieve specific objectives with and through other people (other characters, in this case). These exercises should have you speaking and moving at one time, in a concerted and integrated effort to achieve specific character goals.

L E S S O N   1 4

Shakespearean Language

UNFAMILIAR WORDS AND STRANGE CONSTRUCTIONS

One of the first problems actors face in Shakespeare is the language — specifically, that it's often difficult, and usually not like our own. Thus the need to have word notes in previous exercises.

What would we do without word notes, for example, when faced with Biondello's description of Petruchio in *The Taming of the Shrew*?

> Why, Petruchio is coming, in a new hat and an old jerkin; a pair of old breeches, thrice turn'd; a pair of boots that have been candle-cases, one buckled, another laced; an old rusty sword ta'en out of the town-armory, with a broken hilt, and chapless; with two broken points: his horse hipped with an old mothy saddle, and stirrups of no kindred; besides, possessed with the glanders, and like to mose in the chine; troubled with the lampass, infected with the fashions, full of windgalls, sped with spavins, rayed with the yellows, past cure of the fives, stark spoiled with the staggers, begnawn with the bots; swayed in the back, and shoulder-shotten; near-legged before, and with a half-cheek'd bit, and a headstall of sheep's leather, which, being restrained to keep him from stumbling, hath been often burst, and new-repaired with knots; one girth six times pieced, and a woman's crupper of velure, which hath two letters for her name fairly set down in studs, and here and there pieced with packthread.
>
> (III.ii.42ff.)

We probably get the general idea of this speech without using explanatory notes, but what about the specifics? Even the veteran classical actor (or scholar!) will have to spend several hours at the dictionary on this one.

Shakespeare began his writing career more than 400 years ago. It was at the beginning of the era of modern English, but many traces of Middle and even Old English remained, both in spoken conversation and literary writing.

Shakespeare's rural background, and his Bankside (slum district) London experience, also provided him with a rich indigenous vocabulary that might now — but for his works — be all but forgotten.

So, while the average modern reader can probably stumble through a first reading of unedited Shakespeare, such a reader will encounter many real difficulties in the language. Many words will be strange, or at least strangely used, and many expressions will seem excessively quaint, peculiar, or "literary."

There were no standard dictionaries when Shakespeare began writing. The first English dictionary, a *Table Alphabeticall* of "hard words," was published in 1604, near the end of Shakespeare's writing career. And there were no formal rule books (style manuals) on grammar or sentence construction. Shakespeare and like authors were therefore creating language and inventing syntax as much as they were following rules of usage. Shakespeare himself seems to have invented dozens of words (such as "incarnadine" and "exsufflicate"), and perhaps hundreds of word compounds (such as "shoulder-shotten" and "near-legged"). More than 10,000 words — fully a quarter of the words in English at the time — were created during the Shakespearean era. It is useful, then, to remember that Shakespeare was not only writing plays, he was helping to create the modern English language.

But strange words and quaint expressions are not the only stumbling blocks to reading Shakespeare. The modern reader will also find thousands of variations in the word order and sentence structure, as well as in the spelling of words and the punctuation of phrases, for Shakespearean English was far more fluid in syntax, grammar, and in orthography than is formal speech or writing today. Parts of speech had been named but were not fully systematized. Nouns, for example, were often used as verbs, and when Hugh Evans says, "I will description the matter to you" (*Merry Wives of Windsor*, I.i.222), or Cleopatra says of Octavius "He words me, girls, he words me" (*Antony and Cleopatra*, V.ii.193), these characters are speaking within the allowable framework of normal Elizabethan discourse.

Noun cases were also less formalized in Shakespearean English, where the objective case (for example, "me") was sometimes nominative (as in "methinks") and sometimes dative (as "the cloudy messenger turns me his back," or in Petruchio's comically misunderstood "knock me here." Petruchio means knock on this door *for* me; Grumio takes him to mean "beat me here" and refuses to do it). We needn't be grammarians to appreciate the acting problems that these constructions create. The English language is an organic and ever-changing medium of expression, and in Shakespeare's time it was growing more rapidly than ever before. Actors must "grow back" to it, and "grow forward" with it, in order to capture its organic momentum.

All to the good, says the literary scholar, who in Shakespeare's work sees the history of our language, sees English words and word usage in the process of taking their current forms. Nevertheless, for the beginning actor the resulting problems must be carefully approached and surmounted. Let's look at the problems individually.

First, there are the words (like Biondello's "jerkin"), contractions (like "ta'en"), and terms (like "infected with the fashions") that have simply passed out of popular usage and are unknown today. The actor has to learn their meanings, and *convey* those meanings to an audience who does not have the luxury of bringing footnotes to the performance.

Second, there are words that, while they remain common, have developed new meanings over the centuries, and sometimes lost their old ones. These words create even bigger problems than those in the first category because you don't always know that you don't know what they mean — or what they meant when Shakespeare wrote them. When Othello says, for example:

> He that is robbed, not wanting what is stol'n . . .
> (*Othello*, III.iii.340–341)

he is referring, not to a robbed man who doesn't *desire* what has been stolen, but to a robbed man who does not know that he's been robbed (who is not yet *missing* what is stolen: "wanting" in the sense of "lacking" or "missing"). A contemporary actor (and therefore a contemporary audience) may mistakenly assume the opposite meaning from a first, too-casual reading or hearing of this line. (You may also remember this characteristic Elizabethan usage from Joan of Arc's line in *Henry VI*: "Because you want the grace that others have" discussed in Lesson 13.)

Similarly, when Juliet pleads "Wherefore art thou Romeo?" (that baleful line of high school drama competitions), she is not asking *where* Romeo is, but *why* he has to be named "Romeo" — that is, why must he be a member of the hated Montagues? There is, despite a hundred thousand readings to the contrary, no comma after "thou" in Juliet's plea. And when Hamlet cries out "I'll make a ghost of him that lets me!" he is saying he'll kill the person who tries to *stop* him, *let* meaning "hinder" in those days.

Third, Shakespeare also wrote in a time when the second person singular (also called "intimate") pronouns, principally "thou" and "thee," were still in occasional use, and when third person verb conjugations often had "-eth" endings. To many beginning actors, it seems frustratingly quaint to say "thou art a fool," or "the bird of dawning singeth," or even Hamlet's "I have that within which passeth show."

Add to this the common use of the emphatic "do" with ordinary verbs, so that "he bestrides" becomes "he doth bestride," and Shakespeare may sometimes seem at first glance every bit as ancient as the 400-year span of time doth make him.

Happily, there are solutions to all these problems. First, let's stop calling them problems. They are challenges. Understand that Shakespeare had no trouble being clear, comprehensible, and even simple and ordinary. His two published letters (they are to Henry Wriothesly, the Earl of Southampton, in dedication of his published poems) are absolutely straightforward pieces of writing that contain between them only one word ("moiety") that would not be understood by any high school student in America.

Moreover, at the great emotional moments of his plays, his language is shockingly simple:

ROMEO (*when Tybalt is killed because Romeo tried to intervene in the duel*): I thought all for the best.

CORIOLANUS (*as his mother has successfully intervened in his effort to defeat the Romans*): O mother, mother, what have you done?

LADY MACBETH (*reflecting, in her dream world, on her murder of Duncan*): Yet who would have thought the old man to have so much blood in him!

KING LEAR (*dying, holding the body of Cordelia*): Pray you, undo this button. Thank you, sir. Do you see this? Look on her, look, her lips, Look there, look there.

Why then do we see so many unfamiliar words elsewhere in the plays? It is because Shakespeare *enriched* the theatre with inventive, expressive, *dramatic* language, and extended the possibilities of the theatre by brilliantly shaping and expanding its linguistic base.

Remember Lady Macbeth's line from Lesson 2:

Come thick night, and pall thee in the dunnest smoke of hell.

Shakespeare could easily have said "the darkest smoke of hell." "Darkest" would have been clearer to his 17th-century audience, and it would be clear to us. But clarity isn't everything. "Dunnest" has a thudding sound, and a wealth of hidden meanings. As a color, dun is a dark gray-brown with tones of red, an image of dirty smoke issuing from red coals, a muffled Hell. To "dun" also means to make increasingly persistent demands, as Lady Macbeth will soon do to her husband. And "dun," as we have already seen, sets up the "done," in Macbeth's subsequent "If it were done when 'tis done, then 'twere well if it were done quickly," as well as his "I have done the deed," following the assassination, and Lady Macbeth's final wrap-up: "what's done cannot be undone." So this "dunnest" smoke ("done-est") becomes a highly metaphorical drumbeat in the play, whereas "darkest" is merely descriptive.

Obviously, the job of the actor is to rise to the level of Shakespearean language, not merely to reduce the language to a pedestrian level of clarity, or a merely superficial, single-level contemporary meaning.

Shakespeare's vocabulary was immense; it is estimated that he used more than 20,000 root words in his plays, almost half of all the words then existing in English. No writer before or since has so mastered the lexicon of his or her own tongue.

His plays contain thousands of precise allusions: some 70 trees, 75 flowers, 90 nautical terms, 125 four-footed animals, 175 birds, and 250 mythological characters. He quoted or cited from 42 books of the Bible (he was ecumenical; his citations include references from 18 books of the Old Testament, 18 of the New, and 6 from the Apocrypha!) as well as from over 100 literary and historical works. His plays contain phrases, lines, speeches, and sometimes whole scenes in French, Welsh, Latin, and Italian. *No one* in his original audience could have understood, certainly not at one hearing, all the words in his plays — and his plays were, consequently, written with that in mind. Indeed, many of the obscure and difficult words in Shakespeare were *meant* to be obscure and difficult; they were obscure and difficult in Shakespeare's day as well as ours.

To Shakespeare, or at least to Hamlet, a large vocabulary was a gift from heaven; distinguishing us from the animals:

> What is a man,
> If his chief good and market of his time
> Be but to sleep and feed? A beast, no more.
> Sure, He that made us with such large discourse,
> Looking before and after, gave us not
> That capability and godlike reason
> To fust in us unused.

So to play a Shakespearean character, you must master a "large discourse" simply to be human. Being properly verbose, in Shakespeare, is not to be affected, but to be alive, to be *real*.

Thus, since Shakespeare's vocabulary was immense, *your* vocabulary must expand to meet it. Shakespeare's characters expand the limits of language. They reach for language: They *invent* words, they seek the perfect word and the perfect expression for their purposes and thoughts. They rise to the occasion of Shakespeare, in other words.

WORD CHOICE AND CHARACTER PSYCHE

How on earth do you rise to these occasions? You do so by making a single working assumption: that it is not Shakespeare who chooses the character's words, rather it is the *character himself* (or herself) who creates the language of the part. In other words, each character chooses his or her words, and in playing the character, you have to play the character's linguistic creativity, or the character's "thinking."

We call this a "working assumption" not because it's true, but because it helps the work process. Of course, we know that Shakespeare, in fact, chose the words and wrote them down. But you the actor, in playing the thinking of the character, must assume that your character has chosen them. That is, that it was *Biondello* who decided to say "shoulder-shotten" instead of "dirty-armed" or "muddy." Making this assumption allows you to say not only something about the horse, but something about Biondello.

Your job, then, is to create the illusion that it is your character, not the author, who chooses the words (makes the word choices) of your role. How do you do this with Shakespeare?

First, of course, you look up all the unfamiliar words. This looking up might very well start with looking down — for most Shakespearean plays are published with footnotes at the bottom of the page that define or "gloss" (as from a glossary) troublesome obscurities. Beyond the footnotes, there are book-sized Shakespearean dictionaries and glossaries, as well as a magnificent multivolume reference work, *The Oxford English Dictionary*, which traces the history of every word in the English language, showing how its meaning has evolved since its first usage. The *OED*, as it is commonly called, is available in most scholarly libraries (a revised edition was published in 1989), and it is an invaluable aid to understanding Shakespeare. A reference library is at your disposal somewhere, and some reference materials are listed in the bibliography of this book.

Only when you know what the character is trying to say can you "choose" the words with the necessary passion and conviction. But watch out for footnotes. They can only provide semantic assistance, contemporary (and generally pedestrian) synonyms for words dense in complex associations. *The "meaning" of a word is not the word*. Only the word is the word. Words have sounds and shapes, and convey allusions and etymological associations. To reduce Shakespearean words simply to their glossed meanings is to reduce Shakespearean language — and Shakespearean drama — to banality.

An example of this complexity is found in act V of *Hamlet*, when King Claudius proposes a toast to Hamlet, and as he does so, he poisons the drink, saying:

And in the cup an union shall he throw . . .

We know from footnotes that "union" meant "pearl," and many beginning actors simply play it as though it meant only that.

Well, "union" does mean "pearl," but it also means "unified state," which is what Claudius is hoping to achieve. If Shakespeare had wanted simply to say "pearl," he would have said "pearl." That he said "union" means he wanted us to think about more than just "pearlness." Claudius had earlier called his wife "the imperial jointress of this warlike state"; in killing Hamlet with a "union" he could also firm up the "joint" rule that he has hoped to achieve. (Hamlet had said the time was "out of joint"; if true, Claudius hopes to be the one to correct it — but on his, not Hamlet's, terms.) Perhaps Claudius was also thinking, unconsciously at least, of impaired union when he said that Ophelia was "divided from herself and her fair judgement"; the "union" that brings Hamlet's death will end his similar agony. Shakespeare (thankfully, in my opinion) lived in the prepsychiatric era and never theorized directly about mental states; even to discuss "unconscious thinking," as I have done above will probably raise eyebrows in some quarters. But Shakespeare's knowledge of the human psyche was profound, and the profundity comes out, as often as not, through the word choices of his characters, through their chosen modes of expression that reveal vast worlds about their mental preoccupations — even those preoccupations of which they themselves are only dimly aware.

We don't have to settle on a final meaning of "union" in Claudius's speech. The acting point is that Claudius, seen as a complex human being, has to *reach* for the difficult word "union," rather than just fall back on the easy, and commonplace, word "pearl"—and in reaching for the word he reaches back into his own mind, which is filled with unconscious preoccupations of murder, escape, lust, guilt, mental breakdown, civil strife, and restored unity. Specific interpretations will vary, but the structural point is universal: The footnote gloss is *not a substitute* for the word itself; it is just a tool to help you use the word more precisely, more forcefully, and more effectively.

When you know the meaning of the words and the sense of the speeches, much of the character's meaning can be conveyed by other than sheer semantics: by context, of course, and by *acting*—by tone of voice, inflection, movement, focus, expression, feeling, and gesture—by total engagement in a *speech act*. Words have meaning only in the context of speech acts anyway, and if you integrate the semantic meaning of the words with an overall speech act—into a total communication of the character's goal-oriented action, together with a tactical interplay calculated to succeed in that action—the *dramatic meaning* of a speech will always be powerfully transmitted.

The words, familiar and unfamiliar alike, will be seen as they should: as part of your character's creative effort to achieve his or her goal.

Dramatic meaning is far more than a literal, dictionary definition. Dramatic meaning includes all the elements of spoken communications: the sound of the words, the movements of the actors, and the subtextual elements of acting—character goals, tactics, actions, and emotion. When, secure in the literal meaning of the Shakespearean text, you convey dramatic meaning through an expressive performance, the effect can be both verbally rich and theatrically compelling, and the four centuries between Shakespeare's age and our own "are melted into air, into thin air" (*Tempest*, IV.i.150).

We don't really have to know the dictionary meaning of "begnawn with the bots" or "shoulder-shotten," do we? Certainly not if in playing Biondello you can use your imagination and talent to portray a horse inflicted with appropriately gruesome ailments. Biondello's speech, as obscure as its words may be, can prove a theatrical tour de force even for a beginning actor, who has the talent, energy, commitment, and imagination to "bring down the house" with it. (And bring down the house is what that speech is calculated to do; it brings down Baptista's house, being the teasing that precedes the taming—it softens Katherine up for the confrontations and indignities to follow.)

So, unfamiliar words should be played *as though they were unfamiliar*. You should choose them yourself, and reach for them in the back of your mental vocabulary storehouse—*not* simply rattle them off as though you used them every day. We should get the feeling that Claudius has never *said* the word "union" in his life; that he is, in trying to dignify the occasion, attempting to come up with a fancier word for "pearl"—and his unconscious leads him to a fancier word that is also related to his mental anguish.

■⌐▨⌐▨⌐▨⌐■ EXERCISE 14-1

Play these unfamiliar words by choosing and reaching for them rather than just rattling them off. Find a *reason* why you would use a more difficult word than you usually would:

1.   POLONIUS: I'll sconce me even here.

(*Hamlet*, III.iv.5)

"Sconce" means "hide" or "ensconce." Show off your discretion and learning to the Queen.

2.   PISTOL: Therefore, Caveto be thy counsellor.

(*Henry V*, II.iv.55)

"Caveto" means "Be careful." Show off your knowledge of Italian, and your swashbuckling practicality, to your tavern friends.

3.   OLIVIA: Rudesby, be gone!

(*Twelfth Night*, IV.i.54)

"Rudesby" means "ruffian." Since you are talking to your (drunken) uncle in public, reach for just the right word to humiliate him without bringing down the whole family.

4.   URSULA: Yonder's old coil at home.

(*Much Ado About Nothing*, V.iii.97)

"Old coil" is something like "big to-do," with a hint of things spiralling to a conclusion or "coiling up," which is precisely the case. Choose the perfect word to excite them (Beatrice and Benedick) with the happenings at home, to cause them to leave their little love-chat, but also not to alarm them overmuch — you bring good news.

"THOU ARTS" AND THE LIKE

As for Shakespeare's "thou art's" and "canst thou's," and the overall 16th- and 17th-century tones of the language, with its Old English and Middle English holdovers — these often have a plot purpose you can put to use.

The second person singular ("thou"), which is still in common usage in French ("tu") and German ("du"), serves several functions. It is, first of all, intimate: the pronoun of lovers (Juliet to Romeo: "if thou dost love," "so thou wilt woo," "lest that thy love," "I joy in thee," "I give thee mine," and "give it thee again!").

The intimate address was also customary in "talking down," as a master talking to a servant. When Valentine and Speed discuss Silvia in *The Two Gentlemen of Verona*, Valentine, the master, addresses his servant Speed in the second person singular: "Dost thou know my lady Silvia? . . . Hast thou observed that? . . . Dost thou know her? . . ." Speed answers with the more "polite" address "you": "She that you gaze on? . . . She is not so fair as, of you . . . You never saw her. . . ."

The intimate was also used for formal address, or for a parody of formal address, as in *Twelfth Night,* where Sir Toby is advising how to write a forged, mock-eloquent letter to the social climbing Malvolio:

TOBY: . . . if thou "thou'st" him some thrice, it shall not be amiss.

And it can be used to intensify a verbal assault, particularly to someone lower than you on the social scale:

LEONTES: You lie, you lie.
I say thou liest, Camillo, and I hate thee.

In this case, King Leontes mixes the common and intimate forms, building his anger from the formal "you lie," to the informal, and hence more cutting and demeaning, "thou liest."

There was no *absolute* rule on when to use "thou" and when to use "you" in Shakespeare's day. Shakespeare's company sometimes used the terms interchangeably. The Folio version of *Othello,* for example, transforms many of the Quarto's "thou's" to "you's"—but also a few "you's" to "thou's." The "thee's" and "thou's" were apparently on their way out when Shakespeare was writing, so we mustn't get too dogmatic about specific usages.

In any event, thou's and thee's quickly become less disruptive with time and practice in speaking Shakespeare, as they are simply part of the "world" that you enter when you begin to act this particular playwright. In this way, "acting Shakespeare" is the same as "acting Tennessee Williams" or "acting David Mamet." These authors, too, have a "language" particular to themselves, and even a style of grammatical construction which is different from that, say, on a modern college campus. That their writings are somewhat closer to our daily linguistic constructions does not change the fact that you will have to "enter" the world of these playwrights as well in order to play their characters.

The next lesson will give you more opportunities to develop character word choice.

SUMMARY OF LESSON 14

Shakespeare's language, which dates from the beginning of what we now know as Modern English, is filled with obscure words, archaic expressions, and spelling and grammar that are both often out of date today. This presents special challenges, and special opportunities, to the modern actor. Shakespearean characters, rather than appearing to be trapped in quaint phrasings, should be seen as creating a new language; as reaching for better and better means of expression; as rising to the occasions that their author has given them. Shakespeare's characters must be seen as inventing their own speeches, not following or reciting them, and as performing complete speech acts with their word choice, their sentence structure, and their creative use of language.

L E S S O N   1 5

Word Choice

Here are three longer exercises in "entering" the sometimes unfamiliar world of Shakespearean language. You will learn to choose and reach for new words while acting them, just as your characters do, and probably just as Shakespeare did while writing them.

EXERCISE 15-1

You are explaining to your friends why you — a male — will not marry. (A companion exercise more appropriate to females follows.)

> BENEDICK: That a woman conceived me, I thank her; that she brought me up, I likewise give her most humble thanks: but that I will have a recheat winded in my forehead, or hang my bugle in an invisible baldrick, all women shall pardon me. Because I will not do them the wrong to mistrust any, I will do myself the right to trust none; and the fine is (for the which I may go the finer), I will live a bachelor.
> (*Much Ado About Nothing*, I.i.239ff.)

We learn from footnotes that a "recheat" is a hunting horn, "winded" means "blown" (as a horn is blown), a "baldrick" is a belt, and "fine" means the "summary," or total. But the footnotes give little sense of the richness of the language, or the whimsicality of Benedick's verbal and physical expression.

Let's first walk our way through this speech. We'll divide it into three parts. First, build the two initial lines up to a platform: (step 1) "that a woman conceived me, I thank her," (step 2) "that she brought me up, I likewise give her most humble thanks." You are now on a platform for part two.

Second, analyze the sexual metaphors in the middle. The "recheat winded" could mean a horn blasting in your ears (that is, a wife nagging at you), or a double horn (cow horns) poking out of your forehead — these refer to the cuckold's horns, a traditional Elizabethan gag.

The sheer sound of "recheat," however, also sends thoughts of your future wife's "repeated cheating" rattling in your brain — quite apart from any literal meaning. She will probably "cheat and recheat," is Benedick's unconscious musing.

How about your "hanging your bugle" in an "invisible baldrick"? A bugle is bright, loud, shiny, engaging; the metaphor suggests marriage will make you invisible, silent, dull, isolated. You will be forced to silence your trumpeting, it will be the end of the hunt (for women); you will blow your final "taps" to romance and heroics.

It's also a metaphor for castration. The lockerroom sense of "hang my bugle" and the bawdy sound of "baldrick" both suggest Elizabethan (and contemporary) expressions for penis and testicles. "Balldrick" manages to combine no less than three different vulgarisms referring to the male sex organs. "Hang my bugle in an invisible baldrick" is an obvious double entendre for the emasculated male.

Not convinced? Try changing the line to "put my guitar into an invisible belt." Get the picture now? In the popular 1957 musical comedy, *The Music Man*, a character brought down the house every night simply by her disdainful, gravelly voiced repetition of a French novelist's somewhat obscenely euphonious name: "Balllll-zac!"

Try this middle part of Benedick's speech, then, with a gesture describing the "recheat winded" (you can pronounce "winded" either "wine-did" or "whinn-did," depending on your interpretation), and with a knowing look (an elbow in the ribs?) on the bugle-baldrick line. But *invent* these metaphors, don't merely recite them. Play the speech as though improvising it, word for word, on the spot. *Search for* the individual words, particularly "bugle" and "baldrick." Show off your masculinity and wit, and your freedom from any woman's urging, with the line. Play the words more to amuse and entertain your friends than to make your point about marriage (which you don't in fact believe anyway — indeed, you will be married by week's end).

In the final third of the speech, and with attention to the antithesis ("will not do them the wrong"/"will do myself the right"), point up your "fine"– "finer" pun by jumping off the platform for your final conclusion, which is "I will live a bachelor." That's what the whole speech leads up to:

> for the fine is, for which I will go the finer, [*jump down*] I will live a bachelor.

And at the moment you say it, you believe it! But that's until Beatrice shows up again.

EXERCISE 15-2

BEATRICE: Not till God make men of some other metal than earth. Would it not grieve a woman to be overmastered with a piece of valiant dust? To make an account of her life to a clod of wayward marl? No,

uncle, I'll none: Adam's sons are my brethren; and, truly, I hold it a sin
to match in my kindred.
(*Much Ado About Nothing*, II.i.62ff.)

You are explaining to your uncle why you will not marry. This is, of course,
a companion piece to Exercise 15-1.

Beatrice could have called Benedick (for that's who she's thinking of) a
lump of clay instead of a "clod of wayward marl," for the expressions mean
pretty much the same thing, but that would have meant that Beatrice spoke
in banalities, and great stage lovers don't do that — or they are only banal
lovers. Beatrice not only wants to convince her uncle she will not marry
Benedick, she wants to convince him, and the rest of her family, that she is a
brilliant woman, a captivating wordsmith, and, potentially, a great lover —
for whom they should provide a great husband. So Beatrice reaches for ideal
language at the same time (and for the same reason) as she reaches for an
ideal man.

Notice the downward build to obscurity: from "earth" to "valiant dust"
to "wayward marl." Create that build by reaching farther and farther to find
the precise word that represents Benedick (whom to you is a faithless suitor)
and shows off your own verbal talent as well. Amuse and entertain your
family with your word choice ("metal," "overmastered," "wayward," and
"marl"); your verbal and tonal (downward) building; your dissonant antithesis (sons/sin), and your clever biblical allusion at the end.

▰▱▰▱▰ EXERCISE 15-3 ANTIGONUS

> Your king believes his wife is an adulteress. You, a loyal minis-
> ter, believe he is wrong and that some "villain" has lied to him, so you tell
> him so.

> ANTIGONUS: You are abused, and by some putter-on
> That will be damned for't: would I knew the villain,
> I would land-damn him! Be she honor-flawed —
> I have three daughters: the eldest is eleven;
> The second and the third, nine and some five:
> If this prove true, they'll pay for it. By mine honor
> I'll geld 'em all: fourteen they shall not see
> To bring false generations . . .
> (*The Winter's Tale*, II.i.150ff.)

Look at the words closely. "Abused" is here used to mean "been told a lie
to," as if Leontes's ear had been abused. "For't" is a contraction for "for it."
(There are many such contractions in Shakespeare, often to maintain the
scansion [see Lesson 16], but also because spoken Elizabethan English was
a highly contracted language.)

"Putter-on" is a made-up word compound, a version of which ("put-on") is in use today. "Honor-flawed" is another made-up compound. Compounding words like this was a bit more common in Shakespeare's day than in our own.

"Be she honor-flawed" means, essentially, "If she should prove honor-flawed." Antigonus turns at that point to tell what he would do in that event. The syntax is irregular, in that he has to more or less "back up" to tell about his daughters:

> Be she honor-flawed—
> [Well, what *will* I do? Hey, I know, I'll do something to my daughters. But Leontes doesn't know I have any daughters! I'll guess I'll have to tell him first.]
> I have three daughters . . .

This halting and retrenchment is common enough in speaking, but not in formal rhetoric; you will have to think through the speech (and to back up), just as Antigonus does. You will have to play not only your character's thought, but your character's thinking. No rattling off or reciting Shakespearean poetry here: Your charge is to stumble through the speech *just as Antigonus stumbles through it*. And to create compound words where you just can't find simple ones that say what you want to say. And go back to tell about your daughters so you can then explain how you'd "geld 'em." This speech is a struggle for Antigonus so it must be a struggle for you.

"Land-damn" is a third compound, but, while the two words making it up are common enough, their combination is very puzzling. Indeed, scholars have been debating what Shakespeare meant here for at least 200 years, with no clear answer in sight. (It probably means "to take away the property of," but could also mean "to abuse with rancor" or "to stop the urine of." Quite a varied list of possibilities.)

In the same way, while "geld" is a common word (specifically meaning castration, particularly of farm animals), how can Antigonus possibly apply it to his daughters? Scholars continue to wrestle over this one, too.

So don't simply say these words: create them. Create the greatest punishment you can think of: greater than execution, greater than torture, greater than perpetual damnation. You will . . . uh . . . *land-damn* the son of a gun and you will . . . uh . . . *geld* your own daughters if you're wrong about this!

You reach for the right words—and end up with the wrong ones. So your speech is semantically meaningless, but your *dramatic* meaning is quite powerful. Speaking angrily (perhaps for the first time in your life) to your king, (your *king*, whom you have served so loyally!!!) you reach (imperfectly) for language violent enough and phrases precise enough to express your profound disagreement.

Memorize and play this speech of Antigonus, choosing and reaching for words just beyond his (and your) usual mode of expression. Curse the putter-on; but, as cursing is not part of your general nature, try to find appropriate curse words (and come up with "land-damn" and "geld").

Impress the King with your seriousness of purpose and eloquent attack on the putter-on. (By the way, you are wrong here, too; there is no putter-on. But you don't know that.) Struggle to find the precise punishment you would mete out to this villain. Create the very language of your speech, and try to bring cadences of accusation into your voice to drive your points home.

In playing the speech this way, you should bring the full expressive force of your voice, posture, movement, and gesture to the fulfillment of these goals.

■▎◤▎◤▎■ EXERCISE 15-4 BIONDELLO

Now you're ready to tackle Biondello's description of Petruchio at the wedding. (Biondello can easily be played by a woman, so don't beg off for gender reasons.)

Look at the speech at the beginning of Lesson 14. Get a well-edited text of the play and study the meaning of the unfamiliar words, of which there will be at least thirty (unless you're an Elizabethan linguist already).

After you know the meaning of the words, at least as far as you can gather (some words are unglossable), read the speech aloud a few times to get the general feel of the words.

Understand that your listeners — Katherine's family — know as few of these words as you do. After all, Katherine's people are city folk; they have no more knowledge of what a broken-down horse would look like than you would of the parts of a broken-down airplane engine. What does Baptista, Katherine's father, know of bots? Or glanders?

The point of this speech is that Petruchio is doing something incredible, something virtually *inexpressible*. So your goal is to explain that something unexplainable is going on. *Show* as much as tell what this horse looks like, smells like, sounds like, and how she staggers. Use your imagination, your energy, your mimetic talent (talent for mimicry), and your (understandable) anxiety.

Enjoy it. It's a comedy.

SUMMARY OF LESSON 15

Shakespeare's language, being 400 years old, is sometimes obscure and strange to modern eyes and ears, but can be played powerfully and eloquently if the actor integrates the language with the speech acts of his or her character. Unfamiliar words, whose meaning the actor must first look up in a footnote or dictionary, should not then be rattled off simply as a synonym for the more common word or expression, but should be performed as an effort to reach for richer and more precise language. Actors playing unfamiliar words must also play the character creating — *choosing* — such means of expression.

L E S S O N   1 6

Scansion: A Primer

Scansion is the science, or perhaps the art, of "scanning" the poetic text to find the appropriate speaking meter. Before discussing it further, however, a bit of recent history will provide some necessary perspective.

From the 1930s through the early postwar period, a variation of the Stanislavsky "system" of acting prevailed in the United States. This variation itself had several branches, the chief one being the teachings of the Actor's Studio, which was founded by Harold Clurman, Elia Kazan, and Cheryl Crawford, and was shortly thereafter (from 1948) headed by Lee Strasburg. This was a naturalistically oriented acting method (called simply, in America, "*The* method"), and it urged the actor to find the inner truth of the role in "himself" (or "herself," although feminine gender words rarely appeared in the literature of the period).

The popularity of "the method" reached a peak in the 1950s and early '60s, when American realism was the order of the day, both on stage and in films. However, the downside of the peak was not long in coming. In 1953, Marlon Brando, the most celebrated "method" actor of his time, proved less than completely adequate to the demands of Mark Antony in a film of *Julius Caesar* (particularly opposite the veteran English performers John Gielgud and James Mason, playing Cassius and Brutus), and American actors began a wholesale retreat from Shakespeare and other classical writers. A decade later, Elia Kazan challenged the classics for the new Lincoln Center Company — and lost — with a production of *The Changeling* (by Phillip Massinger) that was so disastrous as to abruptly end his stage-directing career, and spell the doom of the then-current management of the Center.

It was only then perhaps that theatre people recollected that Stanislavsky himself had met failure in his productions of Shakespeare as well, and that "the method" was not in itself sufficient training for performing in these works rich with linguistic nuance, rhetorical splendor, and near-infinite stylistic variety.

The result was a major change in the direction of Shakespearean actor training that continues today. Two important influences helped bring about this change.

First, a number of young American actors, such as Stacy Keach and Richard Chamberlain, went to England to study classical acting at places like LAMDA (the London Academy of Music and Dramatic Art), RADA (the Royal Academy of Dramatic Art), and in the English provincial repertory system. There they studied, among other things, voice development and verse speaking, which had remained (and still remain) key elements of British acting instruction.

Indeed, elocution in its various forms, and the reading aloud of Shakespearean texts, are traditional and key elements of *all* British secondary education—for young persons planning to become lawyers, doctors, journalists, and diplomats, as well as actors. Keach came back from England to play Hamlet in Joseph Papp's new Shakespeare Festival in New York's Central Park, and the effect of his classical training was widely and immediately noticed and admired.

Second, a nationwide movement for strictly American instruction in Shakespearean acting and verse-speaking (though often with an English accent) quickly sprang up to meet the challenge of increased interest in classical production.

B. Iden Payne, an English-born director, exerted enormous influence both from his post at the University of Texas and at the pioneering Oregon Shakespeare Festival, where he directed. Classes in scansion were soon mandatory at acting conservatories, such as the Juilliard School in New York (run by English-born John Houseman and French-born Michel St. Denis) and the American Conservatory Theatre in San Francisco (under William Ball). The speech and voice teachings, and the resulting textbooks—of Cecily Berry, Kristin Linklatter, and Edith Skinner (and their subsequent disciples)—spread across the United States, until few serious acting programs (and *no* serious classical acting programs) failed to integrate professional voice/speech instruction into the curriculum.

This shift in emphasis has proven extraordinarily beneficial, but with one drawback. It has made scansion, in some quarters, appear to be the savior of Shakespeare—a science whose laws determine the success or failure of a Shakespearean venture. It is not that at all. No, the starting point for a study of scansion must be this: It is a *tool* to help unlock the mysteries and project the splendor of dramatic verse. It is *not* a system of laws that determine exactly how verse should (or must!) be spoken.

Enough history: Let's get on with it. What follows is a basic primer on English scansion.

STRESS

In speaking, syllables are sounded with varying force, which we call "stress." The force is largely muscular, coming from the pressure of the diaphragm and the abdominal and intercostal muscles, and from the energy we put into our articulators: tongue, lips, and jaw. Most of this is governed by unconscious mental activity, and its roots are buried deep in linguistic structures we have been developing since infancy.

The speaking stress appears in several guises. Primarily, it involves a slightly increased volume, caused by a stronger pulse from the abdominal musculature. But it also involves a sharper articulation, since more energy goes into the articulators as well (this is what happens when we "spit out" or "chew on" a word or syllable), and it can also involve a slight pitch change (usually upward) and a rhythm change (usually a slight acceleration).

Speaking stress is natural and instinctual; in ordinary speech we stress about half of our syllables without thinking at all about it. The stresses are used to create meaning ("turn RIGHT and then go EAST another block"), emphasis ("she's a JERK"), intensity ("I wanna go HOME!"), articulation ("ANtidisestablishmenTARianism"), and musicality ("DAHling, i THOUGHT you'd NEver COME!").

Spoken English combines naturally stressed and unstressed syllables, often in apparently random order. In multisyllable words, the stress is ordinarily implicit in the word itself: "Applesauce" is stressed on the first syllable, "intended" on the second, "elementary" on the third, and "Kalamazoo" on the fourth.

Sometimes the stress is determined by the part of speech: "Impact" stressed on the first syllable is a noun; stressed on the second syllable it's a verb. And sometimes the stress is determined by the word's meaning: the noun "content," when stressed on the first syllable, refers to something contained (as in the "CONtent of a speech"): stressed on the second syllable the word refers to a state of satisfaction ("I am conTENT").

Single syllable words are stressed according to contextual emphasis. "I want to go to bed" is normally stressed "i WANT to GO to BED," because "want," "go," and "bed" are the operative words of the sentence. Context is not just what comes before a word, but what comes after, as with "in" in these two sentences:

I'M GOing IN.

I'M GOing in the GARden.

English is considered a "stress-pulsed" language, because the pulse pattern of its stresses create its basic rhythm: sort of a "carrier wave" for semantic meaning. The natural rhythms of prose require a regular alternation of stressed and unstressed syllables.

IN the beGINning, god creATEd HEAVen and EARTH.

do NOT pass GO, do NOT collect TWO HUNdred DOLlars.

PLAY it aGAIN, Sam. (Or, PLAY it aGAIN, SAM — depending on your attitude about Sam.)

Not all languages are similarly stressed, by the way. French, for example, is syllable-pulsed, not stress-pulsed. French emphasis is made by lengthening the vowel, not amplifying the muscular pulse occasioned by stressing the syllable. French verse-speaking follows much different principles than those articulated here.

THE VERSE FOOT

Verse is essentially a regularizing of the seemingly random stress pattern of prose. The basic unit of verse is the **foot,** which is a repeating combination of stressed and unstressed syllables. It is the repeating nature of the foot that makes verse regular. In a line like Richard's

> Cannot a plain man live and think no harm. . . ?

or Olivia's

> He might have took his answer long ago.

most speakers will naturally read it with a "da DAH" pattern, thus stressing the second, fourth, sixth, eighth, and tenth syllables, as:

> can NOT | a PLAIN | man LIVE | and THINK | no HARM
> he MIGHT | have TOOK | his ANS | wer LONG | aGO

The "da DAH" unit is the repeating combination, or the foot.

Scanning Marks

Notice in the examples above that feet are divided by a vertical line [|]. Notice also that stressed syllables are printed in capital letters, and unstressed syllables (even when capitalized in ordinary writing) are in all lowercase. These indications are called **scanning marks,** and lines printed this way are said to be *scanned* for meter. Punctuation is also normally not given in these examples.

When scanning already printed text, other methods can be used. The most common is to place a downslash (`) over stressed syllables, and a dipped arc (˘) over those unstressed:

> ˘ ` ˘ ` ˘ ` ˘ ` ˘ `
> Cannot a plain man live and think no harm
> ˘ ` ˘ ` ˘ ` ˘ ` ˘ `
> He might have took his answer long ago

Another is to place a straight apostrophe (') before each stressed syllable:

> Can'not a 'plain man 'live and 'think no 'harm
> He 'might have 'took his 'answer 'long a'go

You may use either when you begin scanning text lines in the next lesson.

The Iambic Foot

The "da DAH" unit is the basic foot used in these lines. It also happens to be the basic foot of Shakespeare, and almost all English verse. It's called the **iamb,** or the **iambic foot,** and is defined as a verse foot with two syllables, the second stressed relatively more than the first. It is the heartbeat of Shakespeare.

THE VERSE LINE: LENGTH AND RHYTHM PATTERNS

The length of each poetic line is determined by its number of feet. Olivia's line above is a *pentameter* because it has five feet. Since it has five iambic feet, the line is defined as **iambic pentameter.**

Blank Verse

Blank verse, which is the basic medium of Shakespearean dramatic writing, is *unrhymed iambic pentameter* — a five-foot iambic line not rhyming with any adjacent line. Iambic pentameter is a relatively natural English line, even in ordinary prose speech. For example:

i THINK | i'll HAVE | some HAM | and EGGS | toDAY . . .

This is a normal real-life remark — it's you ordering breakfast at the coffee shop — that just happens to be iambic pentameter; you are ordering in blank verse. Add:

for OTH | erWISE | my DOG | will PASS | aWAY.

and you would, albeit somewhat inanely, be speaking an iambic pentameter rhyming couplet.

Other Iambic Lines

Two-footed and three-footed iambic lines (iambic dimeter and iambic trimeter, respectively) are considered primitive verse forms, common in medieval drama; they are sometimes called (pejoratively) *doggerel*. Shakespeare uses them mainly as satire, as:

Iambic Dimeter:

asLEEP | my LOVE?
what, DEAD | my DOVE?
(Bottom, as "Pyramus" in the play within the play in *A Midsummer Night's Dream*, V.i.331)

Iambic Trimeter:

> doubt THOU | the STARS | are FIRE
> doubt THAT | the SUN | doth MOVE
> doubt TRUTH | to BE | a LIAR;
> but NE | ver DOUBT | i LOVE.
>
> (Polonius, reading the presumed poetry of Hamlet, written in madness to Ophelia, in *Hamlet*, II.ii.116)

Iambic Tetrameter

Shakespeare rarely uses this form, which has four feet, but he lets Orlando use it in his ridiculous verses to Rosalind in *As You Like It*:

> thus ROS | aLIND | of MAN | y PARTS
> by HEAV'N | ly SY | nod WAS | deVISED
> of MAN | y FACE | s EYES | and HEARTS
> to HAVE | the TOUCH | es DEAR | est PRIZED
> (III.ii.156–159)

> (Thus Rosalind of many parts
> By heav'nly synod was devised
> Of many faces, eyes, and hearts
> To have the touches dearest prized.)

Iambic Hexameter

This is the classic six-footed Alexandrine line favored by French poets and playwrights:

> Le MOND | e CHÈRE | agNES | est UNE | éTRAN | ge CHOSE
>
> (Le monde, chère Agnes, est une étrange chose.)

This is Arnolphe in Molière's *School for Wives* (if you can read broken-up French). But remember, don't stress the capitalized syllables in French, or they'll know you're an American. Just draw out the vowels.

Other Verse Feet

Iambic is the most common rhythm of most English verse, and it is far and away the most common rhythm of Shakespearean dramatic poetry. But other verse feet are also used in poetry, and in Shakespeare.

Trochaic feet ("trochees") are two-syllable units with the accent on the *first*. Trochees are usually seen as variations within an otherwise iambic line; they are generally considered to have a primitive sound when they constitute the basic line pattern. Henry Wadsworth Longfellow's "Hiawatha," which takes a patronizing tone toward Native Americans, is written in trochaic tetrameter ("BY the SHORES of GITCHeeGOOme"). Orlando's silly poems to Rosalind in *As You Like It* are satirized by a variation of a trochaic tetrameter pattern (with a single stressed syllable, followed by a definite pause, as the last foot):

IF a | HART do | LACK a | HIND
LET him | SEEK out | ROS a | LIND
IF the | CAT will | AF ter | KIND
SO be | SURE will | ROS a | LIND.
(III.ii.107–110)

The dropped last syllable in the last foot causes the pause at the end of the line, and creates a singsong syncopation that, in this case, indicates the primitive quality of Orlando's versifying. It is of these trochaic tetrameters that Rosalind remarks "the feet were lame and could not bear themselves without the verse, and therefore stood lamely in the verse" (III.ii.178–180).

But King Lear's lament that Cordelia will come no more:

NEVer | NEVer | NEVer | NEVer | NEVer
(*King Lear*, V.iii.306)

is a famous Shakespearean example of trochaic pentameter that is *not* primitive. Reversing the metric pattern of the preceding blank verse lines, Lear's trochees make a heartbreaking declaration of nullity.

Anapestic feet ("anapests") have three syllables, with the third stressed: "da da DAH." Shakespeare used many anapests, sometimes in succession. The following lines, after an initial iamb, are in anapestic tetrameter:

BOYET: Why ALL | his beHAV | iors did MAKE | their reTIRE
to the COURT | of his EYE | peeping THOR | ough deSIRE.
(*Love's Labor's Lost*, II.i.234–235)

You can see Shakespeare reaching for a syllable in using the two-syllable "thorough" as a variation of the more common single syllable "through." Put the word "through" there and the line seems awkward. Why? Because it doesn't *scan* easily.

Other poetic units may be defined. **Dactylic feet** are three syllables with the first stressed (DAH da da, or "broccoli"). **Spondaic feet** ("spondees") are feet with two equally stressed syllables (the first two words of Adriana's "Ay, Ay, Antipholus . . ." in *Comedy of Errors*). These and other defined feet find their way into Shakespearean verse, but their analysis tends to be more academic than practical for most actors.[17]

The Caesura

Verse lines are not always entirely continuous, and a slight break, called a **caesura,** often breaks the line somewhere in the middle. Often this is marked by punctuation. In an iambic pentameter line, a caesura may occur after the second or third foot, or sometimes even after the first or fourth.

---

[17] The bibliography lists several sources for a more expanded study.

Thus:

> ISABELLA: That Angelo's forsworn, is it not strange?
> (*Measure for Measure*, V.i.38)

A caesura, marked with a doubled vertical line (||), is marked below:

> that ANG|eLO'S| forSWORN|| is IT | not STRANGE

In the iambic hexameter Alexandrine line, in French verse, there is *always* a caesura after the third foot. Look back at the Molière example, where the caesura comes after "Agnes."

Common Variations in Iambic Pentameter

When blank verse first appeared in Elizabethan drama, in the 1560s, it was absolutely regular (see the example of *Gorboduc* in Lesson 6). That was almost immediately seen to be stultifyingly rigid, and no serious or lasting English drama has ever been so rigorously syncopated. Indeed, the vast majority of Shakespeare's verse lines are *not* perfect examples of iambic pentameter.

Four major variations are common in all the plays. Most common is the use of the **feminine ending,** or the *triple ending*. In scansion, lines that end on a stressed syllable, such as iambic lines, are called "masculine"; lines that end on an unstressed syllable are called "feminine." Very often Shakespeare adds an unstressed eleventh syllable to an otherwise regular iambic pentameter line, such as the previously encountered (Lesson 3) line of Richard III:

> they DO | me WRONG | and I | will NOT | enDURE | it

This is an example of a feminine ending. So is Hamlet's:

> i THINK | it WAS | to SEE | my MOTH | er's WED | ding

Both these feminine endings create anticlimaxes of a sort. Richard's (Gloucester's) gives the false hope that he is going to end the line where he should, saying ". . . I will not endure!" When he goes on to say "I will not endure it," he reverses their hope—he *will* endure, they will not. Hamlet's feminine ending creates a beautifully sad understatement of his dismay.

Second is the use of a **substituted trochee,** very often at the beginning of a line, as in Polonius's greeting to Gertrude:

> MADam | i SWEAR | i USE | no ART | at ALL

The trochaic variation is a *turning device*—useful for starting up a new thought, calling somebody's attention, or giving a burst of authority.

A feminine ending, plus a substituted trochee on "that is," together with the most famous caesura in dramatic literature, distinguishes Hamlet's:

> to BE | or NOT | to BE | THAT is | the QUES | tion

Third is the **dropped syllable**. Notice Ophelia's description of her meeting with Hamlet:

He FALLS | to SUCH | per U | sal OF | my FACE
As HE | would DRAW | it. | LONG | stayed he SO

The first of Ophelia's lines is regular (the three previous lines are regular also), but the second breaks the pattern. "It" is an unstressed word that, together with its following pause, occupies a foot by itself. "Long" is both stressed and held (for a "long" time), taking the fourth foot to itself — and the line ends with an anapest. The break in verse, of course, mirrors Ophelia's broken concentration as she tries to describe the long stare Hamlet has given her.

And fourth is the **added syllable**. Goneril, speaking to her father, says:

as YOU | are OLD | and REV | 'rend you SHOULD | be WISE

Perhaps Shakespeare intended an awkwardness in this metrical pattern, which is regular but for the fourth foot, which is anapestic — and then only by suppression of the second syllable of "reverend."

These "irregular" lines are discussed further in the next lesson, which is on how to *use* scansion. In the meantime, don't be thrown by the word "irregular" into thinking that such lines are somehow abnormal. Together, they constitute the *majority* of Shakespearean lines. Indeed, it could be said that Shakespeare only created the iambic "heartbeat" of a regular metrical pattern in order to exploit the possibilities of working countless variations on this basic theme — countless "heartbreaks" and other arrhythmias. Shakespeare's greatest lines are almost always "irregulars." Or else it would be: "To be or not to be, is that my quest?"

Split Lines

Often blank verse lines are divided among speakers, creating a wonderful sense of accelerated action:

CLAUDIUS: The bark is ready, and the wind at help,
The associates tend, and every thing is bent
For England.

HAMLET: For England!

CLAUDIUS: Ay, Hamlet.

HAMLET: Good.

CLAUDIUS: So is it, if thou knew'st our purposes.
(*Hamlet*, IV.iv.47ff.)

End Stops

There is usually some sense of a momentary wait at the end of a verse line. In singsong verses, such as Orlando's poetry to Rosalind, this is a rigid beat. Often the end stops are deliberately forced with *end rhymes,* such as:

HELENA: Good troth, you do me wrong, good sooth, you do,

In such disdainful manner me to woo
But fare you well: perforce I must confess
I thought you lord of more true gentleness.
(*A Midsummer Night's Dream*, II.ii.129)

Although there is no punctuation after "confess," there is a clear sense of a line pause there. Indeed, in this speech you can see Shakespeare deliberately padding the sense with syllables ("more true gentleness" instead of "more gentleness," a redundant "good sooth," and so on) just to maintain the pentameters — and to trivialize, comically, Helena's concerns).

In unrhymed verse, particularly in Shakespeare's more mature plays, the end stop can be very, very small, or even nonexistent, particularly when there is no punctuation. Indeed, it should probably be called an end "hold," because where it works best the actor basically holds the last syllable for a split second, and delicately makes a liaison from it into the first syllable of the next line, as in:

She loves me, sure; the cunning of her passion
Invites me in this churlish messenger.
(*Twelfth Night*, III.ii.23–24)

There is a tiny beat in which you "flick" the last *n* of "passion" into the *i* of "invites me" — for although no punctuation divides these words, and the syntax surely runs them together, the last syllable of "passion," lifted slightly and held for the tiniest extra moment, makes a poetic bridge to the next line.

End Rhymes

Shakespeare uses end rhymes for several purposes, some of which you have already seen. There are poems within the plays, such as Hamlet's to Ophelia and Orlando's to Rosalind. There are also poetic passages standing on their own, such as Helena's "good troth" speech above. In many of the early comedies particularly, long speeches of couplets create a generally amusing and pleasing light romantic pattern. But Shakespeare used rhyme in tragedies as well. *Romeo and Juliet* contains many rhyming passages; Romeo's and Juliet's first lines together, in fact, are in the form of an Italian sonnet, divided between them:

ROMEO: If I profane with my unworthiest hand
      This holy shrine, the gentle fine is this, —
My lips, two blushing pilgrims, ready stand
      To smooth that rough touch with a tender kiss.

JULIET: Good pilgrim, you do wrong your hand too much,
      Which mannerly devotion shows in this;
For saints have hands that pilgrims' hands do touch,
      And palm to palm is holy palmers' kiss.

ROMEO: Have not saints lips, and holy palmers too?

JULIET: Ay, pilgrim, lips that they must use in prayer.

ROMEO: O, then, dear saint, let lips do what hands do;
They pray; grant thou, lest faith turn to despair.

JULIET: Saints do not move, though grant for prayers' sake.

ROMEO: Then move not, while my prayer's effect I take.
  (*Romeo and Juliet*, I.v.95ff.)

In this play, Shakespeare uses rhyming passages not only in the direct exchanges of the lovers, but to give a romantic drive to the machinations of the surrounding plot:

ROMEO: Then plainly know my heart's dear love is set
On the fair daughter of rich Capulet:
As mine on hers, so hers is set on mine:
And all combined, save what thou must combine
By holy marriage: when and where and how
We met, we wooed and made exchange of vow,
I'll tell thee as we pass: but this I pray,
That thou consent to marry us today.

FRIAR LAWRENCE: Holy Saint Francis, what a change is here!
Is Rosaline, whom thou didst love so dear,
So soon forsaken? young men's love then lies
Not truly in their hearts, but in their eyes.
  (*Romeo and Juliet*, II.iv.57ff.)

Shakespeare used considerably less rhyme in his later plays, but he used end rhymes for at least five reasons throughout his career:

1.   To end a scene and/or to occasion an exit:

MACBETH: I go, and it is done; the bell invites me.
Here it not, Duncan, for it is a knell
That summons thee to heaven, or to hell.
  (*Macbeth*, II.ii.71–72)

This is the "travelling music" (in Jackie Gleason's immortal phrase) that Shakespeare, lacking the modern techniques of a dropping curtain or a lighting fade-out, uses to give closure to a scene. Sometimes the "exit" implied by the rhyming couplet is a character's final "life exit," as:

KENT: I have a journey, sir, shortly to go;
My master calls me, I cannot say no.
  (*King Lear*, V.iii.321–322)

The "journey" Kent refers to is his death.

2.   To make an especially pithy or aphoristic statement:

ALBANY: How far your eyes may pierce I cannot tell
Striving to better, oft we mar what's well.
  (*King Lear*, I.iv.336–337)

PRINCE: Bear hence this body and attend our will:
Mercy but murders, pardoning those that kill.
(*Romeo and Juliet*, III.i.201–202)

3.   To make a prediction or a spiritual curse:

BRABANTIO: Look to her, Moor, if thou hast eyes to see.
She has deceived her father, and may thee.
(*Othello*, I.iii.292–293)

4.   To indicate an abstract, rather than a realistic, character:

TIME: I, that please some, try all, both joy and terror
Of good and bad, that makes and unfolds error,
Now take upon me, in the name of Time,
To use my wings. Impute it not a crime
To me . . .
(*The Winter's Tale*, IV.i.1ff. Time's use of rhyme is especially prominent, as it is the only rhyme in the entire play.)

5.   To end a play:

FRIAR LAWRENCE: For never was a story of more woe
Than this of Juliet and her Romeo.
(*Romeo and Juliet*, V.iii.309–310)

ALBANY: The weight of this sad time we must obey.
Speak what we feel, not what we ought to say.
The oldest hath borne most: we that are young
Shall never see so much, nor live so long.
(*King Lear*, V.iii.323–327)

SUMMARY OF LESSON 16

This lesson is a primer on scansion, covering its history in actor training in the United States during the past decades, and its basic principles, including the marking of stress, feet, foot length, caesuras, end stops, rhymes, and the basic pattern and variations on iambic pentameter: the "heartbeat" of Shakespeare's verse.

But how do you *use* scansion? That is the subject of the next chapter.

LESSON 17

Using Scansion

And now we're into the thick of it. How does the actor *use* scansion? How do you *employ* poetic meter? Why should you learn how to scan texts for feet, stress, rhythm, and emphasis?

There are several answers, but you should understand that none of them are purely scientific. Indeed, scansion, which may seem at first to be highly technical (in the wrong hands, it certainly can be reduced to such), is in fact a deeply complex mystery, located somewhere between the realms of physiology, psychology, aesthetics, mathematics, and linguistics. You must never think of it as some sort of binary system or Morse code, with everything reduced to various configurations of stressed and unstressed syllables, so many dots and dashes.

Scansion is not a book of laws, but a *useful tool*. It is fundamentally inexact. Who is to say if the lines we earlier classed as basically anapestic:

Why ALL | his beHAV | iors did MAKE | their reTIRE

is not in fact basically dactylic?

Why | ALL his be | HAViors did | MAKE their re | TIRE

There are, it turns out, many ways to scan a verse, and the only "rule" is to find those that are truly helpful for the actor.

EXERCISE 17-1 FIND THE HEARTBEAT

Basically, iambic verse provides a "baseline" rhythm to the spoken text. This is the "heartbeat" of verse-speaking: a regular underlying "bum BUM, bum BUM, bum BUM, bum BUM, bum BUM." Alone, this heartbeat signals the fundamental pulse of life.

Organize the following speech, which is Margaret's curse on Richard from Lesson 11, by identifying the feet and defining the stressed and unstressed syllables. Place a vertical line (|) between the feet, a downward slash

(ˋ) over the stressed syllables, and a dipped arc (ˇ) over the unstressed syllables. For example:

My train | are men | of choice | and rar | est parts

Recall from Lesson 16 that this is one of the standard ways of noting scansion.

OK, go ahead. The lines are numbered for reference later:

1. Thou elvish-marked, abortive, rooting hog!

2. Thou that wast sealed in thy nativity

3. The slave of nature and the son of hell!

4. Thou slander of thy mother's heavy womb!

5. Thou loathed issue of thy father's loins!

6. Thou rag of honor! thou detested —

Now, check the answer below to see if you got it right.

The normal way of scanning these lines is as follows:

1. Thou el|vish-mark'd, | abor|tive, roo|ting hog!
2. Thou | that wast sealed | in thy | nati|vity
3. The slave | of na|ture and | the son | of hell!
4. Thou slan|der of | thy mo|ther's hea|vy womb!
5. Thou loa|thed is|sue of | thy fa|ther's loins!
6. Thou rag | of ho|nor!   thou | detes|ted — ? ?

How did you do? Consider the explanation below.

In Margaret's six lines, the first, third, fourth, and fifth are "regular" iambic pentameter. This is Margaret's "heartbeat." You can see how the regularity of her beat keeps Margaret on the attack; how it helps her build her argument, summon her energy, capture the attention of the court, and capitalize on her knowledge and verbal authority.

TERMINAL -ED SUFFIXES

Recall from Lesson 11 that on the fifth line you were asked to pronounce "loathed" not as we do in normal speech today, but with two syllables, as "loathe-ed." This is to maintain the structural build in those three lines, focused toward the climactic final "rag of honor" conclusion.

Conversely, "marked" in the first line must be pronounced as just one syllable — as "mark'd" — if the line is to scan as iambic pentameter. Pronounce it "mark-ed" and Margaret's heartbeat goes off. The same with "sealed" in line two. Whether or not a terminal -ed suffix is pronounced depends on the meter of the entire line, not just on that of the word itself.

If you read the speech as indicated here — with "mark'd" and "seal'd" but also with "loathe-ed" — you will see the structural power of building these iambic pentameter lines on top of each other.

It is to maintain regularity on such lines that we sometimes hear certain syllables, normally collapsed in modern prose, boldly pronounced in spoken (and acted) verse:

HAMLET: The time is out of joint; O curse-ed spite
          That ever I was born to set it right.
(*Hamlet*, I.v.189–190)

and

CHORUS: O for a Muse of fire that would ascend
         The brightest heaven of inven-tchi-on.
(*Henry V*, I.i.1)

EXPANDED SYLLABLES

The terminal -ed is an extra or expanded syllable — a metrical adjustment to maintain the line. You don't have to pronounce these expanded syllables: the *-ed*'s (as we call them in the Shakespeare acting trade) or the *tchi-on*'s. You can break the scansion altogether in order to get a more cutting, modern sound. But you lose something too. There are choices to be made here, not just rules to be followed.

Many modern directors will have nothing to do with terminal -ed's, or with any "meter syllables" not found in modern spoken prose. They consider these extra syllables simply too old-fashioned and/or effeminate and/or "classical" for use in contemporary productions. I'm often one of them myself.

Many other directors, however — and nearly all literary critics — feel that leaving out the -ed's is simply an ignorant mistake; that the actors and directors who do so simply don't know how to "do Shakespeare." I'm often in this camp too! Both viewpoints need to be reckoned with.

It is true that a more biting tone can often be gained by "taking out the -ed's," but some of the power and romantic energy of the text is inevitably sacrificed when they disappear. The text can become more halting and awkward; comprehensibility may be lost, as well as dignity. Occasionally, we even retain them in modern ceremonial prose: "blessèd" is an example. There is a trade-off, in other words, and a decision must be made on the basis of what is gained and what is lost by modifying the regularity of the iambs.[18]

But don't start making your choices now. For the rest of this section, put the -ed's *in* (when they belong in) so that you can discover the power of regular verse. Later, you can decide whether (and/or under what circumstances) to take them out.

COMPRESSED AND CONTRACTED SYLLABLES

Shakespeare sometimes compresses or contracts syllables to make the meter work. "Fire," which in most circumstances is a two-syllable word (rhyming with "higher") is compressed into a single long syllable in "O for a Muse of fire," above. Juliet's line at II.ii.109 appears in most modern texts as

O swear not by the moon, the inconstant moon

which scans as the eleven-syllable:

o SWEAR | not BY | the MOON | the in CON | stant MOON.

But in the First Folio of Shakespeare the line is printed in ten syllables:

O swear not by the moon, th'inconstant moon

which is scanned as a regular iambic pentameter line:

o SWEAR | not BY | the MOON | th'inCON | stant MOON

with "th'in" contracted into one syllable.

Expanded and compressed syllables are everywhere in Shakespeare; to be employed when a regular verse line is metrically desired.

Now let's go back to Margaret's speech. Line two in Margaret's speech above begins irregularly, with a single stressed syllable ("thou"), followed by an anapest ("that wast sealed") before resuming the iambic pattern. The break in regular iambics serves to break the build that ends in ". . . rooting hog," and to begin another build that escalates up to the "rag of honor" line.

---

[18]As I indicated above, as a director myself I have both taken them out and kept them in, in just about equal measure, depending on the nature of the play and on the style of production. Sometimes I have managed to have it both ways: In a *Hamlet* that was set in the Weimar years (the 1920s), I took the -ed's out of the play but retained them in the play-within-the-play. Yes, I winced at Hamlet's "O curs'd spite" and Claudius's "O lim'd soul"—thirty years of hearing "curse-ed spite" and "lime-ed soul" had set fixed channels in my brain—and there's no question but that something was lost by the deletion. But in that particular production, something stronger was gained. This is not the place to discuss that, however. You have to learn how to work with the -ed's in, as Shakespeare intended, before deciding to take them out.

And, of course, the last line of Margaret's speech is broken by Richard, who substitutes her name where his was to go:

MARGARET: Thou slander of thy mother's heavy womb!
Thou loathed issue of thy father's loins!
Thou rag of honor!   Thou detested —

RICHARD: Margaret!

MARGARET: Richard!

Richard's brilliant interposition of Margaret's name, instead of his own, "works" as effective drama because Margaret's perfectly regular iambic cadence leaves an exactly defined "space" for her intended final curse — but Richard maddeningly slips in there first. It's as if Margaret had maneuvered twenty minutes for a spot in a parking lot — and then Richard snuck in and grabbed it when her head was turned.

Notice also that the "space" isn't even big enough for two syllables: just for one stressed one. Margaret had clearly been intending to break the bounds of her iambs with her final line, and make a feminine ending:

Thou rag of honor!   Thou detested Richard!

This makes Richard's filling of that space all that much more a violation, for it violates Margaret's planned violation. These are two reckless speakers, each trying to set the other up for catastrophe! It's all prefigured in the scansion.

Without the regular metrical patterning, Richard's interruption would simply be crude and immature; he could only outshout her. *With* the patterning, he can demonstrate his masterful (and engaging) skills at manipulation.

Now try Margaret's speech, using your metrical analysis to build the cadenced arguments, and to leave the "space" for your partner to fill in with your name.

FOLLOWING AND VIOLATING THE PATTERN

By patterning the syllables around a regularized alternation of pulses, Shakespeare was also able to create meaning through sound structure (a linguistic "music"), as well as through semantics (meaning). He did this both by following the meter, and by violating it.

By following it, he was able to build cadences, arguments, and levels of agreement difficult to establish otherwise. You can see that in the regular lines of Margaret's speech, and you should practice it.

▪▩▨▩▨▪ EXERCISE 17-2 OPHELIA

1.   Scan and practice these four lines of Ophelia, telling your father how Hamlet grabbed you and stared at you:

He took me by the wrist, and held me hard;
Then goes he to the length of all his arm;
And with his other hand there o'er his brow,
He falls to such perusal of my face . . .

The lines are essentially regular, with perhaps a spondee replacing an iamb on "there o'er." Or perhaps not. In any event, you have a very solid baseline in these beginning clauses of Ophelia's speech.

But the most important reason for establishing a baseline is the effects you gain by *violating* or *changing* it. These you should have found, and should try now.

2.   Continue with the same speech. Here's the whole thing:

He took me by the wrist, and held me hard;
Then goes he to the length of all his arm;
And, with his other hand thus o'er his brow,
He falls to such perusal of my face
As he would draw it. Long stayed he so;
At last, — a little shaking of mine arm,
And thrice his head thus waving up and down, —
He raised a sigh so piteous and profound,
That it did seem to shatter all his bulk,
And end his being: that done, he lets me go;
And, with his head over his shoulder turn'd,
He seemed to find his way without his eyes;
For out o' doors he went without their help,
And, to the last, bended their light on me.

Look at the pattern of stresses. The first four lines are, as you've seen, essentially regular iambic pentameters. But, as we saw in Lesson 16, line five, "As he would draw it. Long stayed he so" is a nine-syllable line, with an imposed silence after the unstressed "it." We can call this a "stressed silence," since it replaces what would be, in the scansion, a stressed syllable.[19] The silence virtually howls out its presence; it is the silence of Hamlet staring crazily at Ophelia; it is the silence of Ophelia not knowing how to respond.

The next four lines are equally regular iambic pentameter, and line ten also continues the iambic pattern for its first five syllables. But then again it breaks, after "And end his being." Again there is a stressed silence, whereupon the line — and Ophelia's recounting of the episode — begins again, very slowly and softly: "that done, he lets me go." This time the line has an added syllable, not including the stressed silence.

The pattern of these first ten lines is quite powerful: four lines building up to a climactic platform on "As he would draw it," and then a stunning

---

[19] It's also called a "silent beat."

pause, which allows for a major cutback. Then a second four-line regular build, starting higher than the first one started (but not as high as the first one ended), that reaches an even higher platform — and an even more breathtaking silence on "And end his being."

And then — death being about as high as one can go (and foreshadowing thoughts that Hamlet will play upon in "to be or not to be") — there is an enormous cutback in this tenth line to a quiet, awkward, anticlimactic, extrasyllable conclusion: "that done, he lets me go."

In summary, we have four regular iambic pentameters, leading to climax and cutback, followed by four more regular iambic pentameters, leading to a bigger climax and a bigger cutback. This is followed by four near-regular but undeniably clumsy lines, well showing Ophelia's shaky grasp of reality.

"Over" and "bended" are clearly trochees, so that the first and last lines of this concluding sequence (lines eleven and fourteen) are nonbuilding, stammered, and weakly broken in their regularity, as if spoken by a helplessly sobbing girl. The great climaxes are past: Hamlet will "draw" her (there's a sense that Hamlet will draw her "out," too, for she is not entirely forthcoming to him at this point), and Hamlet will die. Now, in telling of his departure, Ophelia can only narrate how the prince staggered out of her room — and faded out of her life.

Try the speech, and try, to the extent possible, to let the scansion tell the story and relay your feelings. For this exercise, work on the *words,* not on your emotions. Relate the story of Hamlet's grabbing you and leaving you, and try to reach the climaxes that the story and the verse provide.

VERSE AND PROSE

The variation from verse to prose, or prose to verse, makes a subtextual statement all its own. Generally, as you would imagine, verse (in Shakespeare) is used in more elegant company; prose is the commoner language of the lower class. Prince Hal speaks prose in the Boar's Head Tavern with Falstaff and his drinking buddies, but verse in the court. Iago, in *Othello,* regularly uses prose to his dimwitted friend, Roderigo, and then switches to verse when talking to the (more cultured) audience in soliloquy:

> IAGO: Meet me by and by at the citadel: I must fetch his necessaries ashore. Farewell.
>
> RODERIGO: Adieu. [*Exit.*]
>
> IAGO: That Cassio loves her, I do well believe it.
> That she loves him, 'tis apt and of great credit. . . .
> (*Othello,* II.i.291ff.)

█▧◢▨◢█ EXERCISE 17-3

Read Iago's lines above (you can skip over Roderigo's "Adieu," or have a partner say it) and get the feel of the shift from prose to verse.

When you feel comfortable with this, try, with a partner, both sides of this earlier Iago/Roderigo exchange:

IAGO: Thou art sure of me: go, make money: I have told thee often, and I re-tell thee again and again, I hate the Moor: my cause is hearted: thine hath no less reason. Let us be conjunctive in our revenge against him: if thou canst cuckold him, thou dost thyself a pleasure, me a sport. There are many events in the womb of time, which will be delivered. Traverse; go; provide thy money. We will have more of this to-morrow. Adieu.

RODERIGO: Where shall we meet i'the morning?

IAGO: At my lodging.

RODERIGO: I'll be with thee betimes.

IAGO: Go to; farewell. Do you hear, Roderigo?

RODERIGO: What say you?

IAGO: No more of drowning, do you hear?

RODERIGO: I am changed: I'll go sell all my land.

IAGO: Go to; farewell! put money in your purse!

[*Exit Roderigo.*]

Thus do I ever make my fool my purse;
For I mine own gained knowledge should profane,
If I would time expend with such a snipe,
But for my sport and profit. I hate the Moor;
And it is thought abroad, that 'twixt my sheets
'Has done my office: I know not if 't be true;
But I, for mere suspicion in that kind,
Will do as if for surety.
(*Othello*, I.iii.371ff.)

The prose exchange between Roderigo and Iago is wickedly colloquial, dense with plotting and aphoristic philosophy ("there are many events in the womb of time . . ."). The switch to the regular metrics of blank verse show that Iago, his friend out of the way, is preparing to return to the court and military life where he can make his forces work. Notice that the words "I hate the Moor" occur in both the prose and verse sections. Where they appear in the verse, they follow the first break (on "profit") in the iambic regularity, forcing a bold transition in the speech, and harkening us back to the earlier prose section; they also show that Iago's hatred for the Moor (Othello) is wholly out of keeping with the courtly argument (about Roderigo) that he is making up to that point. Change that line to

But for my sport and fun. I hate the Moor

And the transition is all but overlooked.

Shakespeare's alternation of prose and verse has many variations and subtleties. The island monster Caliban, for example, speaks verse in *The Tempest,* while court hangers-on Stephano and Trinculo speak prose; though this may seem at first glance unlikely, it indicates Caliban's mystical origins and the inner triviality of the courtiers underneath their finery. King Lear alternates between verse and prose, almost speech by speech, in act IV of *King Lear,* demonstrating the chaos of his broken mind. In the third act of *A Midsummer Night's Dream,* fairy Queen Titania romances Bottom the Weaver in verse, while Bottom responds to her stolidly in prose, creating a hilarious comic counterpoint. There are no "rules" as to when Shakespeare uses prose or verse, only dramatic opportunities. We're dealing with creative genius here, not literary arithmetic.

Broken Verse

Broken verse — verse in which the iambic line simply stops in midsentence or even midword — is a powerful indicator of mental breakdown. King Lear's wild stammers are immensely moving because they are set against an iambic baseline:

> LEAR: . . . No, you unnatural hags,
> I will have such revenges on you both,
> That all the world shall — I will do such things —
> What they are, yet I know not; but they shall be
> The terrors of the earth. You think I'll weep;
> No, I'll not weep —
> I have full cause of weeping; but this heart
> Shall break into a hundred thousand flaws,
> Or e'er I'll weep. — O fool, I shall go mad!
> (*King Lear,* II.iv.281ff.)

"That all the world shall . . ." begins as a perfect iambic pentameter line that simply falls apart when Lear can't figure out how to finish his own sentence. What *shall* the world do? He honestly doesn't know.

Lear tries to get back on track with "I will do such things . . ." but then realizes he has no idea what exactly he will do, being a king no longer. His helplessness is mirrored by his inability to continue the heartbeats of his line. "Hysterica passio," he cries at one point: a Latin name for a fluttering heart.

▚▞▚▞ EXERCISE 17-4

Study Lear's speech and memorize it. Perform it, creating the mental breakdown in this exercise simply by the broken verses rather than by emotional hysteria. See how the scansion can help create the situation you find yourself (Lear's self) in.

Broken Prose

In *Othello,* Othello is so consumed with raging jealousy that his lines break down first into broken verse, and then into broken prose:

OTHELLO: Hath he said any thing?

IAGO: He hath, my lord; but be you well assured,
No more than he'll unswear.

OTHELLO: What hath he said?

IAGO: Faith, that he did — I know not what he did.

OTHELLO: What? what?

IAGO: Lie —

OTHELLO: With her?

IAGO: With her, on her; what you will.

OTHELLO: Lie with her! lie on her! — We say lie on her, when they belie her. — Lie with her! that's fulsome. — Handkerchief — confessions — handkerchief! — To confess, and be hanged for his labor; — first, to be hanged, and then to confess. — I tremble at it. Nature would not invest herself in such shadowing passion without some instruction. It is not words that shake me thus: — pish! — noses, ears, and lips. — Is't possible? — Confess — handkerchief! — O devil! —
(IV.i.29ff.)

This collapse is shocking, particularly in light of the sonorous and regular verses we have come to expect from Othello. It is made even more shocking by Iago's calm adherence to the regular metrics of the pentameters. *Iago* shows no hysteria here, and Othello trusts him because of it.

GENERAL IRREGULARITY

It's important to keep in mind (1) that the vast majority of Shakespeare's verse lines are *not* regular, and (2) that the more he wrote, the less regular his verse lines became.

In the late plays, it's hard sometimes to find even a single regular line. Look at this speech of Leontes in *The Winter's Tale*. Leontes believes his wife is unfaithful, that she is having an affair with his best friend, Polixenes ("Sir Smile," he sarcastically calls him), and that he, Leontes, is now a cuckold — and wearing the "forked" horns that symbolize cuckolding. Leontes dismisses his son from the room in order to discuss, with the audience, cuckolding in society (but his boy hides and Leontes discovers him at the end of the speech):

LEONTES: Inch thick, knee deep; o'er head and ears a forked one.
Go, play, boy, play: thy mother plays, and I
Play too; but so disgraced a part, whose issue
Will hiss me to my grave: contempt and clamor
Will be my knell. Go play, boy, play. There have been
(Or I am much deceived) cuckolds ere now,
And many a man there is (even at this present,

Now, while I speak this) holds his wife by the arm
That little thinks she has been sluiced in his absence
And his pond fished by his next neighbor, by
Sir Smile, his neighbor: nay, there's comfort in't,
That other men have gates, and those gates opened,
As mine, against their will. Should all despair
That have revolted wives, the tenth of mankind
Would hang themselves. Physic for it there's none;
It is a bawdy planet, that will strike
Where 'tis predominant; and 'tis powerful, think it,
From east, west, north, and south, be it concluded,
No barricado for a belly. Know't.
It will let in and out the enemy
With bag and baggage. Many thousand on's
Have the disease, and feel it not. How now, boy?
(*The Winter's Tale*, I.ii.186ff.)

The irregular verse here is extreme: in part to show Leontes's great mental distraction, and in part to show his preoccupation with anarchy and social disorder. Leontes earlier says, "I have *tremor cordis* [that is, heart palpitations] on me, my heart dances," and the verse here brilliantly echoes his cardiac near-arrest. But this sort of verse is quite typical of late Shakespeare. *All* of Shakespeare's characters in the later plays wrestle as much with language as they struggle with destiny.

Notice how the broken verse is punctuated with bold, simple phrases and images: "knee deep," "thy mother plays," "bawdy planet," "east, west, north, and south," and "bag and baggage." The rhythm of this speech is a rhythm of ideas as much as stressed syllables. This is typical of Shakespeare's most mature playwriting.

◤◤◤ EXERCISE 17-5

   Scan Leontes's speech. Which are the regular lines? Try reading the speech a few times. What value is there in the occasional regularity? What setups are there for the many violations? Can we even talk of violating the norm when the violations so outweigh the norms?

THE TENSION OF VERSE

   These exercises should lead us to a deeper understanding of the usefulness, and the challenge, of verse drama.
   Great verse drama exists in *dynamic tension:* It lies between meter and meaning; between poetic stress and rhetorical emphasis; between the regularity of verse and the chaos of physical phenomena (and human existence).

If we look at the first line of Ophelia's speech in Exercise 17-2:

He took me by the wrist, and held me hard

we can easily see that, while "by" scans with a stress, it is not a word that Ophelia would ever emphasize. And while the scansion of the line reads

he TOOK me BY the WRIST and HELD me HARD

the rhetorical emphasis might be more like

he TOOK me by the WRIST and HELD me HARD

or even

he TOOK ME by the WRIST and HELD ME — hard

How does the scansion work with the rhetoric?

It works by maintaining a subtle tension between them. Where poetic stress and rhetorical emphasis join together, as in "wrist," the conveyance of the image is solid, powerful, unwavering. Where they are somewhat apart — say in the word "me" (both times) — there is a quaver of uncertainty. It's at those moments of dissonance that feeling and vulnerability come through with brilliant delicacy. An understated "hard" in the line above, against our expectation (from the meter) that it will be strongly stressed, conveys Ophelia's anxiety as much or more than any furrowed brow or teary expression.

You are not going to learn that from this book — or from any other book — because the tension we're speaking of must be *heard* and *felt* as well as understood from a technical viewpoint. You must see Shakespeare, and hear Shakespeare, and read Shakespeare aloud to get the music of his meter, and see how it dances with the meaning of his text. This is a lifetime study for actors, and what they get out of it depends probably on instinctual and intuitive abilities as well. But your study will prompt your instincts, and your practice will shape your intuitions. Start now.

THE MUSIC OF VERSE

Verse is an artifice, but so is language; so is speaking; so is drama. Verse, language, drama: These are all methods by which human beings have tried to organize phenomena and make use of the world. They are among our tools for understanding the universe, coming to terms with human nature, and reducing our extraordinary life perceptions and experience to comprehensible and manageable units.

Shakespeare's characters — like Shakespeare himself and those who perform in and attend plays — are trying to conceptualize the world. They/we are all trying to manage their/our lives and their/our destiny; trying to create an orderly language with which to understand the world and to control what in human existence can possibly be controlled.

Ordinary language suffices for ordinary tasks ("pass the bread"); but more complexly structured and sculpted language is required for dealing persuasively with matters of state, divinity, love, and death. Shakespeare did not shrink from those grand occasions. He rose to them, and he did so better than anyone else.

His language, working on a blank verse baseline, is both dense and light at the same time: dense because it contains so much information, observation, and analysis; light because its structure brings us meaning on several levels at the same time, overburdening us in no single one of them.

Verse communicates to us without our having to think about it. Hearing well-articulated verse is like floating downstream, where we can just go with the current—speeding up at the rapids, slowing down at the still waters, and moving through an ever-changing field of perceptions, with all our senses fully unburdened and alive.

If you, the actor, can hear the music of the verse, and can let it flow freely, with your mind and hands and voice free to act the part at the same time, you will be able to rise to the same occasions Shakespeare did. You will be able to pass on the Shakespearean current so that the audience can float downstream with you, instead of struggling to paddle upstream, and thereby miss the scenery (and the pleasure).

And that's why and how you should study scansion—not to learn how to tap out five beats to the line, but to explore the tension between those five beats in your mind, and the five beats that sometimes come, sometimes halt, sometimes go around the other way, and sometimes get lost in a character's *tremor cordis*.

ᐁᐅᐁᐅᐁ EXERCISE 17-6

Go back to any of the speeches you worked on in Lesson 13, the gallery of Shakespearean characters. Scan the speeches and analyze the scansion according to the principles in this lesson and the one preceding.

See if you can let the scansion float you through these texts, adding strength and body to your work on them up to this point.

SUMMARY OF LESSON 17

This lesson describes a basic means of scanning a text: determining the feet; finding the stressed syllables; expanding, compressing, or contracting syllables to maintain the regular scanning (in some cases); determining the baseline or "heartbeat" of blank verse—and then *using* the scansion, as Shakespeare intends, by either following or violating the basic and established patterns. A discussion of the proper tension between meaning and meter, rhetorical emphasis, and poetic stress, concludes the lesson.

Shakespearean Rhetoric

Rhetoric is the deliberate arrangement of language for *persuasiveness* and *effectiveness*. It is not an empty or an abstract art, and it is not restricted to aesthetics. In the terrible days of World War II, when London was subject to massive bombardments, English national survival was almost wholly secured by the speeches of Winston Churchill, the prime minister. By sheer *rhetoric*. Churchill's legendary exhortations —

> What is our aim?
> I can answer in one word: victory —
> Victory at all costs,
> Victory in spite of all terror;
> Victory, however long and hard the road may be!
> For without victory —
> There is no survival!
> (speech before the House of Commons, May 1940)

and

> We shall not flag nor fail.
> We shall go on to the end.
> We shall fight on the seas and oceans,
> We shall fight with growing confidence and growing strength in the air,
> We shall defend our island whatever the cost may be,
> We shall fight on the beaches,
> We shall fight on the landing ground,
> We shall fight in the fields and in the streets,
> We shall fight in the hills,
> We shall never surrender!
> (speech before the House of Commons, June 1940)

and

168

This is not the end.
It is not even the beginning of the end.
But it is,
Perhaps,
The end of the beginning.
(radio address, 1942)

proved stronger in the end than a hail of Nazi missiles. The English spirit held firm, the country refused to capitulate, and England remained uninvaded and unconquered.

In the same way, a new era in American and world politics was initiated by a young president who begged, in his inaugural address,

My fellow Americans:
Ask not what your country can do for you,
Ask what you can do for your country.
My fellow citizens of the world:
Ask not what America will do for you,
But what together we can do for the freedom of man.
(John F. Kennedy, inaugural address, 1961)

And racial relations in the United States began an irreversible move toward integration when a civil rights leader wrote from jail:

Injustice anywhere is a threat to justice everywhere.

And then spoke of his dreams before a million persons gathered in front of the Washington Monument:

I have a dream! that one day, in the red hills of Georgia, the sons of former slaves and the sons of former slaveowners will be able to sit down together at the table of brotherhood;

I have a dream! that my four little children will one day live in a nation where they will not be judged by the color of their skin but the content of their character;

I have a dream! . . .
(Martin Luther King, August 1963)

In these cases, there can be no question but that — reversing the old cliché — words spoke louder than actions. And that words *were* actions. Words alone, effectively arranged and spoken with both passion and conviction, will change minds, direct and redirect national policies, and save (or take) lives. Spoken words have often been the most crucial actions of human history, and their impact often transcends the ages. We in America can still be roused to patriotic fervor with Patrick Henry's defiant retort to the British:

Is life so dear, or peace so sweet, as to be purchased at the price of chains and slavery? Forbid it, Almighty God! I know not what course others may take, but as for me, give me liberty or give me death!

Or the close of Abraham Lincoln's Gettysburg Address:

> ... that we highly resolve that these dead shall not have died in vain, that this nation, under God, shall have a new birth of freedom, and that the government of the people, by the people, and for the people shall not perish from the earth.

Strong political and patriotic rhetoric has power not only in its own time, but for centuries that follow. People have laid down their lives for words such as these.

Certain rhetorical devices are in use in this political oratory. **Alliteration**, the repetition of initial consonants, builds a momentum of repeated sounds: "purchased at the price," "the dead shall not have died," "the sons of former slaves and the sons of former slaveowners." The **rhetorical question**, a question that you plan to answer yourself, sets up the audience: "What is our aim?" asked Churchill, and then told his listeners what "our" aim should be. And **metaphor** is a powerful evocation of fervent feeling: "the table of brotherhood," "citizens of the world," "however long and hard the road."

We have seen all of these devices in Shakespeare many times:

Alliteration:

> O happy horse, to bear the weight of Antony.
> (Cleopatra, from Exercise 3-3)

Rhetorical Question:

> O Charmian,
> Where think'st thou he is now? Stands he or sits he?
> (Cleopatra, same exercise)

Metaphor:

> Though others have the arm, show us the sleeve.
> (Luciana, from Exercise 5-2)

and

> Now is the winter of our discontent
> Made glorious summer by this sun of York ...
> (Gloucester, from Exercise 5-4)

Shakespeare was, among many other things, one of the great rhetoricians of the English language. His history plays are exemplars of political rhetoric: so much so that "anti-Stratfordians" (persons who think other authors wrote Shakespeare's plays) suggest "Shake-Spear" was a made-up name for this chronicler of the warlike kings in English history.[20] Shakespeare's rhetoric

---

[20] The current author does not subscribe to the anti-Stratfordian viewpoint. However, the debate, which has been formally argued before a panel of justices of the U.S. Supreme Court, will prove at the very least a fascinating diversion for students interested in Shakespeare and his times.

certainly served patriotic purposes for the Tudor and Stuart monarchies of England during his lifetime (he was on the payroll of both Queen Elizabeth and King James during his entire career), and his fervent speeches on behalf of the English national character played a significant role — particularly in the delivery of Laurence Olivier — in the British survival effort during World War II (as we saw in Lesson 8). Indeed, there were times when it seemed that Churchill and Shakespeare were the only weapons England had.

But rhetoric is not only political. Rhetoric is a comprehensive speech act, with many applications: intellectual, social, aesthetic, and theatrical. Rhetoric can be philosophically argumentative, socially persuasive, and wonderfully entertaining. It both enhances the speaker and elevates the listener; it brightens the message and both shapes and animates the communication. It makes plays *playful;* it makes us realize that Shakespearean actors (they were called "players" in his day) were always playing with their words, creating a theatre of creatively playful language that encapsulated both action and ideas.

Wit and wordplay are the soul of rhetoric, the glory of sprightly conversation and eloquent discourse. "Practice rhetoric in your common talk," Tranio advises Lucentio in Shakespeare's *Taming of the Shrew.* The educated person, Tranio suggests, should make rhetoric part of the workings and enjoyment of life itself. Our goal, at least, is to make it part of acting in the Shakespearean theatre. So let's take Tranio at his word. How do we "practice" rhetoric?

BASIC RHETORIC

Most rhetoric employs *repetition* in various ways:

1.   For building a *progression* ("We shall fight on the beaches, We shall fight on the landing ground"),

2.   or for pointing out an *antithesis* ("Give me liberty or give me death").

Sometimes a *double antithesis* makes a particularly neat rhetorical conclusion: "injustice anywhere . . . justice everywhere" and "beginning of the end . . . end of the beginning."

Most such repetition indicates a level of *contrivance.* It is clear that the speaker has deliberately selected and arranged his or her words, and didn't just speak entirely spontaneously. This level of contrivance calls attention to the speaker as well as the subject. In political rhetoric, the "subtext" of rhetoric is "I will lead you." Churchill's statements, therefore, say *both:*

We shall fight them . . . (text)

and

"By phrasing my words so eloquently, I am showing myself as the best person to lead you in that fight" (subtext)

Rhetoric thus shows off the speaker as well as the speaker's ideas. It shows the speaker as intelligent, authoritative, confident, eloquent—and sometimes witty and sexy as well.

Rhetoric, particularly in its witty or romantic guises, is often called *wordplay,* as it is a "playing with words." As such, it is naturally dramatic, for it is part of "playing." Actors are, of course, "players" and what they play mostly with is words.

Shakespearean wordplay uses many rhetorical devices. Most were isolated and identified in Shakespeare's own day, achieving a prominent position in the curricula of the grammar schools that Shakespeare and most young men of the time attended. The most important are listed and discussed below.

Few modern Shakespearean actors ever learn all these technical names, but you should at least get to know what the major rhetorical devices look and sound like.

Ploce is the most general term for a patterned *reuse* (repetition) of words within the same phrase or speech:

> ROMEO: Love goes toward love, as schoolboys from their books,
> But love from love, toward school with heavy looks.
> (*Romeo and Juliet,* II.ii.157–158)

and

> PRINCESS: You do the king my father too much wrong
> And wrong the reputation of your name . . .
> (*Love's Labor's Lost,* II.i.154–155)

There are many specific variations of ploce. **Anaphora** is a series of phrases that *begin* identically, such as Churchill's:

> We shall fight on the beaches
> We shall fight on the landing ground

This is sometimes combined with **isocolon,** a series of phrases of the same length, as in Lincoln's:

> of the people,
> by the people,
> and
> for the people,

In Shakespeare we see all the time:

> Was ever woman in this humor wooed?
> Was ever woman in this humor won?
> (*Richard III,* I.ii.226–227)

and

O'er courtiers' knees, that dream on court'sies straight,
O'er lawyers' fingers, who straight dream on fees,
O'er ladies' lips, who straight on kisses dream . . .
(*Romeo and Juliet*, I.iv. 72–74)

Notice in this example not only the initial repetitions, but the internal ones: of "dream" and "straight," and the repeated plural possessives—"courtiers' . . . lawyers' . . . ladies'"—at the second word position of each line.

Epistrophe is the opposite of anaphora: these are lines or phrases that *end* with the same word:

Come, gentle night; come, loving, black-browed night.
(*Romeo and Juliet*, III.ii.20)

Thou told'st me they were stol'n unto this wood;
And here am I, and wood within this wood.
(*A Midsummer Night's Dream*, II.i.191–192. "Wood" is a pun, with the first and third meaning "forest," and the second meaning "blockheaded.")

Parison is a mixture of repetition and antithesis: matching word against word. Martin Luther King's was one:

Injustice anywhere is a threat to justice everywhere.

and so is Helena's:

You both are rivals and love Hermia;
And now both rivals to mock Helena.
(*A Midsummer Night's Dream*, III.ii.155–156)

Some other rhetorical devices (*figures* they are also called) are common to Shakespearean wordplay, particularly in the earlier plays. **Antimetabole,** for example, is the repetition of words in inverted order:

Some true love turn'd, and not a false turn'd true.
(*A Midsummer Night's Dream*, III.ii.90)

Anadiplosis means giving the word that ends one clause the first, or near the first, position in the next:

ISABELLE: I am a woeful suitor to your honor.
Please but your honor hear me.
(*Measure for Measure*, II.ii.30–31)

Epizeuxis (which we first saw in Lesson 10) is a phrase or word repeated in immediate succession, usually with an escalating emphasis:

LEAR: O Lear, Lear, Lear, beat at this gate, that let thy folly in . . .
(*King Lear*, I.iv.292–293)

Epanolepsis is a line beginning and ending with the same word:

Weigh oath with oath and you will nothing weigh.
(*A Midsummer Night's Dream*, III.ii.131)

Polyptoton is an example of modified ploce; the second word is not identical with the first, but is from the same root:

I followed fast; but faster he did fly.
(*A Midsummer Night's Dream*, III.ii.416)

Asteismus is one speech picking up a word and giving it a different application:

BOLINGBROKE: . . . Convey him to the tower!

RICHARD II: Oh good, Convey! Conveyers are you all . . .
(*Richard II*, IV.i.316–317)[21]

And, of course, there are puns. Technically called **paronomasia**, puns are words used in different and often contradictory senses, as in the exchange:

WIDOW: He that is giddy thinks the world turns round.

PETRUCHIO: Roundly replied.

KATHERINE: Mistress, how mean you that?

WIDOW: Thus I conceive by him.

PETRUCHIO: Conceives by me! — How likes Hortensio that?

HORTENSIO: My widow says, thus she conceives her tale.

PETRUCHIO: Very well mended. — Kiss him for that, good widow.

KATHERINE: "He that is giddy thinks the world turns round" —
I pray you, tell me what you meant by that.

WIDOW: Your husband, being troubled with a shrew,
Measures my husband's sorrow by his woe:
And now you know my meaning.

KATHERINE: A very mean meaning.

WIDOW: Right, I mean you.

KATHERINE: And I am mean, indeed, respecting you.
(*The Taming of the Shrew*, V.ii.19ff.)

Punning double entendres of "conceive" (to understand, to get pregnant) and "mean" (intend, cruel) are combined here with rhyme, alliteration, and anadiplosis to make a battle of wits, a battle fought in wordplay. Such puns are comic, of course, ("the lowest form of humor," we are sometimes told), but they are also used by Shakespeare at crucial moments in the tragedies, as by Lady Macbeth, planning the assassination of King Duncan:

LADY MACBETH: If he do bleed,
I'll gild the faces of the grooms withal,

---

[21]For this definition and example, and a few others in this section, I am indebted to Harold Brooks' excellent introduction to the Arden edition of *A Midsummer Night's Dream* (New York: Methuen, 1979), especially pp. xlv–xlvix.

For it must seem their guilt.
(*Macbeth,* II.ii.54–56)

and by the dying Mercutio:

. . . ask for me tomorrow and you will find me a grave man.
(*Romeo and Juliet,* III.i.102)

In *The Winter's Tale,* Leontes makes a grimly ironic triple pun, speaking to his son:

Go play boy. Thy mother plays and I play too . . .
(I.ii.187)

The first "play" means "have fun," the second means "is having an affair," and the third means "pretend not to notice." It is extraordinary playwriting skill that compresses this highly complex idea into one seemingly simple (and wryly amusing) line.

FIGURES OF SPEECH

Figures of speech are grander literary devices also common to Shakespeare, and effective in his dramatic rhetoric.

The **simile** is a classic figure of speech in which two dissimilar things are directly compared to one another; the comparison is generally made by the words "like" or "as." "Here is your husband, like a mildew'd ear," Hamlet says savagely to his mother. "Let virtue be as wax and melt in her own fire," he continues. Both are similes.

Similes in the theatre must be dramatic, not merely narrative or descriptive. When Henry V says to his army:

I see you stand like greyhounds in the slips,
Straining upon the start.
(*Henry V,* III.i.31–32)

his simile ("you stand like greyhounds") does not merely state a fact, it must be a speech act, an attempt to compel his soldiers into action. Far from actually describing his soldiers with this simile (having just been repulsed in their first effort, the soldiers probably look more like cows slumbering in the shade than greyhounds straining at their leashes), Henry is rousing them. He is trying to make them *become* "like greyhounds." Henry's goal is to make his men accept his simile—to induce and inspire them to risk their lives. It will take all his authority, courage, and seductive charisma to do this. His soldiers *will become* straining greyhounds to please him if he earns their admiration and respect. They will rise to his occasion—if he rises to Shakespeare's!

Metaphor, which is an *implied* simile, a comparison drawn without the connecting word "like" or "as," is also firmly in the Shakespearean canon, of course. Shakespeare, in fact, is its greatest master. When Henry moves beyond the greyhound simile with

> The game's afoot!

he switches to metaphor, alluding to the French army as so many rabbits.

Because it is indirect and implied, the metaphor is more powerful than the simile. The English soldiers are only *compared* to greyhounds; but they are subtly induced into thinking the French army *actually is* but "game" to be hunted.

Shakespearean metaphor runs the gamut from the commonplace:

> CLAUDIO: There, Leonato, take her back again;
> Give not this rotten orange to your friend.
> (*Much Ado About Nothing*, IV.i.33–34)

to the trenchant:

> HAMLET: Nay, but to live
> In the rank sweat of an enseamed bed
> Stewed in corruption, honeying and making love
> O'er the nasty sty!
> (*Hamlet*, III.iv.91–94, to his mother, describing her lovemaking with her husband, the "mildew'd ear . . .")

to the profound:

> MACBETH: Life's but a walking shadow, a poor player
> That struts and frets his hour upon the stage
> And then is heard no more . . .
> (*Macbeth*, V.v.24–27)

Shakespeare is also a frequent user of **alliteration,** which he borrowed and refined from the medieval theatre. His alliteration is sometimes simple and subtle:

> PRINCESS: Such short lived wits do wither as they grow.
> (*Love's Labor's Lost*, II.i.54)

sometimes comic and satirical:

> HOLOFERNES: The preyful princess pierced and prick'd a pretty pleasing pricket . . .
> (*Love's Labor's Lost*, IV.ii.57)

and sometimes bitter:

> KENT: Your eldest daughters have foredone themselves,
> And desperately are dead.
> (*King Lear*, V.iii.291–292)

Alliteration creates a pattern of sound that, in conjunction with verse stress and meaning emphasis, creates a rolling momentum through many speeches, a momentum that can be accelerated or halted, depending on the alliterative practice. Holofernes' *p* words propel a wilful and clever articulation; Kent's *d* words toll the death knell for the evil Regan and Goneril.

OTHER RHETORICAL, DRAMATIC, AND LITERARY DEVICES

Many other devices will be passed over with just a mention here, including the following.

Apostrophes are short speeches given to absent persons, or things, or gods. "O happy horse, to bear the weight of Antony" (Cleopatra) is an apostrophe to a horse.

Asides are comments delivered directly to the audience. When Viola, disguised as Cesario, turns to us to admit

> Pray God defend me! A little thing would make me tell them how much I lack of a man.

she is obviously speaking *aside,* so that the characters on stage cannot hear.

Soliloquies are whole speeches given directly to the audience, such as Richard's opening "Now is the winter of our discontent" (Exercise 5-4). Sometimes, as with Hamlet's famous "To be or not to be" soliloquy, these speeches may be presumed to be the character's "thinking aloud."

Dialects are speech regionalisms. Fluellen, in *Henry V,* is written in Welsh dialect; Edgar, in *King Lear,* adopts a West country dialect when he disguises himself to his blind father. In England, it has been traditional for many years to play low comic parts in a Cockney dialect, although they are not necessarily written that way.

ANTI-RHETORIC

Not all of Shakespeare's characters speak with rhetorical splendor, however. Just as Shakespeare often breaks his verse line (as we saw with King Lear in Lesson 17) in order to show the chaos and confusion of a mind struggling with incipient disorder, so Shakespeare also creates characters whose rhetorical skills fail them, often at crucial moments. Don John, the bastard brother of Don Pedro in *Much Ado About Nothing,* is mortally embarrassed when, at the beginning of the play, his brother and Leonato exchange fulsomely flowery greetings to each other, leaving the less articulate John all but speechless. All John can manage, when the eyes of the court turn to him for his response, is the rhetorically feeble "I thank you. I am not of many words, but I thank you." As the court chuckles at his obvious discomfort, John seethes inwardly, plotting revenge. In a good production of this play, John's villainy — and he is, indeed, the play's villain — can be shown to stem from this moment of rhetorical insufficiency and public humiliation.[22]

Many of Shakespeare's characters, like those of some modern American authors, are at least occasionally inarticulate, and their speeches may be marked with rhetorical awkwardness: pauses, slips of the tongue, and *influencies,* or speech halts. Some such characters may stop in midsentence, afraid to continue:

MESSENGER: [*Bringing bad news to Antony*] And to Ionia, whilst —

ANTONY: "Antony" thou wouldst say.

MESSENGER: Oh, my lord.

ANTONY: Speak to me home! Mince not the general tongue!

(*Antony and Cleopatra,* I.ii.107–109)

Sometimes characters fail to complete their sentences, letting their thoughts just trail off:

HAMLET: For if the sun breed maggots in a dead dog, being a good kissing carrion — Have you a daughter?

(to Polonius, *Hamlet,* II.ii.181–183)

LEAR: Fiery? The fiery Duke, tell the hot Duke that —
No, but not yet, maybe he is not well.

(*King Lear,* II.iv.105–107)

IAGO: Nothing my Lord; or if — I know not what.

(*Othello,* III.iii.36)

Shakespeare's characters may stammer:

CLARENCE: Who sent you hither? Wherefore do you come?

2ND MURDERER: To, to, to —

CLARENCE: To murder me?

BOTH MURDERERS: Aye, aye.

(*Richard III,* I.iv.176–179)

MISTRESS QUICKLY: I shall never laugh but in that maid's company: but (indeed) she is given too much to alicholy and musing: but for you — well — go to —

(*Merry Wives of Windsor,* I.iv.162–165)

---

[22] Don John is often played as an abstract villain, whose evil comes from nature (in Renaissance terms: from a "humour" in his makeup) rather than from psychological bases. But if the actor plays this moment of embarrassment as the final straw in a lifetime of humiliation, it could help create a character whose behavior emanates quite understandably from the situation the audience actually observes at the beginning of the play.

They may bluster:

> HOSTESS: Thou wo't, wo't thou? thou wo't, wo't ta? do, do, thou rogue!
> Do, thou hemp-seed.
> (*2 Henry IV*, II.i.54–55)

> EMILIA: Villainy, villainy, villainy!
> I think upon 't: I think: I smell 't: O villainy!
> I thought so then: I'll kill myself for grief:
> O villainy, villainy!
> (*Othello*, V.ii.194–196)

And sometimes, as when Macduff hears of his wife's murder, they are utterly silent.

All of these "mincings of the general tongue" stand in contrast to the expert rhetoric of characters who, at least in their prime, create brilliant linguistic structures, imposing (for a time at least) a sense of intellectual order on what is ultimately a phenomenologically chaotic universe.

These tongue-mincings: these stammerings, trail-offs, influencies, blusterings, and silences of the (momentarily?) inarticulate, provide the humanizing context for Shakespeare's brilliant literary creativity. And they provide the *tension* that must always exist between essence and existence — specifically, in this case, between the created rhetoric of dramatic language (constructed, ordered, communicative, rational, conclusive) and the natural clumsiness of life's ordinary conversation (organic, arbitrary, expressive, emotional, circular).

Shakespeare often used other aspects of *anti-rhetoric* that actors must learn to play with and perhaps master. Dialects, which we discussed earlier, is one. Speech **malapropisms** — that is, the use of the wrong word — is another. Malapropisms are named after the character Mrs. Malaprop in Richard Sheridan's 18th-century *The Rivals*. Speech **mannerisms** are another. These are the peculiar and habitual usages of individual characters. They help to identify a character, setting him or her off from the "standard" social and cultural codes of the play.

Dogberry in *Much Ado About Nothing* is Shakespeare's most famous malapropist and speech mannerist:

> DOGBERRY: Dost thou not suspect my place? dost thou not suspect my years? — O that he were here to write me down an ass — but, masters, remember that I am an ass! Though it be not written down, yet forget not that I am an ass. — No, thou villain, thou art full of piety, as shall be proved upon thee by good witness. I am a wise fellow; and, which is more, an officer; and, which is more, a householder; and, which is more, as pretty a piece of flesh as any in Messina; and one that knows the law, go to; and a rich fellow enough; go to; and a fellow that hath had losses; and one that hath two gowns, and every thing handsome about him. — Bring him away. — O that I had been writ down an ass!

Dogberry's famous malapropisms ("piety" instead of, perhaps, "iniquity"), his repeated irrelevances (such as "go to" and "which is more") and his foolish constructions, saying the opposite of what he means ("remember that I am an ass!") provide a virtual composition of character through faulty word choice and clumsy rhetoric.

MOCK-RHETORIC

Shakespeare also *mocks* rhetoric, showing how an overreliance on language and wordplay can destroy human relationships. Indeed, this is one of the themes of *Love's Labor's Lost,* where Berowne learns to distance himself from his own "taffeta phrases," and "figures pedantical." And in *Much Ado About Nothing* (a play very much about rhetoric itself), when Benedick finally learns to leave the battle of wits with his friends ("I will leave you now to your gossip-like humor"), his rejection of rhetoric is a decision to experience the fullness of real life and human love.

Thus, characters who use rhetoric falsely, or as empty pretension, are subject to jibes:

TOUCHSTONE: Learn this of me: to have is to have; for it is a figure in rhetoric that drink, being poured out of a cup into a glass, by filling the one, doth empty the other.
(*As You Like It,* V.i.44–46)

Or satire:

POLONIUS: Madam, I swear I use no art at all.
That he is mad, 'tis true: 'tis true, 'tis pity;
And pity 'tis, 'tis true: — a foolish figure;
But farewell it, for I will use no art.
(*Hamlet,* II.ii.97–100. "Art" here means rhetoric and "figure" means figure of speech.)

Shakespeare's mastery of rhetoric presents, therefore, a complex challenge. It can both add and subtract to a character's dignity, depending on how it is meant, how it is received, and how it is performed. You must fully understand Shakespeare's intentions behind his rhetoric before you can either rise or sink to its levels in performance — before you can *play* rhetoric.

How do you play rhetoric? Remember that merely knowing the names for a few figures of speech does little if anything to help you play them. What's important is how to *use* them.

Playing rhetoric is just that — a matter of *playing.* It is here, more than anywhere, that the notions of "play" as both a theatrical and a childhood activity (a playhouse and a playground activity) come together.

In using rhetoric, you are trying to inspire as well as describe; to entertain as well as to move; to attract as well as to persuade. Rhetoric and wordplay both demand an audience: the person or persons you are playing to. And they demand that you inspire/entertain/attract that audience with the contrivance of your speech — with your word choice — as well as with your content.

EXERCISE 18-1

Learn and deliver the political speech fragments at the beginning of this lesson. Try to capture — and raise — the spirits of your listeners.

Try to *impress* them with your command of the language and your *work* in compressing the most meaning into the fewest words.

Try to *entertain* them with your clever word choices, paradoxes, and balanced phrases.

Try to *inspire* them with your carefully built cadences.

EXERCISE 18-2

Read, with one or several partners, the Kate–Petruchio–Widow–Hortensio dialogue above. Don't take parts; just read alternate speeches around a circle. Try to "outclever" each other. "Point" the puns; that is, make them pay off by forcing a laugh, or a groan, from the group.

Make up business to "point" your puns further.

EXERCISE 18-3

Go back to the passages you worked on in Lesson 13: the gallery of Shakespearean characters. Analyze those speeches for their rhetorical figures and devices, as you have learned them here. How can you "point" these speeches, using emphasis and scansion where appropriate, to make the words "play"? How can you point them physically: with movement, costume (your blanket), prop (your yardstick), and gesture?

Prepare one (or more) of these speeches with this in mind.

EXERCISE 18-4

Tackle the Dogberry speech above, remembering that Dogberry is not trying to be stupid or silly. He is trying to be impressive, a "wise fellow!" The stupidity (as well as the humanity) comes from doing what we all do: trying to impress others with our intelligence, correctness, and fair-mindedness. Dogberry just tries too hard, and he's not up to it.

Try the Polonius speech in the same manner. Impress the queen with your charming cleverness, your affable naturalness; indeed, with your lack of "artifice." Don't try to show Polonius's failure: Shakespeare will take care of that for you!

SUMMARY OF LESSON 18

Rhetoric, the deliberate arrangement of language for effectiveness and persuasiveness, is a powerful political force; it is also entertaining and enlightening. Shakespeare is its dramatic master, and his plays are filled with rhetorical devices that become complex speech acts: a dramatic use of crescendoing oratory, figures of speech, and linguistic wordplay that both defines his characters and stimulates the inner action of the plays. But Shakespeare's rhetoric is balanced within the plays by frequent elements of anti-rhetoric: stammerings, speech faults, and silences, as well as an occasional mocking of characters who are overreliant on rhetorical contrivance. The actor plays within a tension that Shakespeare creates between the rhetorical brilliance of certain language constructions and the more inarticulate chaos and confusion of ordinary life.

Speeches Into Scenes

Thus far we have been working almost exclusively with single speeches, though speeches often addressed to a group of persons (such as "the court").

It is time to turn our attention to scenes. Scenework, of course, is not merely you delivering speeches to an acting partner and listening to what comes back at you. In a scene, you are trying to pursue a goal by *affecting your scene partner's attitude and/or behavior*. And your partner is doing the same with you.

This is *interaction*. And since your speeches are speech acts, in a scene you are engaged in a comprehensive linguistic and physical interplay — *with someone else*.

▆▆▆▆ EXERCISE 19-1

Half of your group should memorize one part of the following dialogue, the other half the other.

CITIZEN 1: Neighbor, well met: whither away so fast?

CITIZEN 2: I promise you, I scarcely know myself:
Hear you the news abroad?

CITIZEN 1:   Ay, that the king is dead.

CITIZEN 2: Ill news, by'r lady, seldom comes the better:
I fear, I fear, 'twill prove a giddy world.
(*Richard III*, II.iii.1ff.)

You and your partners are English citizens (of either sex), and you both have just heard that the king, Edward IV, has died. You also know that there are serious national problems ahead: The king's legal successor is a juvenile, incapable of ruling on his own, and "full of danger is the Duke of Gloucester" who is (you presume) now angling for the throne. Note that "seldom comes the better" is a proverbial expression meaning "change is rarely for the better."

"Play" the dialogue, improvised and unrehearsed, with a series of partners.

Don't let the apparent simplicity of the scene delude you into just rattling off the lines. Analyze the scene: What is happening here?

Now you are going to have a "director." Learn and play the scene with the following stage directions:

[Citizen 2 is off right; Citizen 1 is off left. Citizen 2 enters running, sees Citizen 1 offstage and stops. Citizen 2 turns back and starts to run right, but Citizen 1 enters from left and, stopping at center, calls to Citizen 2.]

CITIZEN 1: Neighbor!

[Citizen 2 stops, turns, recognizes Citizen 1, and reluctantly crosses to center to embrace his/her neighbor.]

CITIZEN 1: Well met!

[Citizen 2 grins nervously, then again starts to escape — this time downstage right. Citizen 1 hollers after him/her.]

CITIZEN 1: Whither away so fast?

CITIZEN 2:

[Stops. Turns. Tries to answer but fails. Looks around, sees nothing. Then, with an embarrassed laugh at himself/herself]

I promise you, I scarcely know myself!

[Citizen 1 laughs indulgently. Citizen 2 looks around carefully to see if there are any government spies about; then, deciding there are none, crosses back to Citizen 1.]

CITIZEN 2: Hear you the news abroad?

CITIZEN 1:

[Booming out, delighted to be in on the gossip, and showing off his/her superior knowledge]

Ay, that the king is DEAD!

[With an emphasis on "dead," letting Citizen 2 know he/she, not being very fond of Edward IV himself/herself, is very happy at this particular turn of events.]

CITIZEN 2:

[Terrified, rebuking his/her neighbor's delight, and silencing him/her — to avoid being overheard by spies]

Ill news, by'r lady!

[Citizen 1 protests weakly; Citizen 2 explains his/her rebuke by reference to an old proverb; thus showing off his/her folk wisdom.]

Seldom comes the better!

[Citizen 1 turns away, reflecting on the folk wisdom, and realizing for the first time that the successor to Edward IV might be worse than the old king. Citizen 2 presses his/her advantage:]

I fear . . .

[Citizen 2 gives Citizen 1 a heightened epizeuxis — a repeated phrase built up to a higher level — to turn him/her around.]

I FEAR! . . .

[Citizen 1 turns around to hear what follows. Citizen 2 chooses his/her words carefully and speaks sententiously so as to impress Citizen 1 with an eloquent and final summing up of the present situation.]

'twill prove a . . . giddy . . . world!

The "directed" stage directions lead to just one way of playing this "simple" scene. They create several aspects of interaction not immediately apparent when the scene is read from the page:

1.   A *difference of opinion* between the two characters. This is essential to create the *opposition* necessary for drama to take place. If both characters had identical opinions, and had identical information, there would be no need for either of them to speak, and no interesting (or dramatic) interaction would take place.

2.   A *different goal* for each character. Citizen 2 wants to run away, Citizen 1 wants to show off his/her knowledge of (and opinions about) current events with a neighbor.

3.   A *change* of opinion in the characters caused by the action of the scene. In this case, Citizen 1 is sobered by Citizen 2's version of events known to them both, but Citizen 2 is calmed (arrested from flight) by Citizen 1's relaxed attitude.

4.   Physical *action* that reflects the change of opinion and the "thinking" (the "*inner action*") of the characters in the scene.

Action (physical and inner) and change are intrinsic to drama — Shakespearean and all other as well. Every scene should feature these four aspects of character interaction.

In addition the scene shows:

5.   A *change in tone,* from the hurried interrogations of the first two speeches to the thoughtful word choice ("Ill news"), sententious philosophizing ("seldom comes the better"), and eloquent phrase-making ("'twill prove a giddy world") of the last speech.

6.   A *change in rhythm,* from the scattered confusion of speech two ("I scarcely know myself") to the finality of the direct factual declaration of speech three ("the king is dead"). Note that "I scarcely know myself" carries somewhat of an implied double meaning: (1) in context — "I don't know why I'm running" — and (2) out of context — "I don't know who I am." Both converge to create the sense of deep personal uncertainty and insecurity when a king dies without a clear succession, the king in Shakespeare's day being not only the political but the spiritual leader of the country.

7.   A *coming together* of the two characters, who begin going in different directions (physically as well as intellectually) and who end up in some sort of harmony. Scenes may go in the opposite direction as well, but they ordinarily go one way or the other; stage relationships should not remain static.

8.   A *sense of the outside world*. Where is Citizen 2 headed? Where did he/she come from? We have a sense of geography, even if it is never stated. There is news "abroad," meaning in the offstage environment to the left and right of the characters. "By'r lady" gives us a character in heaven above to oversee events as well. When Citizen 2 ends by referring to a "giddy world," we already have previewed some of the geography of that world; the characters make it live in our minds by considering it in their words.

These latter four aspects, while not always present, give tone, shape, variety, credibility, and a more involving sense of dramatic action to any scene.

As you play the scene with multiple partners, notice how much of the interaction cues come from the text and its analysis, and how much comes from the personal variation in your acting partners — how much, in other words, stems from the innate "personality" of the characters as portrayed by different actors. Some aspects of the scene wll be relatively unchanged from one pairing of actors to another; others will change considerably. The size, sex, litheness, vocal authority of each actor will — and should — invariably affect the scene.

■▞▞▞▞■ EXERCISE 19-2

Learn the other part. Reverse roles, and play the scene again around the room (that is, with all the other partners).

LINE LINKAGE

Let's look at one portion of the text in the previous scene closely:

CITIZEN 2: . . . Hear you the news abroad?

CITIZEN 1:   Ay, that the king is dead.

Obviously, this is question and answer. If it were improvised speech, the questioner would undoubtedly end his question with a rising inflection — that is, with a distinct upward rise in pitch on the last syllable:

                            broad?

Hear you the news a ↗

Oddly, however, most beginning actors, incorrectly[23] read the line with a *falling* inflection:

Hear you the news a ⬊
                broad?

When answered with the flat declarative:

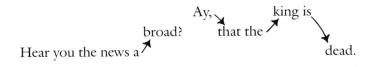

the overall rhythm is monotonous, unenergized, and undramatic. It also sounds unspontaneous.

On the other hand, when inflected upward, the exchange is more energetic and lifelike:

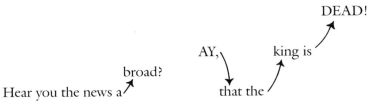

And if the first citizen ends his or her line on an upglide as well, the exchange becomes absolutely infectious:

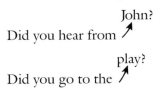

The raised pitch on "DEAD" will be a good prompt for the second citizen's "Ill news . . ." rejoinder.

Inexperienced actors often read lines (particularly questions) with falling rather than rising inflections primarily because they are insecure; and falling inflections sound, in their ears, more authoritative, superior, and "Britishy." All they really are is lifeless. You ask questions because you want to provoke answers. Overhear a spontaneous conversation among your friends; listen to the inflections in their questions.

           John?
Did you hear from ⬈

          play?
Did you go to the ⬈

---

[23] This is one of the rare times I will say a reading is "incorrect." That's shorthand, of course; there are no absolute rules here. But this seems to me a reading that comes only from actor nervousness, which is very common, and not from any effort, conscious or unconscious, at playing from a character's goal or objective.

Rising inflections *provoke* responses; they demand some sort of action. Rising inflections, therefore, give rise to exciting dialogue exchanges, and points that hit home on the other side, to the other character. They link your lines to your partner's response, and his or her lines to *your* response, and for this reason are called **line linkage** devices. They tie speeches in a scene to each other. Dramatic dialogue is not merely a series of speeches given in sequence. It is an integration of speech acts: a series of questions and answers; questions and new questions; provocations and responses; provocations and responses-that-themselves-become-provocations.

Not only questions should end with rising inflections, but *most lines* that ask for a response should end that way as well. And most lines ask for a response. One of the aspects of any exciting scene — in Shakespeare or any other writer — is the continuing provocation: the characters questioning, demanding, and urging the actions of each other.

ATTACKS AND FOLLOW-THROUGHS

Effective line linkage usually requires strong *attacks* at the beginning of every speech and strong *follow-throughs* at the end of every speech.

The attack is the first syllable of your speech. It must get your speech started, but — just as importantly — it must also make everybody else on stage *stop* speaking. It must demand attention and focus on what you are about to say. All speaking (in life) includes a hidden demand for surrounding silence and attention. All speeches (in life) somehow indicate, through tone of voice and physical behavior: "OK, everybody, shut up now and listen to me!" In life, this is no problem: We learn it from infancy. In the theatre, where the other actors are prevented from speaking (because it's somebody else's line), we have to work at it a bit harder. We have to pretend (act) that we are *earning* the right to speak, not just accepting it from the playwright.

Shakespeare, blessedly, helps us at every turn. The vast majority of his speeches begin with *one-syllable words,* which are the easiest to attack.[24]

The follow-through (the last syllable or syllables of your speech) need not always include a rising inflection, but it must include a substantial energy pulse: a demand, an invocation, a provocation to the acting partner. It is the follow-through that "hooks" your listener and compels him or her into responsive action.

Strong attacks and follow-throughs are crucial to the success of any scene, but never more crucial than in Shakespeare. Therefore:

Start your speech by silencing others, and

---

[24] More than 90 percent of Shakespeare's speeches begin with one-syllable words; this is an astonishing statistic. (See my *Acting Power*, p. 73.) You can check this statistic by opening a volume of Shakespeare at random, and scanning the first word of each speech on the page. Where Shakespeare uses a multi-syllable word for the attack, it is usually the name or title of the character addressed, or a turntaking command or exclamation such as "prithee" or "marry!"

End your speech by forcing others into some sort of appropriate action, or response.

Do this for each speech!

CUING

Directors often spend the last week of rehearsal begging the actors to "pick up their cues." It is certainly true that the silences between speeches rarely convey much that is dramatic or interesting to an audience, no matter how much they may satisfy the actor.

In Shakespeare, it is usually quite important to "act on the lines" rather than to try to act in the pauses between the lines. Since Shakespeare accomplishes so much with his words, the psychological contortions you go through during your silences may fail to make any impact whatsoever (even though they make you feel like you're acting up a storm).

There are two kinds of cues: a line cue and an action cue. The **line cue** is the one you know; that's the last word on the speech preceding yours, the one you memorize along with your line so you know when to start speaking.

The **action cue,** however, is perhaps even more important; that's the moment in the preceding speech when your character *decides to speak,* and begins forming a response.

If you are playing the Second Citizen, for example, and you hear the First Citizen's

Hear you the news abroad?

your line cue is "abroad." You don't speak until that word is completed. But your action cue is "news." At that point you know very well what the First Citizen's question is going to be, and you're already framing your answer. You may even know by "Hear you . . ."

So you are preparing to speak *during,* not after, the cue line. By the time of your line cue, the word ("Ay") is already formed in your mouth, you have air in your lungs: You are impatient to speak. And your line comes bounding out. This is a good, fast cue. Most lines are like this. In most good dialogue, you are preparing to speak well before the actual line cue arrives; you are inhaling on, not after, your partner's line. You may even be working hard not to interrupt your partner.

Good cuing takes these factors into account, and makes dialogue not a syncopated alternation of speeches, but a driving set of queries, provocations, and responses, almost overlapping each other, from characters eager — even impatient — to speak their minds.

Now repeat Exercise 19-2, with attention to attacks, follow-throughs, and action cuing. Though the scene is very short, you should be able to practice all of these in both of the parts.

▉▚▞▚▞▚▉ EXERCISE 19-3

Divide students into three groups, with each group learning one role in the three-person citizen scene of which the earlier exercises were only the beginning. Then "mix and match" partners in playing the scene. If you wish, you may change the word "sir" to "miss" if addressed to a female actor, and the word "masters" to "neighbors" if addressed to one or more women.

Try to create the eight aspects of a good scene, discussed above, with each performance of this three-person scene. And try to achieve strong attacks, follow-throughs, and action cuing with each speech as appropriate.

FIRST CITIZEN: Good morrow, neighbor: whither away so fast?

SECOND CITIZEN: I promise you I scarcely know myself:
Hear you the news abroad?

FIRST CITIZEN: Ay,—that the king is dead.

SECOND CITIZEN: Ill news, by'r lady; seldom comes the better:
I fear, I fear 'twill prove a giddy world.
    [*Enter another Citizen.*]

THIRD CITIZEN: Neighbors, God speed!

FIRST CITIZEN: Give you good morrow, sir.

THIRD CITIZEN: Doth the news hold of good King Edward's death?

SECOND CITIZEN: Ay, sir, it is too true; God help, the while!

THIRD CITIZEN: Then, masters, look to see a troublous world.

FIRST CITIZEN: No, no; by God's good grace his son shall reign.

THIRD CITIZEN: Woe to that land that's governed by a child!

SECOND CITIZEN: In him there is a hope of government,
That, in his nonage, council under him,
And, in his full and ripened years, himself,
No doubt, shall then, and till then, govern well.

FIRST CITIZEN: So stood the state when Henry the Sixth
Was crowned in Paris but at nine months old.

THIRD CITIZEN: Stood the state so? No, no, good friends, God wot;
For then this land was famously enriched
With politic grave counsel; then the king
Had virtuous uncles to protect his Grace.

FIRST CITIZEN: Why, so hath this, both by his father and mother.

THIRD CITIZEN: Better it were they all came by his father,
Or by his father there were none at all;
For emulation now, who shall be nearest,
Will touch us all too near, if God prevent not.
O, full of danger is the Duke of Gloucester!

And the queen's sons and brothers haught and proud:
And were they to be ruled, and not to rule,
This sickly land might solace as before.

FIRST CITIZEN: Come, come, we fear the worst; all will be well.

THIRD CITIZEN: When clouds are seen, wise men put on their cloaks;
When great leaves fall, then winter is at hand;
When the sun sets, who doth not look for night?
Untimely storms make men expect a dearth.
All may be well; but, if God sort it so,
'Tis more than we deserve, or I expect.

SECOND CITIZEN: Truly, the hearts of men are full of fear:
You cannot reason almost with a man
That looks not heavily and full of dread.

THIRD CITIZEN: Before the days of change, still is it so:
By a divine instinct men's minds mistrust
Ensuing danger; as, by proof, we see
The waters swell before a boisterous storm
But leave it all to God. — Whither away?

SECOND CITIZEN: Marry, we were sent for to the justices.

THIRD CITIZEN: And so was I: I'll bear you company.   [*Exeunt.*]

Word notes: "God wot" means "God knows." "Marry" is a mild oath, a euphemism for "By the Virgin Mary."

Perhaps you didn't expect your first scene in this book on Shakespeare to be among unnamed "citizens" in Richard III, but these are the roles you, as a beginning actor, are most likely to get when you first make your way into a Shakespearean company.

And they are *wonderful* roles for scenework — first, because you have here the entire role (these characters appear nowhere else in the play; this scene contains their entire parts), and second because the scene has all the elements of Shakespeare: action, conflict, feeling, rhetoric, and poetry. Opportunities for true greatness are right here. A superb actor can make a whole audience shiver with "O full of danger is the Duke of Gloucester." Master these parts, and leave until later the greater glories of Romeo, Rosalind, and Lady Macbeth!

Author's aside: I am always amused when beginning actors disdain roles like these, asking for a role they can "sink their teeth into." You can sink teeth, tongue, and jowls into these little parts, and still leave half the meat on the bones. The greatest Shakespearean actors on earth can find these roles immensely rewarding.

A three-person scene is not just half-again bigger than a two-person scene — it's three times bigger. You have at least three two-person scenes in every three-person scene (Citizens 1 and 2, 2 and 3, and 1 and 3), plus you have two levels of communication — interaction and performance — going on

You can use the blanket, rope, and stick costume for your scenes, too. Below left, Benedick and Beatrice in *Much Ado About Nothing* (IV.i. or V.ii.); center, Cleopatra and the Messenger in *Antony and Cleopatra* (II.v.); above right, Lear and the Fool in *King Lear* (I.v.); below right, the comic duel between Viola and Sir Andrew in *Twelfth Night* (III.iv, although this scene cannot be performed without additional actors and some carefully rehearsed staging).

Cleopatra and the Messenger

Benedick and Beatrice

Lear and the Fool

Viola and Sir Andrew

at all times (Citizen 2 speaking to Citizen 3 is an interaction between them; Citizen 2 speaking to Citizen 3, in part for the benefit of Citizen 1 is a performance).

Analyze, as best you can, the relationships among the three characters, and the change in that relationship as the scene progresses.

Analyze the technical elements we have discussed in this chapter, including line linkage and cuing.

Then direct *yourselves,* in the same way you were directed by the author of this book earlier in this lesson, in creating your character's line-by-line changing of goals, changing of opinions, and physical actions.

◼︎▨▨◼︎ EXERCISE 19-4

Employ the same principles from Exercise 19-3 in any of the following "citizen" scenes. By changing a word here and there, when and if necessary, the scenes can be done without respect to gender. In each case you will play the entire role as it exists in the play. (You will, in these scenes, need to become familiar with the play first.)

1. *Coriolanus,* IV.iii. A Roman and a Volcian meet to exchange gossip of Coriolanus's banishment from Rome, and its implications for the Volcians.

2. *Antony and Cleopatra,* IV.iii. Four soldiers stand guard, and hear mysterious noises, forecasting Antony's defeat.

3. *Julius Caesar,* III.iii. Four overwrought Roman citizens encounter Cinna the poet, and, confusing him with Cinna the conspirator, decide to kill him. When Cinna protests that he is Cinna the poet, they decide to kill him anyway, "for his bad verses."

4. *Romeo and Juliet,* I.i. (through to the fight). Samson and Gregory, servants to the Capulets, run into Abraham and Balthasar, servants to the Montagues.[25]

◼︎▨▨◼︎ EXERCISE 19-5

Choose any scene in Shakespeare (there are, of course, thousands), and prepare it with a partner. Keep it short, as simple as possible, and from a play you know fairly well. You may choose any play from Shakespeare's works (from what we sometimes call "the canon"), but it is best to start with lesser known characters who can reasonably be seen as close to your own age.

---

[25] The author began his Shakespearean acting career in the role of Abraham in this scene!

SUMMARY OF LESSON 19

In this lesson, you are encouraged to begin scenework, first by analyzing the process of interchange and line linkage (specifically attack, follow-through, and cuing), and then by finding, where you can, eight things that should or might be present during a scene: a difference of opinion, a change of each opinion, a change of goal, physical action, a change of tone, a change in rhythm, a coming together (or a going apart), and a sense of the outside world impinging on the immediate circumstances. A scene among three anonymous citizens in *Richard III* shows how rich — in terms of dynamic action — such a seemingly "minor" scene can prove when analyzed and "directed." You are encouraged to find, analyze, and "direct" such scenes yourself.

LESSON 20

Storytelling

Plot, or the "story" of the play, does not always get a lot of attention among literary critics or scholarly commentators, but it is at the absolute center of Shakespearean dramaturgy. It is the motive force of the play, driving the actors, integrating the design and technical elements, and drawing in—seducing, shall we say—the playhouse audience.

In performance, the plot compels audience attention and involvement. It is plot and its product, suspense, that creates empathy and makes us care about the characters and what happens to them. It is plot that makes us care, for example, whether Romeo marries Juliet, or whether Birnum wood comes to Dunsinane. This caring is what ultimately makes the play's events *dramatic,* allowing us to appreciate the staging and acting.

No matter how brilliantly executed, acting always depends on the story that is acted. If the story is compelling, the audience will be drawn in by the feelings, actions, and behavior of the characters—and thereby attentive to (and attracted by) your performance. If the audience gets lost in the story, they will "tune out" of the play. They will then no longer care about the characters, and all your histrionic ability will appear as so much empty oratory and staginess.

Plotless performances can be *admired,* much as a foreign artifact can be admired in a museum, but they cannot create the emotional thrill or aesthetic and intellectual satisfaction of realized dramatic art. It's as simple as that. From Aeschylus to Beckett, the great playwrights have also been great storytellers—and actors have to be great story-conveyors.

Shakespeare himself created wonderful stories. While most of his plot lines were borrowed from earlier sources, his taletelling ability—his refinement of those borrowed sources—was absolutely superb. Charles and Mary Lamb's *Tales from Shakespeare,* a narrative recapitulation of the stories of the major plays, has been continuously in print for more than 180 years: testimony to the compelling plots of Shakespeare, even in nondramatic narration. To lose the story of a Shakespearean play is to lose its dramatic heart, and its theatrical heartbeat.

196

One of the first duties of the actors (and directors), therefore, is to *bring out the story* clearly and vividly. If the story is alive, if it's clear, if the play's actions seem to proceed convincingly from appropriate stimuli, and then establish suspense toward their eventual outcome, then, by these accomplishments alone, the play (and the acting) will already be assured of a substantial measure of success.

Is this the actor's job, or the director's? The answer is simple: It is the job of both the actor and director.

Obviously, a director in the current American or European theatre has a major role in elucidating the story line. So, for that matter, does the costume designer, the scenery designer, and the lighting designer. But no director or designer will spend the time in a typical three- to six-week rehearsal period to tell *your* story, particularly if your story happens to be the Third Citizen's or the Second Servant's or Abraham's.

In addition, the director may simply not be very experienced, or very experienced in Shakespeare, or very understanding about the inner structure of the play. Many directors—many *fine* directors—are primarily visually oriented, or musically oriented, or "effects" oriented, and will be concentrating on other things besides what's happening (or not happening) to your character and your situation. Storytelling *should* be a primary concern of every director, but it *must* be a primary concern of every actor!

Telling the story, however, is not easily accomplished, especially in Shakespeare.

First, the audience must hurdle the same problems that we've faced earlier: the often archaic language, the obscure words and constructions, the strangeness of blank verse, and the unfamiliarity (in these days) of many of Shakespeare's historical and mythological references. And the audience doesn't have the reader's option of consulting glossaries or footnotes during a performance, or of pausing over or rereading the most difficult passages.

Second, there's the elliptical and indirect manner in which Shakespearean characters often speak, in which sense is often shaded with elaborate poetic, satiric, comic, and/or ironic tones. What *are* we supposed to make of the servant announcing Laertes' violent rebellion with an extended metaphor of the ocean "overpeering of his list"?

Third, Shakespeare wrote *big* plays, usually with multiple foreign settings and huge casts of characters. *Richard III* has about fifty clearly identified individual characters for the audience to keep straight—along with their genealogical relationships, social/political rankings, and romantic entanglements. *Antony and Cleopatra* has forty-six scenes, thirty-four principal characters, and takes place in two dozen sites in and around Alexandria, Rome, Messina, Misenum, Syria, Athens, Actium, and at various places on the high seas. Neither program notes (which did not exist in Shakespeare's day) nor representational scenery (which didn't either) is of much help in establishing the identity of these characters or locales.

And fourth, our own reading and working with the plays as actors (and directors), and the familiarity this eventually brings, often blinds us to the difficulties the audience will have in comprehending, in one sitting, what it may have taken us months or years to understand.

And so actors often rattle through what seems obvious to them—as the audience scratches its collective head, wondering what we're talking about.

So how do you begin?

As an actor, you must begin by realizing that *the audience doesn't know the play*.[26] They haven't read it; they don't know who's who, or what's where. They don't know who's related to whom, what country the play is set in, who the king here is, or even *if* there's a king. You have to help them find out about all these matters, and sometimes you have to help them over and over again.

Shakespeare gives you some problems here. It's often not clear where we are, or who's about. Frequently characters aren't even named in the dialogue until well after they appear. Macduff, in *Macbeth,* is not identified until well after his first big scene. Sometimes characters are called by several different names: Polixenes, in *The Winter's Tale,* is also addressed as "Bohemia," which is the name of his country, and "brother" (by someone not his brother), and also referred to sarcastically as "Sir Smile." And like so many Shakespearean characters, he also appears in full disguise! In a clumsily directed production, the audience won't be able to identify him at the curtain call. In a carelessly acted one, they won't even care.

You're going to have to provide the road map here. If the audience is to follow the story, you must first point them in the right direction. You must *illustrate* the action of the play, not merely talk them through it.

Shakespeare gives you all the basics, of course. Almost every entrance is made with some sort of announcement ("See where he comes!" or "Look who comes here" or "Here comes two of the house of the Montagues"). One scholar has identified 450 "entrance announcements" in the 37 plays. Place indications are equally spread through the plays ("Get ye all three into the box tree!" "Here is her father's house," "Here the street is narrow") as are environmental conditions ("The air bites shrewdly; it is very cold," "So foul and fair a day I have not seen.") The forest scenes of *A Midsummer Night's Dream* contain no less than twenty-six indications that it's nighttime.

Creating clarity in a Shakespearean (or any other) production is, first, a matter of knowing what you mean, meaning what you say, and *making sense* of what you say—that is, speaking the text clearly. Shakespeare provides the basics, but you have to transmit them forcefully.

Second, clarity is a matter of communicating *visually*—of using movement, gesture, and physical expression to communicate facts and ideas, and

---

[26] All right, *some* of them will probably know the play. Some may even know the play quite well. But you can't count on that; and most of them, let's face it, will know it only vaguely, perhaps from a reading or viewing several years previously. The rest will know nothing of it at all. "The audience" is a collectivity, and you play to all its members, not just to the occasional Shakespearean scholar or enthusiast. You must provide the audience with *the entire play:* the story, the characters, the actions, the lines, the interpretation. Everything.

to move along the story of the play. Visual communication is not more important than spoken sense, but it is more often ignored.

Too frequently, even in professional productions, movement and gesture are simply employed to intensify emotion or to create stage spectacle. These may be valuable, but the primary reason why humans gesture (and why actors playing characters gesture) is to *communicate meaning.* Yet, the movement on stage often does little in this regard; sometimes it does just the opposite.

EXAMPLE: THE TEMPEST

Toward the beginning of *The Tempest,* two principal characters, Prospero and Miranda, come on stage. We gather they are father and daughter, living on a deserted island. But Miranda, we find, is ignorant of her true identity, and Prospero begins telling her their secret family history:

PROSPERO: Twelve year since, Miranda, twelve year since.
Thy father was the Duke of Milan, and
A prince of power.

MIRANDA: Sir, are not you my father?

PROSPERO: Thy mother was a piece of virtue, and
She said thou wast my daughter; and thy father
Was Duke of Milan; thou his only heir . . .

Did you have to read this twice to understand it fully? Most people do. It's apparent—but only after careful reading—that Prospero is saying that he is Miranda's father but was also once the Duke of Milan. Miranda, however, is confused, and so, probably, are we. Prospero, by speaking in a roundabout manner, seems to be evading rather than answering Miranda's question. Moreover, he never *directly* confirms being her father: He never says, for example, "Sure, honey!"

Now consider the poor theatre audience. They can't work out Prospero's syllogism on the page, nor can they ask him to repeat his line until they get it. They may even miss a word or two if somebody should cough, or if the actor should have a muffled delivery. Woe betide them then, for they'll be lost for the rest of the scene, if not for the entire play!

Yet this happens all the time. In a recent production, the actor playing Prospero gestured vaguely rightward as he said "thy father was the Duke of Milan," thereby unintentionally steering most of the audience into thinking that Miranda was actually the daughter of a duke in some country (Milan) somewhere off to the right!

Should we change the wording in order to solve the problem? Should we use, for example:

PROSPERO: Twelve year since, Miranda, twelve year since,
I was the Duke of Milan, and a prince of power.

MIRANDA: Sir, are not you my father?

PROSPERO: Sure I am! But I was once the Duke of Milan, too;
And you my only heir . . .

Of course not. The debasing of the Shakespearean text aside, Prospero's indirection, his syllogistic reasoning, his near-evasiveness is all part of his character, as is his ducal third-person self-reference. Shakespeare wants to establish these speech characteristics right away, and it is your job — the actor's job — to make the meaning clear within this context. And with the Shakespearean text, not some pedestrian alteration.

You can do it. In this case, all it takes is for you to gesture to *yourself* when saying "thy father." This would confirm quite unambiguously that you are both Miranda's father *and* the former Duke of Milan.

It's almost frightening what a difference a simple gesture can make. Pointing to yourself clarifies the story and moves it forward; pointing to your right loses the audience, sometimes for the balance of the evening.

There are literally *hundreds* of examples like this in Shakespeare, where the difference between a mediocre and a great performance may lie primarily in the way a superb performer can clarify the action and vividly elucidate, or bring out, the story (plot) elements, inducing empathy for the characters and, consequently, a strong theatrical impact for the overall production.

ELUCIDATING, NOT INDICATING

Elucidating the text is not a matter of *indicating* the character's action or feeling.[27] It is simply a matter of clarifying the facts and ideas; it is communicating fully, with movement and gesture as well as phrasing and intonation.

That communication is primarily *to the other characters in the play*. Needless to say, Miranda also must understand who her father is, and who the Duke of Milan is. Miranda also has never read *The Tempest*, or even the plot synopsis in the program. Prospero leads the audience into the story by clearly explaining the situation to Miranda. Good storytelling, and effective interaction with your acting partner, are usually the same thing.

Most of the time, explaining things for the audience is the same as explaining things to the persons you're talking to — which is to say the other characters in the play. Elucidating (the word means "making lucid," or

---

[27] "Indicating" is adopting a pose or attitude that indicates (to the audience) the character's emotion — putting on a worried expression, for example, to show the audience that you are afraid. You should be taught, quite correctly, *not* to do this. Rather, you should be taught to play the action of your character. A person in a truly frightening predicament would most likely try to project *fearlessness* by way of self-protection (think of Falstaff in battle, or of Viola and Andrew Aguecheek in their duel). In any event, actors should always play the actions of their characters, and not indicate the emotions they feel the characters should project. But that is not the subject here — elucidating the story is not indicating feelings. Elucidating the story is making your points to the other characters; it is part of the action of every character. It is communicating facts and ideas with force and precision.

"throwing light upon") is simply a process of explaining yourself, of making points, and of making yourself understood, by characters and audience alike.

Actors and directors often tend to take the play's points for granted, mainly because the rehearsal process has made the play pretty well known to them. But you must remember that the audience — *and the characters* — have not rehearsed a play, only the actors and the directors have. So you must elucidate the action of that play fully and without shame. You are not thereby "indicating" emotions, you are rather doing the work of the characters in their situations.

ILLUSTRATING: POINTING THE WAY

The most common way of making yourself understood is to "illustrate" your meaning (*illustrate* also derives from words meaning "throw light upon") by pointing and gesturing.

Prospero's pointing to himself illustrates the fact that by "thy father," he means himself. You can physically point in several ways: with a hand to your breast, or with two hands angled sharply inward, or by pointing at yourself with your finger or thumb. Each of these methods creates a slightly different character, from the sensitive father to the deposed and angry duke.

There are also subtler means of pointing: with your eyes, your eyebrows, a turn of your shoulders, the tilt of your head, even with the projection of your voice. But for the time being, you should employ bolder and less subtle "pointings," as described in the following exercises.

▰▰▰▰▰▰ EXERCISE 20-1

PROSPERO: Thy mother was a piece of virtue, and
She said thou wast my daughter; and thy father
Was Duke of Milan; thou his only heir,
And princess, no worse issued.

This is the speech we have just been examining. Memorize and deliver it "straight," with no movement.

Now perform it, pointing the way (indeed, you will be "overpointing" the way at first).

Imagine Prospero's wife ("thy mother") dead, in heaven; and Miranda to your right. Gesture, on "thy mother" to Miranda's mother in heaven. Point, on "thou (wast my daughter)" to Miranda.

Gesture to yourself on "thy father," and then take an end stop pause.

Gesture distantly to your left, after "Duke of Milan" (as if to a country far across the seas), and then point back to Miranda for the final "thou (his only heir)."

Finally, open the point to Miranda to a caressing gesture on the word "princess," abstractly illustrating with the gesture what makes her a princess.

And drop your gesturing hand at "issued."

Do this in order to make Miranda understand very clearly what you are saying. Imagine she knows absolutely nothing of this; that she is hearing it for the first time; indeed, that she believes something just the opposite.

Place an actor in Miranda's spot, and try to make the actor believe that he or she is what you are saying—that is, a princess—and that you are the deposed Duke of Milan.

Get comfortable with the speech, and the gestures and pointing. Understand that in a performance you will rarely if ever "illustrate" a line quite this much; still, the illustration here should make the story clearer, and more "real," even to you. It should make Miranda's mother a little more vivid in your imagination (locating her in heaven), and should make "Milan" seem like a real place since it has some sort of geographical locus. It should also make the word "princess" take on a more specific and emotional (and less fairy tale) connotation in your mind.

The result will be your telling Prospero's story far more clearly and compellingly to those among your overhearers (in the audience or elsewhere) who are wholly ignorant of it.

◼︎◼︎◼︎◼︎◼︎ EXERCISE 20-2

> DROMIO OF EPHESUS: I have some marks of yours upon my pate,
> Some of my mistress' marks upon my shoulders;
> But not a thousand marks between you both.
> (*The Comedy of Errors*, I.ii.81ff)

You are speaking to Antipholus of Syracuse, the long lost twin of your master, Antipholus of Ephesus. You mistake him for his twin, and he is mistaking you for *your* twin.

He has just asked what you did with the thousand marks he thinks he gave you (he actually gave them to your twin), and you're telling him you don't know what he's talking about. Your line is a pun on "marks" meaning wounds from a beating, and "marks" meaning Ephesian currency.

Say the line "straight," without movement or gesture.

Now try it with the following illustration:

I have some marks of yours
[*Point to Antipholus, at your right, with your right hand.*]

upon my pate,
[*With your left hand, touch your scalp—and show how it hurts.*]

Some of my mistress' . . .
[*With your right hand crossing your body, point to your mistress's house at your left.*]

marks upon my shoulders;
[*Move your left hand to the back of your right shoulder; you should now be almost hugging yourself, with both arms crossed around your body.*]

But not a thousand marks
[*Rub the fingers of your right hand in a "money-counting" gesture, and start moving your right hand towards Antipholus, to your right.*]

between you both
[*Open your arms fully, pointing to Antipholus at your right, with your right hand, and to your mistress's house at your left, with your left hand.*]

Use all these pointings and gestures to show Antipholus, very vividly, that (1) you don't have his money, (2) he and his wife have beaten you quite enough this week, and (3) you don't know what the hell he's talking about!

This is an elaborate (and comic!) pattern of illustration, combining pointing (which establishes Antipholus and the mistress, as well as clarifying the meaning of pate for the few people who may not know it) and gesturing (which establishes that "marks," the last time around, means money).

The illustration not only serves to clarify the story, it physically "ties you up in knots," and, when expertly done, can be an amusing piece of comic business—one that is tied quite specifically to the text, not just added on at the whim of the director. Dromio is indeed "tied up in knots," metaphorically, as the mistaken identities of the play draw him into deeper and deeper confusion.

Work this speech a few times until it feels comfortable to you. Can you play some variations on it? Don't think of it as set business, but as gestures that help you convey your meanings and win your goals. Even the amusing business (showing him you are tied in knots) is a way of entertaining your master (or the person you assume is your master), and preventing him from beating you again.

EXERCISE 20-3

IAGO: Thus do I ever make my fool my purse;
For I mine own gained knowledge should profane,
If I would time expend with such a snipe,
But for my sport and profit. I hate the Moor;
And it is thought abroad, that 'twixt my sheets
'Has done my office: I know not if't be true;
But I, for mere suspicion in that kind,
Will do as if for surety. He holds me well;
The better shall my purpose work on him.
Cassio's a proper man: let me see now;
To get his place, and to plume up my will
In double knavery—How, how?—Let's see:—
After some time, to abuse Othello's ear
That he is too familiar with his wife:—
He hath a person, and a smooth dispose,
To be suspected; framed to make women false.

> The Moor is of a free and open nature,
> That thinks men honest that but seem to be so;
> And will as tenderly be led by th'nose
> As asses are.
> I have't; — it is engendered: — hell and night
> Must bring this monstrous birth to the world's light.

This is one of Iago's great soliloquies in *Othello*. In it, he refers to four people: Roderigo ("my fool"), Othello ("the Moor"), Cassio ("a proper man"), and himself. He also implicitly refers to his own wife, suggesting that "'twixt my sheets, [Othello has] done my office" (that is, slept with my wife). In the speech, Iago develops his plan, sharing it with the audience at the same time, to keep Roderigo as his money source (as his "purse"), and to convince Othello that Cassio has been having an affair with Othello's wife.

Learn the speech, and "place" the three men in specific spots: Roderigo, who has just left you, directly upstage or behind you, Cassio off to your left, and Othello off to your right. Also place your "sheets," as in an upstairs apartment above and behind you on the left.

Determine who the pronouns "he," "him," and "his" refer to in every reference (note that the word " Has" in the sixth line is a contraction for "He has"), and point or physically gesture toward the appropriately placed "character" each time he (or she) is named or referred to.

Vary in manner your pointing and gesturing, and, when appropriate, let the gesture flow into a more illustrative expression, as the identification of the character becomes a description of the character, as:

> Thus do I make my fool [*Point to the departing Roderigo*] . . . my purse [*Clench your fist*]
>
> Cassio's [*Point at him*] . . . a proper man [*Let the point turn into a prissy gesture, such as holding a teacup with the thumb and forefinger with the pinkie raised.*]
>
> The Moor [*Point at him*] . . . is of a free and open nature [*Let the point evolve into a openhanded gesture, your palm up.*]
>
> That thinks men honest that but seem to be so,
> And will as tenderly be led by the nose . . . [*The open hand closes, as on a leash attached to Othello's nose.*]
>
> As asses are . . . [*Jerk the leash sharply, as to move a stubborn ass.*]

Try this speech on friends unfamiliar with the play, who will make up Iago's audience. Can they understand what you're saying? Can they follow the story? If they don't know the play, give them enough background to know whom your talking about. *Illustrate* your soliloquy until you can confidently deliver it so even a stranger will know just what you are planning to do.

■▧◩▧◩■ EXERCISE 20-4

      Choose and prepare any longish expository speech (ten lines or more) from the first scene of any Shakespearean play, or from any scene that requires no prior explanation in order to be understood. Perform the speech before a group (such as an acting class), illustrating it so fully that the group can follow your thoughts precisely and, when called to do so, can explain exactly what you said and meant. "Place" the characters you are referring to in specific spots, and try to create a physical score to illustrate the meaning as clearly as possible.

      A side note: This is good practice for giving Shakespearean auditions. Much of the time, directors watching student auditions in Shakespeare have little or no idea of what the actors are trying to get across—the words just fly by. It's not that the actor doesn't understand the text, but that the actor isn't elucidating or clarifying or illustrating the text, and the director is reduced to taking notes on vocal strength, movement capability, and other technical aspects. The best auditions *get the director involved in the story*, even when the speech is only one or two minutes long.

      It is, of course, quite possible to become overelaborate at illustrating your lines, but don't worry about this now. The *impulse* to make clear, and to use your movement and gesture in precise integration with your delivery of the text, is something you should work to develop. The text may be the dominant force in your performance, but you must play the character—and must communicate the character's struggles—as a complete physical and emotional person, not just as a talking head.

PLAYING YOUR DECISION MAKING

      Along with illustrating the text, there's a second method for increasing your storytelling effectiveness while acting Shakespeare or any other playwright.

      That's playing your decision as it's being made, not simply reporting on its having been made. Playing the *act* of decision making.

      The above speech by Iago is a classic in this, because it is obvious that Iago is making his plans here, right before our eyes. Having him mull over alternatives in his mind ("let me see now . . . how? how?") puts us right inside his mind—where all the suspense lies. This is like the camera "point of view" in films, where the camera gets behind the eyes of the character and the audience sees what the character sees.

      All performances can be sharpened if the actors remember to *make decisions* on stage, not merely follow prearranged patterns established by the playwright and director. This is particularly important on the famous speeches: Hamlet's "to be or not to be" soliloquy, for instance, or Macbeth's "tomorrow and tomorrow and tomorrow" reflection, which all too often are given just as set speeches the characters have recited from memory. *You* are giving them from memory, of course, but the character must be shown to be thinking them up right on the spot. And the way to be sure you show that is to always be considering alternatives — the words and actions the characters *don't* end up saying or doing. The words and actions characters consider but reject.

Sometimes characters talk about the actions they reject: "Now I might do it," Hamlet says before deciding not to kill Claudius in act III. But more often they only think about them. Therefore, you have to *think:* to decide and choose before our eyes. You have to decide to come onto the stage, to speak, to shut up, to sit down, to leave. And you have to *choose* to speak (as Dudley Knight says, "Until an actor truly considers the very real availability of just shutting up, she or he will not confront the specific reasons why the character keeps going"),[28] and *choose* the exact words that you speak — from among thousands of alternatives. You have to make the play up as you go along, just as the character does.

◥◤◢◤◢◣ EXERCISE 20-5

In this street scene, Olivia, a young widow, comes upon her drunken uncle, Sir Toby, attacking a young man in her front yard. The young man is Sebastian; Olivia thinks it is Cesario, with whom she is infatuated. Cesario is actually Viola, Sebastian's twin sister in male disguise. Believing that the handsome "Cesario" has finally come to visit her, Olivia sends Toby packing, and invites the young man (who has never seen her before) inside.

> OLIVIA: [*To Sir Toby*] Will it be ever thus? Ungracious wretch
> Fit for the mountains and the barbarous caves,
> Where manners ne'er were preached! out of my sight! —
> Be not offended, dear Cesario.
> Rudesby, be gone! [*Sir Toby leaves.*]
> [*To Sebastian*] I prithee, gentle friend,
> Let thy fair wisdom, not thy passion, sway
> In this uncivil and unjust extent
> Against thy peace. Go with me to my house;
> And hear thou there how many fruitless pranks
> This ruffian hath botched up, that thou thereby
> Mayst smile at this: thou shalt not choose but go:
> Do not deny. Beshrew his soul for me,
> He started one poor heart of mine in thee.
> (*Twelfth Night*, IV.i.407ff.)

---

[28] *On Stage Studies*, Summer 1989, p. 47.